The Church in Act

The Church in Act

Lutheran Liturgical Theology in Ecumenical Conversation

Maxwell E. Johnson

Fortress Press
Minneapolis

THE CHURCH IN ACT

Lutheran Liturgical Theology in Ecumenical Conversation

Cover image: Thinkstock / Brussels – Last super of Christ from Saint Antoine church; sedmak

Cover design: Alisha Lofgren

Library of Congress Cataloging-in-Publication Data

Print ISBN: 978-1-4514-8883-8

eBook ISBN: 978-1-4514-9668-0

The paper used in this publication meets the minimum requirements of American National Standard for Information Sciences — Permanence of Paper for Printed Library Materials, ANSI Z329.48-1984.

Manufactured in the U.S.A.

This book was produced using PressBooks.com, and PDF rendering was done by PrinceXML.

Contents

Preface

In 2004, I published a collection of several of my essays in a volume entitled *Worship: Rites, Feasts, and Reflections*,[1] which dealt with a variety of topics in liturgical history and theology, two of which appear again here in a revised form, namely, "The Real and Multiple Presences of Christ in Contemporary Lutheran Liturgical and Sacramental Practice," and "Eucharistic Reservation and Lutheranism: An Extension of Sunday Worship?" And, while an ecumenical theme was certainly a characteristic of that previous volume, this particular collection is characterized not only by an ecumenical orientation, but, particularly, by my own confessional stance as a *Lutheran*. As will become clear, in fact, the writings selected for this collection were chosen precisely because they reflect my Lutheran-based liturgical theological conversation with others. Indeed, as one who has had the privilege of teaching liturgical studies in Roman Catholic institutions over the past twenty years plus, first at the School and Department of Theology, Saint John's University, Collegeville, Minnesota, from 1993 to 1997, and since then as a member of the Department of Theology at the University of Notre Dame, I have been directly involved on a day-to-day basis in what has become, especially in light of the now fifty-year-old Roman

1. *Worship: Rites, Feasts, and Reflections* (Portland: The Pastoral Press, 2004).

Catholic *Constitution on the Sacred Liturgy* at the Second Vatican Council, an ecumenical liturgical conversation in the church and in the academy between Lutherans and Roman Catholics, Anglicans, Eastern Rite Christians, Orthodox and Catholic, and, increasingly, others, among undergraduates, graduate students, and faculty colleagues.

If, however, the subtitle of this volume, *Lutheran Liturgical Theology in Ecumenical Conversation*, makes that orientation rather obvious, it needs to be said also that the title of this volume, *The Church in Act*, is likewise grounded in a rather strong Lutheran confessional position, namely, Article VII of the *Confessio Augustana* or *Augsburg Confession* (1530), which offers what most certainly can be termed a *liturgical* definition of the church: "It is also taught among us that one holy Christian church will be and remain forever. This is the assembly of all believers [or 'saints'] among whom the Gospel is preached in its purity and the holy sacraments are administered according to the Gospel."[2] The "church in act," then, is the church constituted, called into existence, by the very "act" it is called and empowered by the Spirit of God to do, that is, to assemble together in order to proclaim the gospel in its purity and administer the sacraments of the gospel, according to that gospel. Roman Catholic liturgical theologians like to quote Jesuit Cardinal Henri de Lubac's famous statement that "the Eucharist builds the Church and the Church makes the Eucharist,"[3] but *Augustana* VII says basically the same thing, although not limited to the Eucharist. So also, the late Lutheran liturgical scholar S. Anita Stauffer (d. 2007) echoed a parallel approach when she said, "The Church is never more the Church than when it worships."[4] And,

---

2. Theodore Tappert, ed., *The Book of Concord: The Confessions of the Evangelical Lutheran Church* (Fortress Press: Philadelphia, 1959), 32.
3. See Henri de Lubac, Corpus Mysticum: *The Eucharist and the Church in the Middle Ages,* trans. Gemma Simmonds, CJ, with Richard Price and Christopher Stephens, *Faith and Reason: Philosophical Enquiries* (Notre Dame: University of Notre Dame Press, 2007).

along similar lines, Russian Orthodox liturgical theologian Alexander Schmemann once wrote, "Christian worship, by its nature, structure and content, is the revelation and realization by the Church of her own real nature. And this nature is the new life in Christ—union in Christ with God the Holy Spirit, knowledge of the Truth, unity, love, grace, peace, [and] salvation."[5]

Leitourgia, liturgy or worship, of course, is not all that the church does or enacts in the world, but it is, nevertheless, the very word and sacrament *source* from which the church—which is called also to live faithfully in the world in acts of *martyria* (witness), *diakonia* (service), and *didascalia* (teaching)—finds revealed its God-given identity and self-understanding. While Lutherans may have a distinct theological understanding of the "purity" of the gospel and of what constitutes the "right" administration of the sacraments, the very fact that similar terminology is used by others to define the church points us toward a potential common ecumenical liturgical-ecclesiological understanding.[6]

The first chapter in this collection, Chapter 1, "Baptismal Spirituality in the Early Churches and Its Implications for the Church Today," places Baptism and a baptismal spirituality, or baptismal orientation to life in Christ, at the foundation of the Church and its worship. This chapter was originally delivered as a plenary address at the 1999 Institute of Liturgical Studies at Valparaiso University, Valparaiso, Indiana.[7] Not only does it reflect my own scholarly

---

4. S. Anita Stauffer, *Re-Examining Baptismal Fonts*, video recording (Collegeville: The Liturgical Press, 1991).

5. Alexander Schmemann, *Introduction to Liturgical Theology*, 2nd ed. (Crestwood, NY: St. Vladimir's Seminary Press, 1975), 23.

6. This approach is developed further below in chapter 9, "*Satis est*: Ecumenical Catalyst or Narrow Reductionism?," 221-39.

7. "Baptismal 'Spirituality' in the Early Church and Its Implications for the Church Today," in *Worship, Culture, and Catholicity 1997–1999*, ed. Rhoda Schuler, Institute of Liturgical Studies Occasional Papers #10 (Valparaiso, IN: Institute of Liturgical Studies, 2005), 188–211.

interests in the Rites of Christian Initiation, in other words, Baptism, "Confirmation," and First Communion, about which I have written several books and articles,[8] but this particular chapter underscores the variety of baptismal theologies, and, hence, differing baptismal spiritualities, in early Christianity, including the rich diversity of biblical images that will come to cluster around Romans 6 and John 3:5 as participation in Christ's death as well as adoption and new birth in water and the Holy Spirit. This chapter also provides a critical look at contemporary Lutheran and other adaptations of the adult catechumenate.

Chapter 2, "The Holy Spirit and Lutheran Liturgical-Sacramental Worship," also had its origins at a scholarly conference, "The Spirit in Worship and Worship in the Spirit" at the Institute of Sacred Music and Yale Divinity School in 2008.[9] While portions of this chapter are naturally concerned with the role of the Holy Spirit in the Rites of Christian Initiation, a principal component is the relationship of the Holy Spirit to the Lord's Supper or Eucharist. Here, particular theological attention is given to what is called the "Spirit epiclesis" in the eucharistic prayer, including a comparative study of its theology and placement in eucharistic prayers throughout the broad history both of Eastern and Western liturgical texts, including frequently ignored texts from within the Lutheran liturgical tradition.

The third, fourth, and fifth chapters in this volume all focus primarily as well on various topics having to do with the Eucharist.

8. See *The Rites of Christian Initiation: Their Evolution and Interpretation*, rev. and expanded ed. (Collegeville, MN: The Liturgical Press, Pueblo Books, 2007); *Images of Baptism* (Chicago: Liturgy Training Publications, 2001, reprinted by Ashland City, TN: Order of Saint Luke Publications, 2013); revised and expanded edition of E. C. Whitaker, *Documents of the Baptismal Liturgy*, Alcuin Club Collections 79 (London: SPCK; Collegeville: Pueblo, 2003); and, as editor and contributor, *Living Water, Sealing Spirit: Readings on Christian Initiation* (Collegeville, MN: The Liturgical Press, Pueblo Books, 1995).

9. An earlier version appeared as "The Holy Spirit and Lutheran Liturgical-Sacramental Worship," in *The Spirit in Worship—Worship in the Spirit*, ed. Bryan Spinks and Teresa Berger (Collegeville, MN: The Liturgical Press, Pueblo Books, 2009), 155–178.

Chapter 3, "The Real and Multiple Presences of Christ in Contemporary Lutheran Liturgical and Sacramental Praxis," was also originally an invited public lecture, this time as the keynote address for the June 1998 conference, "Church and Eucharist: The Many Presences of Christ," sponsored by the Center for Pastoral Liturgy (now the Notre Dame Center for Liturgy) at the University of Notre Dame.[10] For this I was given the assignment of addressing what *Lutheran* liturgy and sacramental practice might look like if it took seriously the multiple presences of Christ (assembly, word, Eucharist, and ministers) articulated by article 7 of the 1963 Roman Catholic *Constitution on the Sacred Liturgy* (hereafter *CSL*).[11] Arguing that *CSL* 7 itself could easily be read as an affirmation of Lutheran liturgical-theological principles already, this chapter provides both an appreciation for developments in contemporary Roman Catholic and Lutheran liturgical-sacramental practice as well as critique of what is lacking and what remains to be done.

"Eucharistic Reservation and Lutheranism: An Extension of Sunday Worship?" chapter 4, appeared originally in a Festschrift for my colleague, Nathan Mitchell,[12] whose own work on reservation of, communion from, and devotion to the Eucharist outside of the Liturgy, *Cult and Controversy: The Worship of the Eucharist Outside Mass*,[13] has become a modern classic. This chapter surveys a variety of Lutheran practices regarding what is done with the eucharistic

10. This was originally published as "The 'Real' and Multiple 'Presences' of Christ in Contemporary Lutheran Liturgical and Sacramental Practice," in *The Many Presences of Christ*, ed. T. Fitzgerald and D. Lysik (Chicago: Liturgy Training Publications, 1999), 105–120.

11. For the text, see *Vatican Council II: The Conciliar and Post Conciliar Documents*, ed. Austin Flannery, vol. 1, new rev. ed. (Collegeville, MN: The Liturgical Press, 1984), 4–5.

12. *Ars Liturgiae: Worship, Aesthetics, and Practice*, ed. Clare V. Johnson (Chicago: Liturgy Training Publications, 2003), 27–54. It was also presented as a public lecture entitled "Real Presence, Eucharistic Reservation, and Ecumenism," Summer Institute of Christian Spirituality "Soul Food" Lecture Series, Spring Hill College, Mobile, AL, June 6, 2002.

13. Nathan Mitchell, *Cult and Controversy: The Worship of the Eucharist Outside Mass* (New York: Pueblo, 1982).

elements remaining after the Liturgy (practices ranging all the way from irreverent disposal, to reverent consumption, to actual reservation in an aumbry or tabernacle for the communion of the sick) and subjects those practices to critique in light of the current Lutheran rite for the "Sending of Holy Communion"[14] to those unable to be present at public worship, and from the perspectives of Luther and of the history of reservation and communion distribution apart from the Sunday Liturgy in both East and West. I conclude that some form of limited reservation of the Eucharist would seem to be quite permissible from within a Lutheran theological framework.

Chapter 5, "What Is Normative for Contemporary Lutheran Worship? Word and Sacrament as Nonnegotiable," also had its origins in part as a Festschrift essay, this time for Anglican liturgical scholar and friend Bryan Spinks,[15] and, in part, as an invited keynote address for a leadership conference, "Experiencing God Through Preaching and Worship," at the Lutheran School of Theology in Chicago, April 4, 2011.[16] The question of what constitutes a "norm" for Lutheran worship, specifically for the worship of the Evangelical Lutheran Church in America (ELCA), is raised precisely because contemporary Lutheran worship books, such as *Lutheran Book of Worship* (1978), *With One Voice* (1995), and *Evangelical Lutheran Worship* (2006), while published certainly with approval by the church, function today more as "resources for congregational worship" rather than as what might be termed the "authorized worship books" of the church, such as the *Service Book and Hymnal* was in 1958, or as the 1979 *Book of Common Prayer* or the *Missale*

---

14. *Evangelical Lutheran Worship: Pastoral Care* (Minneapolis: Augsburg Fortress, 2008), 81–92.

15. "Is Anything Normative in Contemporary Lutheran Worship?," in *The Serious Business of Worship: Essays in Honour of Bryan D. Spinks*, ed. Melanie Ross and Simon Jones (London: T & T Clark, 2010), 171–84.

16. "What Is Normative in Contemporary Lutheran Worship? Word and Sacrament as Nonnegotiable," *Currents in Theology and Mission* 38, no. 4 (August 2011): 245–55.

Romanum of Pope Paul VI are, respectively, for Episcopalians and Roman Catholics today. This chapter attempts to resolve the question of "normativity" for worship by focusing on what is implied for Lutheran liturgical and sacramental practice in the 1997 ELCA statement, *The Use of the Means of Grace: A Statement on the Practice of Word and Sacrament.*[17] I conclude this chapter by suggesting that in light of this statement if there were no *Lutheran Book of Worship* or *Evangelical Lutheran Worship*, someone would have to invent them in order to fulfill what this statement intends.

There is no question but that the most fruitful ecumenical gift in the past almost fifty years of ecumenical-liturgical convergence and sharing has been the three-year Roman Catholic Sunday and Festival Lectionary, appearing first in the 1969 *Ordo Lectionum Missae*, and adapted now in much of the English-speaking Protestant world within and as the *Revised Common Lectionary.*[18] In chapter 6, "Ordinary Time? The Time after Epiphany and Pentecost: Celebrating the Mystery of Christ in All Its Fullness,"[19] I move from specific issues regarding Baptism and Eucharist to the proclamation of the word in those periods of the liturgical year called by ELCA Lutherans the "Time after Epiphany" and "Time after Pentecost," and called "Sundays of Ordinary Time" by Roman Catholics. The theology of these seasons is, essentially, the theology of Sunday as the original Christian feast day, but how one approaches the Sundays

17. Evangelical Lutheran Church in America, *The Use of the Means of Grace: A Statement on the Practice of Word and Sacrament* (Minneapolis: Augsburg Fortress, 1997). This statement was adopted for guidance and practice by the fifth Biennial Churchwide Assembly of the Evangelical Lutheran Church in America, August 19, 1997.

18. Consultation on Common Texts, CCT, *The Revised Common Lectionary* (Nashville: Abingdon, 1992).

19. An earlier version of this chapter appeared as "*Tempus per annum*: Celebrating the Mystery of Christ in All Its Fullness," *Liturgical Ministry* 17 (Fall 2008): 153–63. This updated version, under the title of "The Extraordinary Nature of Ordinary Time?," was presented as a workshop at The Valparaiso Liturgical Institute, *The Word in Time: Lectionary, Proclamation, and the Church Year*, Valparaiso, IN, April 28–30, 2014.

of these seasons, thanks to the work of Fritz West,[20] depends upon whether or not one employs a "Catholic hermeneutic" of viewing the lectionary and preaching as part of the eucharistic liturgy, an approach shared theoretically also by Lutherans and Episcopalians, or a "Protestant hermeneutic" of viewing the Sunday Liturgy as a preaching service with no Eucharist. At the same time, attention is given here to the relationship between the first reading from the Old, Older, or First Testament and the selected Gospel reading in light of potential theological problems concerning the relationship of Christianity and Judaism.

The next two chapters are both concerned with theological and liturgical issues concerning the Blessed Virgin Mary in an ecumenical context, a topic that has occupied my attention both in my scholarship and teaching for some years as well.[21] Chapter 7, "The Blessed Virgin Mary and Ecumenical Convergence in Doctrine, Doxology, and Devotion," had its origins as an address given to the National Workshop on Christian Unity, Columbus, Ohio, April 8–11, 2013, and is published here for the first time.[22] If this chapter is concerned generally, in light of the various ecumenical dialogues on Mary, with whether or not certain dogmatic questions or devotional practices need any longer be church-dividing within situations of greater communion, chapter 8, "The Virgin of Guadalupe in Ecumenical Context," looks specifically at the place of this particular

---

20. Fritz West, *Scripture and Memory: The Ecumenical Hermeneutic of the Three-Year Lectionaries* (Collegeville, MN: The Liturgical Press, Pueblo Books, 1997).

21. See my "Sub Tuum Praesidium: The Theotokos in Christian Life and Worship Before Ephesus," in *The Place of Christ in Liturgical Prayer: Christology, Trinity and Liturgical Theology*, ed. Bryan Spinks (Collegeville, MN: The Liturgical Press, 2008), 243–267; "The One Mediator, the Saints, and Mary: A Lutheran Reflection," *Worship* 67, no. 3 (1993): 226–38; *The Virgin of Guadalupe: Theological Reflections of an Anglo-Lutheran Liturgist*, foreword by Virgil P. Elizondo, Celebrating Faith: Explorations in Latino Spirituality and Theology Series (Landham, MD: Rowman and Littlefield, 2002); and, as editor and contributor, *American Magnificat: Protestants on Mary of Guadalupe*, ed. Maxwell E. Johnson (Collegeville, MN: The Liturgical Press, 2010).

22. An abridged version of this chapter appears in *Worship* 88, 6 (November 2014): 482–506.

Marian advocation within the changing cultural—Latino/ Hispanic—landscape of American Christianity. Originally presented as the Annual Theotokos Lecture, at Marquette University, Milwaukee, Wisconsin, on November 15, 2009,[23] I argue in this chapter that a place may indeed be found for her within Lutheranism simply because she proclaims the gospel, especially as contained in the words of the *Magnificat*, because, in classic Lutheran theological terms, she embodies for us God's unmerited grace, and because her image and narrative function as a type and model of what the multicultural mestizo church is to become in the world.

The next two chapters deal specifically with ecumenical liturgical issues in relationship to Christian unity. Chapter 9, "*Satis est*: Ecumenical Catalyst or Narrow Reductionism?" a revision of a much earlier essay,[24] was again a plenary address for one of the Institutes of Liturgical Studies at Valparaiso University, Valparaiso, Indiana, this time in 2002.[25] Looking at the frequent Lutheran invocation of the *satis est* principle from *Augustana* VII, in order either to support or challenge Lutheran ecumenical relationships and proposals for Christian unity, I argue, as noted briefly at the beginning of this introduction, for a "liturgical" reading of *Augustana* VII's definition of the church and conclude that what is "sufficient" for the church's spiritual unity should function as a catalyst for pursuing visible Christian unity rather than as a limiting principle restricting that pursuit. Particular attention is given in this chapter to the full

23. An earlier version of this chapter was presented in Spanish, "Santa María de Guadalupe y la Teologia Luterana," to the monks and guests at La Abadía del Tepeyac, Cuautitlán, Mexico, on October 21, 2005, and also as "Introduction: Can Protestants Celebrate the Virgin of Guadalupe?," inJohnson, *American Magnificat*, 1–18.

24. "'*Satis est?*' A Liturgist Looks at the Ecumenical Implications of *Augustana* VII," *Lutheran Forum* 31, 1 (Spring 1997): 12–18.

25. "'Satis Est': Ecumenical Catalyst or Narrow Reductionism?," in *Liturgy in a New Millennium, 2000–2003*, ed. Rhoda Schuler, Institute of Liturgical Studies Occasional Papers #11 (Valparaiso, IN: Institute of Liturgical Studies, 2006), 158–172.

communion relationship between the ELCA and The Episcopal Church as well as to the 1997 *Joint Declaration on Justification* between the Lutheran World Federation and the Roman Catholic Church.

Chapter 10, "Christian Worship and Ecumenism: What Shall We Do Now?" like many of the other chapters in this collection, also began as an invited public lecture, "Liturgy, Ecumenism, and the Pursuit of Christian Unity," presented at Saint Mary Seminary and Graduate School of Theology, for the Week of Prayer for Christian Unity, sponsored by the Roman Catholic Diocese of Cleveland, Ohio, on January 21, 2011.[26] The question of "What shall we do now?" arises from the fact that until the 2011 publication of the translation of the third edition of the *Missale Romanum* of Pope Paul VI, based on the new translation rules contained in the controversial document *Liturgiam Authenticam* in 2001, English-speaking liturgical Christians of several denominations had been sharing with Roman Catholics essentially the same English versions of liturgical greetings and responses, the *Kyrie, Gloria in Excelsis*, Nicene and Apostles' Creeds, *Sanctus*, and *Agnus Dei* within their eucharistic liturgies, as well as the *Te Deum, Benedictus, Magnificat*, and *Nunc Dimittis* at the various hours of daily prayer. This broad ecumenical consensus in the very language of Christian worship has now ceased, at least as far as common texts with English-speaking Roman Catholics go. This chapter offers a critique of this development and its unfortunate ecumenical results and implications, even as it concludes on a more hopeful note for the future.

As noted at the beginning of this introduction, these chapters reflect my ongoing ecumenical conversations with members of other Christian traditions, most especially with Roman Catholic, Eastern and Oriental Orthodox and Catholic, and Anglican Christians. In

26. Another version of this appeared as "Ecumenism and the Study of Liturgy: What Shall We Do Now?," *Liturgical Ministry* 20, *Retrospective: 20 years of Liturgical Ministry* (Winter 2011): 13–21.

so doing I have been guided immensely by the approaches to ecumenism from two contemporary Roman Catholic scholars. First, on the occasion several years ago of his receiving the *Berakah* award from the North American Academy of Liturgy, the great Eastern Rite Catholic liturgiologist, and one of my former teachers, Robert Taft, SJ, made the following statement about ecumenism:

Ecumenism is not just a movement. It is a new way of being Christian. It is also a new way of being a scholar. Ecumenical scholarship means much more than scholarly objectivity, goes much further than just being honest and fair. It attempts to work disinterestedly, serving no cause but the truth wherever it is to be found. It seeks to see things from the other's point of view, to take seriously the other's critique of one's own communion and its historic errors and failings. Like the preamble to Saint Ignatius' *Spiritual Exercises* it seeks to put the best interpretation on what the other does and says, to shine the exposing light of criticism evenly, on the failings of one's own church as well as on those of others. In short, it seeks to move Christian love into the realm of scholarship, and it is the implacable enemy of all forms of bigotry, intolerance, unfairness, selective reporting, and oblique comparisons that contrast the unrealized ideal of one's own church with the less-than-ideal reality of someone else's.[27]

And, second, several years ago, Roman Catholic theologian Hans Küng articulated an ecumenical vision of Christian identity that I still find compelling and one to which I frequently refer. Küng wrote,

a. Who is *Catholic*? Someone who attaches special importance to the Catholic—that is, *entire*, universal, all encompassing, total—Church. In the concrete, to the *continuity* of faith in time and the community of faith in space, maintained in all disruptions.

1. Who is *Protestant*? Someone who attaches special importance in all traditions, doctrines, and practices of the Church to

27. Robert Taft, SJ, "Response to the Berakah Award: Anamnesis," in *Beyond East and West: Problems in Liturgical Understanding*, ed. Robert Taft, SJ, 2nd ed. (Rome: Pontificio Istituto Orientale, 1991), 287.

constant critical recourse to the gospel (Scripture) and to constant, practical *reform* according to the norm of the gospel.

2. But from all this it is clear that "Catholic" and "Protestant" basic attitudes, correctly understood, are by no means mutually exclusive. Today even the "born" Catholic can be truly Protestant and the "born" Protestant truly Catholic in his mentality, so that even now in the whole world there are innumerable Christians who—despite the obstructions of the churches' machinery—do in fact realize a genuine ecumenicity finding its center in the light of the gospel. Being truly Christian today means being an *ecumenical Christian*.[28]

While remaining a confessional and committed Lutheran to the core, I sincerely hope that my own work stands within that ecumenical scholarly approach and understanding articulated by Taft and Küng, and that I emerge in these chapters as one who is indeed a truly "ecumenical Christian," that is, in my case, truly as a Catholic Lutheran, to borrow from my colleague Virgil Elizondo's self-description as a "Protestant Catholic."[29] Indeed, being and becoming "ecumenical Christians" is well summarized in the following litany used each year for the intercessions at Evening Prayer by the monks of Saint John's Abbey, Collegeville, Minnesota, during the Week of Prayer for Christian Unity, January 18–25:

Let us pray that Christians everywhere may heed God's call to become one, holy, catholic and apostolic church, as we say: *Lord, make us one.*
- Lord, bless our brothers and sisters in the Church of Rome; may their preservation of the catholic substance of the faith, their commitment to the historical continuity of the church, and their love for the Eucharist enrich and challenge all Christians.
- Lord, bless our brothers and sisters in the Churches of the East; may they continue to enrich your church by their faith in the Holy Spirit,

28. Hans Küng, *Signposts for the Future: Contemporary Issues Facing the Church* (Garden City, NY: 1978), 94.
29. Justo González, *Mañana: Christian Theology from a Hispanic Perspective*, foreword by Virgilio Elizondo (Nashville: Abingdon Press, 1990), 10.

their love for the Divine Liturgy, and their respect for ecclesiastical tradition.

- Look especially on our brothers and sisters in the Armenian Apostolic Church; may their suffering bear witness to the forgiving love which you have shown us in Christ Jesus.
- Bless our brothers and sisters of the Anglican Communion; may their respect for diversity and individual conscience challenge the whole church, and their treasures of language and music never cease to magnify your holy Name.
- Bless our Lutheran brothers and sisters; may their love for the Scriptures and their faith in your all-sufficient grace help us all to receive your salvation as purest gift.
- Bless our brothers and sisters of the Reformed Tradition; may they continue to edify the church with their preaching and inspire us all by their dedicated work for your kingdom.
- Bless our brothers and sisters of the Free Church Tradition; may their warmth and enthusiasm bring new life to the work and prayer of your church.
- Bless us and all Christians; may we come to that perfect oneness which you have with your Son in the unifying love of the Holy Spirit.[30]

Finally, I wish to express my thanks to the following people who have made this book possible. To my graduate assistant, Mark Roosien, for proofreading the manuscript, to all those who offered helpful comments, responses, and critiques when many of these chapters were delivered originally as public lectures, addresses, or at workshops, and to Michael Gibson of Fortress for seeing this through as a Fortress Press publication.

---

30. *Benedictine Daily Prayer: A Short Breviary*, ed. Maxwell E. Johnson, et. al. (Collegeville, MN: The Liturgical Press, 2005), 1731–32.

Acknowledgements

The author wishes to acknowledge gratefully permission granted for use of the following essays and excerpts:

Abingdon Press for excerpts from *Justo L. González, Mañana: Christian Theology from a Hispanic Perspective* (Nashville: Abingdon, 1990).

Currents in Theology and Mission, for "What is Normative in Contemporary Lutheran Worship? Word and Sacrament as Nonnegotiable," *Currents in Theology and Mission* 38, no. 4 (August 2011): 245–55.

Currents in Theology and Mission for excerpt from José David Rodríguez, Jr., with the assistance of Colleen R. Nelson, "The Virgin of Guadalupe," *Currents in Theology and Mission*, 13, 6 (December 1986).

The Institute of Liturgical Studies, Valparaiso, Indiana, for "Baptismal 'Spirituality' in the Early Church and its Implications for the Church Today," in *Worship, Culture, and Catholicity 1997–1999*, ed. Rhoda Schuler, Institute of Liturgical Studies Occasional Papers #10 (Valparaiso, IN: Institute of Liturgical Studies, 2005), 188–211, and

"'Satis Est': Ecumenical Catalyst or Narrow Reductionism?," in *Liturgy in a New Millennium, 2000–2003,* ed. Rhoda Schuler, Institute of Liturgical Studies Occasional Papers #11 (Valparaiso, IN: Institute of Liturgical Studies, 2006), 158–72.

The Liturgical Press, Collegeville, Minnesota, for "Ecumenism and the Study of Liturgy: What Shall We Do Now?," *Liturgical Ministry* 20, *Retrospective: 20 years of Liturgical Ministry* (Winter 2011): 13–21; "Introduction: Can Protestants Celebrate the Virgin of Guadalupe?," in*American Magnificat: Protestants on Mary of Guadalupe*, ed. Maxwell E. Johnson (Collegeville: The Liturgical Press, 2010), 1–18; "The Holy Spirit and Lutheran Liturgical-Sacramental Worship," in *The Spirit in Worship—Worship in the Spirit*, ed. Bryan Spinks and Teresa Berger (Collegeville: The Liturgical Press, Pueblo, 2009), 155–178; and "*Tempus per annum*: Celebrating the Mystery of Christ in All Its Fullness," *Liturgical Ministry* 17 (Fall 2008): 153–63.

Liturgy Training Publications, Chicago, Illinois, for "Eucharistic Reservation and Lutheranism: An Extension of the Sunday Worship?," in*Ars Liturgiae: Worship, Aesthetics, and Practice*, ed. Clare V. Johnson (Chicago: Liturgy Training Publications, 2003), 27–54.

Lutherisches Verlagshaus GmbH for excerpts from Peter Brunner, *Worship in the Name of Jesus*, trans., M. H . Bertram (St. Louis: Concordia Publishing House, 1968).

Moody Publishers for excerpt from J. Dwight Pentecost, *Romanism in the Light of Scripture* (Chicago: Moody Press, 1962).

Notre Dame Center for Liturgy, Notre Dame, Indiana, for "The 'Real' and Multiple 'Presences' of Christ in Contemporary Lutheran Liturgical and Sacramental Practice," in *The Many Presences of Christ,* ed. T. Fitzgerald and D. Lysik (Chicago: Liturgy Training Publications, 1999), 105–20.

Pax Christi USA for the *Litany of Mary of Nazareth* (Erie, PA: Pax Christi, no date).
  Word and World for excerpt from Bonnie Jensen, "We Sing Mary's Song," *Word and World* 7/1 (1987), 81-82.

Unless otherwise noted, all biblical citations are from the *New Revised Standard Version Bible* (National Council of Churches, 1989).

1

—

Baptismal Spirituality in the Early Church and Its Implications for the Church Today

In an essay entitled "The Sacraments in Wesleyan Perspective," originally published in 1988, British Methodist liturgical theologian Geoffrey Wainwright says, "Without the heartbeat of the sacraments at its center, a church will lack confidence about the gospel message and about its own ability to proclaim that message in evangelism, to live it out in its own internal fellowship, and to embody it in service to the needy."[1] And, second, in an essay appearing originally in 1993, "Renewing Worship: The Recovery of Classical Patterns," he writes that "[a] deeper replunging into its own tradition will, in my judgment, be necessary if the church is to survive in recognizable form, particularly in our western culture."[2] The "heartbeat of the

---

1. G. Wainwright, "The Sacraments in Wesleyan Perspective," in *Worship with One Accord: Where Liturgy and Ecumenism Embrace*, ed. G. Wainwright (New York: Oxford University Press, 1997), 106.
2. G. Wainwright, "Renewing Worship: The Recovery of Classical Patterns," in Wainwright, *Worship with One Accord*, 138.

sacraments" at the very center of the church's life, and the need for "a deeper replunging into its own tradition," provide the overall focus for this chapter, that is, looking at the notion of baptismal spirituality in the early Christian churches and its usefulness or implications for the life of the church today. In doing so, I wish to divide my comments into three sections: (1) Not Early Christian Baptismal *Spirituality* but *Spiritualities*; (2) The So-Called Golden Age of the Baptismal Process; and (3) The Implications or Usefulness of This Spirituality for the Church Today.

Not Early Christian Baptismal *Spirituality*
but *Spiritualities*

It is often said that if early Christianity had used the later Roman Catholic terminology of *Blessed Sacrament* to refer to any of its sacramental rites, it would have used it to refer to Baptism and not to the Eucharist (a term, by the way, actually used by Luther as early as 1519 to talk about Baptism[3]). But, of course, what would have been meant by *Baptism* in this early context was not simply the water bath and trinitarian formula, the later Scholastic precision of *matter* and *form*, or even the Reformation language of *water* and the *word*, but would have included the entire catechetical and sacramental-ritual process by which Christians, in the words of Tertullian, were "made, not born," that foundational and formative experience of church leading, at least in the case of adult converts, from initial conversion and inquiry all the way to full incorporation within the life of the church. That is, this "Blessed Sacrament" of Baptism in early Christianity encompassed what the Lutheran World Federation

---

3. See "The Holy and Blessed Sacrament of Baptism," in *Luther's Works*, vol. 35: *Word and Sacrament* 1, ed. by E. T. Bachmann (Philadelphia/St. Louis: Fortress Press and Concordia Publishing House, 1960), 23–44.

Chicago Statement on Worship and Culture: Baptism and Rites of Life Passage describes as

> a) formation in the one faith (traditionally known as the catechumenate), b) the water-bath, and c) the incorporation of the baptized into the whole Christian community and its mission. This latter incorporation is expressed by the newly baptized being led to the table of the Lord's Supper, the very table where their baptismal identity will also be strengthened and re-affirmed throughout their life.[4]

Such an all-encompassing view of Baptism and the need for solid formation in the Christian faith brought with it several implications for the day-to-day organization of the church itself. While our evidence is not what we wish it would be for the first three centuries of the Christian era, there is no question but that the way of forming new Christians through this ritual process was the task of the whole church itself, all the way from the agapaic life of the community, especially those whose lives witnessed directly to the gospel in the presence of others, to the various ministries needed throughout the catechumenate and within the celebration of the rites themselves. An early church order, the so-called *Apostolic Tradition,* ascribed to Hippolytus of Rome in the early third century (ca. 215), but which is probably neither apostolic, nor of Hippolytan authorship, nor Roman, nor early third century,[5] testifies to this variety of people involved in the process, with special roles assigned to sponsors who

---

4. Lutheran World Federation, *Chicago Statement on Worship and Culture: Baptism and Rites of Life Passage* (Geneva 1998), para. 2.1.

5. For recent studies see Paul F. Bradshaw, Maxwell E. Johnson, and L. Edward Phillips, *The Apostolic Tradition: A Commentary,* Hermeneia (Minneapolis: Fortress Press, 2002); W. Kinzig, C. Markschies, and M. Vinzent, *Tauffragen und Bekenntnis: Studien zur sogennanten 'Traditio Apostolica" zu den 'Interrogationes de fide' und zum 'Römischen Glaubensbekenntnis'* (New York: Walter de Gruyter, 1999); M. Metzger, "Nouvelles perspectives pour la prétendue *Tradition apostolique,*" *Ecclesia Orans* 5 (1988): 241–59; Metzger, "Enquêtes autour de la prétendue *Tradition apostolique,*" *Ecclesia Orans* 9 (1992): 7–36; Metzger, "A propos des règlements écclesiastiques et de la prétendue *Tradition apostolique,*" *Revue des sciences religieuses* 66 (1992): 249–61.

present and testify to the worthiness of the baptismal candidates, to lay and ordained catechists, to deacons, presbyters, and the bishop, who, as the chief pastor, had the responsibility of overseeing the entire process and concluded the baptismal rite itself with a hand-laying gesture of pneumatic blessing and paternity, a kiss, and welcome into the eucharistic communion of the church.[6] Other documents, such as the late first- or early second-century *Didache,* or *Teaching of the Twelve Apostles,* underscore the involvement of the whole community in the prebaptismal fast that would have been undertaken by those preparing for Baptism.[7] Indeed, the royal priesthood of the faithful signified throughout the baptismal process and into which the neophytes were incorporated was regularly exercised in the eucharistic assembly, as we know already from Justin the Martyr in the mid second-century,[8] and from the mid third-century Syrian church order, the *Didascalia Apostolorum,*[9] with various roles for lectors; door keepers; even widows and, possibly, *women* presbyters; cantors; deacons, both male and female; presbyters; and bishops, with the faithful themselves presenting the "gifts" for the Meal and for the poor and offering prayers of intercession for the church and the world. In many ways, the liturgical assembly itself was but the gathering of the church to exercise its common baptismal priesthood before God, in union with the one high priest of the church, Jesus Christ, in the power of his Holy Spirit.

Because of Baptism, that is, the life-shaping direction of the whole baptismal process, it is no wonder that early Christians, especially people like Tertullian and Cyprian in the North African West,

6. Bradshaw, Johnson, and Phillips, *The Apostolic Tradition,* 82–135.
7. For a text of the *Didache,* see Kurt Niederwimmer, *The Didache,* Hermeneia (Minneapolis: Fortress Press, 1998), 59–130.
8. Justin Martyr, *First Apology,* 61.
9. S. Brock and M. Vasey, *The Liturgical Portions of the Didascalia,* Grove Liturgical Study 29 (Bramcote/Nottingham: Grove Books, Ltd., 1982).

Gregory Thaumaturgos (the Wonder Worker) in the Syrian East, and Origen of Alexandria in Egypt, struggled with the question of how to treat serious postbaptismal sin (e.g., what is sometimes referred to as the traditional triad of apostasy, adultery, and murder). And it is no wonder that after such "shipwreck" on the rock of postbaptismal sin, the answer given to this problem was nothing other than a "return to Baptism" itself through the process of public and "canonical penance," a process that mirrored the rigors of the catechumenate itself, and a process understood, in the words of Tertullian, to be a "plank" thrown to the drowning sinner as one more chance, but *only* one more chance, to get it right.[10] If the Eucharist was both the culmination and the ongoing repeatable sacrament of baptismal initiation, then canonical penance was the way of return for the excommunicated, those cut off from eucharistic communion, to the regular sacramental life of the church. Together with catechumens and the "elect," that is, those in the final stages of baptismal preparation, these penitents would be regularly dismissed with prayer and hand laying from the Sunday assembly after the Liturgy of the Word, and, after a designated time of penance (usually determined according to the gravity of their sin), would be reconciled with Christ and the church through the hand-laying absolution of the bishop, an event that in the later Roman tradition would take place with great solemnity on Holy ("Maundy") Thursday. Eucharist, penitence, and, indeed, all of ecclesial life in early Christianity seems to have flowed from the all-encompassing catechetical and sacramental-ritual process of Baptism, just as later evidence for early Christian proclamation of the word stems, in large part, from extant pre- and postbaptismal catechetical homilies.

---

10. Tertullian, *De Poenitentia* 7. On the process of "canonical penance" in early Christianity, see J. Dallen, *The Reconciling Community: The Rite of Penance* (Collegeville, MN: Pueblo, 1986).

Unfortunately, we are not completely certain about the overall *contents* of specific catechetical instruction provided to catechumens within the churches of the first three centuries. From scattered references throughout early Christian writings, however, it is quite clear that some kind of explanation of the Scriptures in relationship to salvation in Christ along with continual ethical or moral formation in the life of the Christian community were essential components of this process. The first six chapters of the *Didache*, for example, describe what is called "The Two Ways," that of life and death. Significantly, the contents of these first six chapters are not concerned with Christian *doctrine* but focus, instead, on the Ten Commandments and the type of ethical-moral life expected from those who are to be members of Christ through Baptism. Similarly, chapter 20 of the *Apostolic Tradition* refers to an examination of those who have completed the catechumenate and now desire to enter the next stage of the process—"election"—leading more immediately to Baptism. Again, the questions they are asked at this point are not questions about doctrine but about the quality of their lives. Chapter 20 directs,

> And when those appointed to receive Baptism are chosen, their life having been examined (if they lived virtuously while they were catechumens and if they honored the widows, and if they visited those who are sick, and if they fulfilled every good work), and when those who brought them in testify on his behalf that he acted thus, then let them hear the gospel.[11]

We Lutherans tend to become a bit uncomfortable with a process that places so much emphasis upon the moral life and, apparently, so little on doctrine. How, we might ask, can someone seek to become Christian if they haven't heard or don't hear the gospel

---

11. Bradshaw, Johnson, and Phillips, *The Apostolic Tradition*, 104.

(cf. Rom. 10:17)? Yet, as recent studies are beginning to show,[12] it is quite possible that in early Christianity, catechumens themselves, as the above text from *Apostolic Tradition* 20 seems to imply, did not "hear," and, hence, were not even introduced to, the "gospel" or Gospels, until they were elected to the final stage of baptismal preparation. Formation thus had more to do with an apprenticeship in learning to *live* as Christians. And, if we are to believe the standard textbook theory that the regular catechumenate in the pre-Nicene church could last as long as three years in duration, this is a rather long time for "converts" not to be introduced to the very central texts of the Christian tradition. Yet, some remnant of this process may, in fact, be contained in the seventh- or eighth-century *Gelasian Sacramentary*, where, during the third week of Lent, the "elect," now by this time clearly infants brought by their parents to public catechesis, received the Gospels themselves by means of an extended introduction to each one by a deacon.[13] While the doctrinal Lutheran in me bristles a bit at this, I wonder if Luther himself didn't intuit this kind of early Christian baptismal process in the very organization of his *Small Catechism*, where instruction in the meaning of the Ten Commandments comes *first* before everything else and, so, *precedes* that of the Apostles' Creed, the Lord's Prayer, and the sacraments.

Nevertheless, if Baptism in early Christianity shaped the whole of Christian life and identity and fostered a "spirituality" or way of life in the Holy Spirit that was ecclesial, ethical, social, and sacramental, the baptismal liturgy, including its eucharistic culmination, as the church's great "School of Prayer," also shaped the teaching or doctrine of the church itself. Although true prayer is always a gift

---

12. See Paul F. Bradshaw, *Reconstructing Early Christian Worship* (Collegeville, MN: Pueblo, 2010), 55–68.
13. See E. C. Whitaker, *Documents of the Baptismal Liturgy* (hereafter, *DBL*), rev. and expanded Maxwell E. Johnson (Collegeville, MN: Pueblo, 2003), 218–21.

of the Holy Spirit (see Rom. 8:26–27 and Gal. 4:6–7) and cannot adequately be "taught," the great gift of the church's liturgical tradition is that it provides both a language and structure *for* prayer. In other words, as early Christianity knew even without written liturgical texts, the way to learn and teach Christian prayer is to learn from the liturgy itself how it is that the church actually prays in its assemblies. Within early Christianity much of this happened simply as the result of the catechumens' ongoing participation in the liturgical life of the church through the daily public gatherings for what came to be called the Divine Office or Liturgy of the Hours and the Sunday eucharistic liturgy. And it is the very structure and contents of this prayer of the church that provided a model for all of Christian prayer, namely, that Christian prayer is "trinitarian" in structure and focus. That is, Christian prayer is addressed *to* God, "our Abba, Father," *through* Jesus Christ the Son, our great high priest and mediator, *in* the Holy Spirit, the Comforter, the Paraclete, the Counselor, who leads us by word and sacrament to confess that Jesus is Lord (see 1 Cor. 12:3). Note, for example, the concluding formula for the Prayer of the Day still in our own worship books: "Through your Son Jesus Christ our Lord who lives and reigns with you and the Holy Spirit, one God, both now and forever." Or, note the concluding doxology at the end of the Great Thanksgiving: "Through him, with him, in him, in the unity of the Holy Spirit, all honor and glory is yours, almighty Father, now and forever. Amen."

Furthermore, an ancient Christian principle, often summarized by the Latin phrase, *lex orandi . . . lex credendi*, states that the "rule of praying establishes the rule of believing." That is, the faith of the church is both constituted and expressed by the prayer of the church. Indeed, the liturgy is not only the "school for prayer," but also the "school for faith," and, as such, serves as a continual formative fitting "text" for all the baptized themselves in their lifelong process of continual formation in the faith. Long before there was an Apostles' or Nicene Creed, or an explicit "doctrine" of the Trinity, it was through the Prayer of Blessing or Thanksgiving over the baptismal waters, through the candidate's threefold confession of faith in the Father, Son, and Holy Spirit in the context of Baptism itself ("Do you believe in . . . ?" "I believe . . . "), and through the great *eucharistia* over the bread and cup of the Lord's Supper, consisting of *praise* to God for the work of creation and redemption, *thanksgiving* for the life, death, resurrection, and ascension of Christ, and *invocation* of the Holy Spirit, that the church professed its faith in the Trinity by means of *doxology* and *praise*. In other words, it was the *Liturgy*—baptismal and eucharistic—that assisted in forming *orthodox* Christian teaching. That is, orthodox trinitarian and christological doctrine developed, in large part, from the church at prayer, as the baptismal-credal profession of faith gave rise to the official creeds themselves; as prayer *to* Christ contributed to understanding his *homoousios* with the Father; as the Holy Spirit's *divine* role in Baptism shaped the theology of the Spirit's divinity in Athanasius, the Cappadocian Fathers, and the Council of Constantinople; and even as early devotion to Mary as *Theotokos* gave rise, in part, to the decree of the Council of Ephesus. While *orthodoxy* means "right thinking" or "right opinion," such right thinking developed, at least in part, from the doxology of the church, where several of our central Christian doctrines were prayed liturgically long before they were formalized dogmatically.[14] Indeed, trinitarian faith was born in the font and nurtured and sustained at the table, good enough reason, in my opinion, to be very cautious today of those who would replace the Liturgy with something else in the name of contemporary "relevance" or "hospitality to seekers"

---

14. See my recent study, *Praying and Believing in Early Christianity: The Interplay between Christian Worship and Doctrine* (Collegeville, MN: Michael Glazier, 2013), where I treat these issues in detail.

or of those who so tinker with classic liturgical formulas that one is left wondering if it is the Triune God of Scripture and the classic tradition who is intended any longer.[15] Careless tinkering with the church's *lex orandi* can have drastic consequences for the church's *lex credendi*.

There is, therefore, not one baptismal spirituality in early Christianity but several complementary baptismal *spiritualities*. In the New Testament itself we are presented with a rich mosaic of baptismal images: forgiveness of sins and the gift of the Holy Spirit (Acts 2:38); new birth through water and the Holy Spirit (John 3:5; Titus 3:5–7); putting off of the "old nature" and "putting on the new," that is, "being clothed in the righteousness of Christ" (Gal. 3:27; Col. 3:9–10); initiation into the "one body" of the Christian community (1 Cor. 12:13; see also Acts 2:42); washing, sanctification, and justification in Christ and the Holy Spirit (1 Cor. 6:11); enlightenment (Heb. 6:4; 10:32; 1 Pet. 2:9); being "anointed" and "sealed" by the Holy Spirit (2 Cor. 1:21–22; 1 John 2:20, 27); being "sealed" or "marked" as belonging to God and God's people (2 Cor. 1:21–22; Eph. 1:13–14; 4:30; Rev. 7:3); and, of course, being joined to Christ through participation in his death, burial, and resurrection (Rom. 6:3–11; Col. 2:12–15).[16] From this mosaic, two will stand out with particular emphasis in early Christianity: Baptism as new birth through water and the Holy Spirit (John 3:5ff.); and Baptism as being united with Christ in his death, burial, and resurrection (Rom. 6:3–11). And, as Christianity developed and spread throughout the diverse cultures of the ancient world, the "one baptism" (cf. Eph. 4:5) of the church was expressed by means of a variety of different liturgical practices and interpretations within the distinct Christian

15. Cf. Wainwright, "The Sacraments in Wesleyan Perspective," 120 and 122.
16. Biblical texts are taken from the *New Revised Standard Version Bible*, National Council of the Churches of Christ, 1989.

churches. For the early Syriac-speaking Christians of East Syria, living in what is modern-day Iraq and Iran, the catechumenate itself was quite minimal, it seems, and the rites themselves *may* have taken place on Epiphany, understood as the great Theophany of Christ in the Jordan, his own baptismal "birth" in the Jordan, a "new birth" rite understood as the means by which the Holy Spirit, through a *prebaptismal* anointing, assimilated the neophyte to the messianic priesthood and kingship of Christ.[17] For the early Greek- and Coptic-speaking Egyptian Christian tradition, known by Clement and Origen of Alexandria, a forty-day prebaptismal catechumenate commencing on Epiphany, again understood as the feast of Jesus' Baptism, seems to have led to Baptism on the sixth day of the sixth week of this post-Epiphany fast (sometime in mid-February),[18] and the rite itself, again focusing possibly on a prebaptismal anointing, appears to have been understood not in terms of death and resurrection imagery but rather as "crossing the Jordan" with our Joshua-Jesus. For Origen himself the imagery of catechumenate and Baptism had little to do with the paschal language of crossing the Red Sea or death and burial in Christ. Rather, for him, the exodus from Egypt signified entrance into the forty-year catechumenate, and it was the Israelites' crossing of the Jordan that functioned as the great Old Testament baptismal typology.[19] In fact, within the

17. On this tradition, see especially the work of G. Winkler, "The Original Meaning of the Prebaptismal Anointing and Its Implications," in *Living Water, Sealing Spirit: Readings on Christian Initiation*, hereafter, *LWSS*, ed. M. Johnson (Collegeville, MN: Pueblo, 1995), 58–81; and the recent study of K. McDonnell, *The Baptism of Jesus in the Jordan: The Trinitarian and Cosmic Order of Salvation* (Collegeville, MN: Michael Glazier, 1996).

18. On this, see Paul F. Bradshaw and Maxwell E. Johnson, *The Origins of Feasts, Fasts, and Seasons in Early Christianity* (Collegeville, MN: Pueblo, 2011), 92–108.

19. On Origen's baptismal theology, see J. Laporte, "Models from Philo in Origen's Teaching on Original Sin," in *LWSS*, 101–17; C. Blanc, "Le Baptême d'après Origène," *Studia Patristica* 11 (1972): 113–24; H. Crouzel, "Origène et la structure du sacrement," in *Bulletin de littérature ecclésiastique* 2 (1962): 81–92; J. Daniélou, *The Bible and The Liturgy* (Notre Dame: University of Notre Dame Press, 1956), 99–113; and J. Daniélou, *Origen* (New York: Sheed and Ward, 1955), 52–61.

first three centuries of the church's existence it was only among the Latin-speaking Christians of the North African churches, and the undoubtedly multiethnic groups that made up the Christian communities living in Rome, where we begin to encounter both the possibility of Baptism at Easter and the concomitant use of Romans 6 theology to interpret such a practice. But even here we should be cautious. Our major evidence for this is Tertullian, who writes,

> The Passover [i.e., Easter] provides the day of most solemnity for baptism, for then was accomplished our Lord's passion, *and into it we are baptized.* . . . After that, Pentecost is a most auspicious period for arranging baptisms, for during it our Lord's resurrection was several times made known among the disciples, and the grace of the Holy Spirit first given. . . . For all that, every day is a Lord's day: any hour, any season, is suitable for baptism. If there is any difference of solemnity, it makes no difference to the grace.[20]

It is thus not known if Easter Baptism was but a *theological* preference for Tertullian himself, which he wished to advocate, or a practice that he actually knew. In fact, our *only* clear reference to Easter Baptism in the first few centuries is Hippolytus of Rome's *Commentary on Daniel*, where he refers to the "Bath" being open at Pascha, but it is not clear if at Rome this was the only occasion or not. For that matter, if Hippolytus himself had anything to do with the *Apostolic Tradition*, it is interesting to note that nowhere in that document is Easter ever referred to as the occasion for Baptism. While the description of Baptism taking place at the end of an all-night Saturday vigil is certainly consistent with Easter Baptism, the document does *not* say that it *was* Easter and, for that matter, all-night vigils were more common in Christian antiquity than in the later tradition.

Similarly, apart from the possibility of a forty-day prebaptismal catechumenate in early Egypt, we simply do not know the length or

20. *DBL*, 10 (emphasis added).

duration of the final preparation period elsewhere, or when during the year it may have taken place. While *Apostolic Tradition* 17 refers to the possibility of a total of three years preparation, other sources suggest a total of three *months*, and contemporary scholarship has argued that a pattern of three *weeks* of final preparation may have been customary in several places.[21]

My point in all this is that today, in spite of the several common elements we might note regarding the baptismal process in the early church, we must be very cautious about assuming a single, universal, normative, and fixed pattern or interpretation of Baptism in early Christianity. Above all, we need to avoid the standard cliché that "the early church baptized at Easter" and knew a process consisting of, for example, a primitive period of catechesis corresponding to what would later become Lent with Baptism at Easter interpreted according to Paul's theology of death and burial in Christ expressed in Romans 6. What we do know about early Christian baptismal practices and interpretation disagrees with that assumption. While a Romans 6 theology of Baptism is important, and certainly cherished by us Lutherans for good theological reasons, we Lutherans simply have to get used to the fact that Paul's baptismal theology was relatively silent in the first few centuries of the church and was only rediscovered in the mid-to-late fourth century.

This silence of Saint Paul in the early centuries should speak volumes about notions of early Christian baptismal spirituality. From the early Syrian—and possibly Egyptian—traditions comes a whole cluster of baptismal images that have little to do with passing from death to life, or with sharing in the dying and rising of Christ through baptism. Such images, noted the late Mark Searle, include seeing the font as *womb*, rather than tomb, literally called the *Jordan*

---

21. See Maxwell E. Johnson, "From Three Weeks to Forty Days: Baptismal Preparation and the Origins of Lent," in *LWSS*, 118–36.

itself in some traditions, images like "adoption, divinization, sanctification, gift of the Spirit, indwelling, glory, power, wisdom, rebirth, restoration, [and] mission."[22] Hence, a spirituality based on Baptism as death, burial, and resurrection is one powerful way of articulating a way of Christian identity, life, and service. A spirituality based on the new birth theology of John 3, or on images of baptismal adoption, is yet another. For the one spirituality, Christ's own death and resurrection is of paramount importance. For the other spirituality, the incarnation itself is viewed as salvific, as, for example, in the words of Athanasius: "God became what we are so that we could be made [*theopoiethomen*] what he is";[23] that is, through Baptism we become by adoption what Christ is by nature. For the one spirituality, Baptism is the *tomb* in which the sinful self is put to death in Christ. For the other spirituality, Baptism is the *womb* through which the Mothering Spirit of God (Spirit is feminine and actually called *Mother* in the early Syriac tradition) gives new birth and new life. For the one spirituality, Adam is to be put to death. For the other spirituality, Adam is to be sought after and rescued from sin, death, and bondage. For the one spirituality, Easter is *the* feast par excellence, the very center of the liturgical year. For the other spirituality, it is the Theophany of Christ in the Jordan at Epiphany, the very manifestation of the Trinity in the waters of the font, that assumes great importance. Indeed, how one thinks of Baptism will shape how one views Christian life and identity. Even if these two views are not contradictory or exclusive, they did and do shape distinct emphases and orientations to which we should pay attention still today.[24]

---

22. M. Searle, "Infant Baptism Reconsidered," in *LWSS*, 385.

23. Athanasius, *De Incarnatione Verbi Dei*, 54.

24. I explore all of this more fully in my book, *Images of Baptism* (Chicago: Liturgy Training Publications, 2001; reprinted by Ashland City, TN: Order of Saint Luke Publications, 2013).

The So-Called Golden Age of the Baptismal Process

We liturgists are often accused of trying to make the contemporary church fit a presumed normative liturgical pattern as it is reconstructed from the various extant sources of the fourth and fifth centuries, that period Johannes Quasten called "the Golden Age of Greek Patristic Literature."[25] I doubt that the Roman Catholic Rites of Christian Initiation of Adults (RCIA)[26] or the recent Lutheran adaptation of the catechumenal process, *Welcome to Christ,*[27] *Renewing Worship: Holy Baptism and Related Rites,*[28] and *Evangelical Lutheran Worship (ELW),*[29] do much to persuade our critics that some kind of modern liturgical repristination of this "Golden Age" is not being intended today. Even the subtitle of Edward Yarnold's revised edition of his *The Awe-Inspiring Rites of Christian Initiation: The Origins of the R.C.I.A.* would seem to provide, quite unintentionally, some fuel for such a critique. And, of course, it is true that our contemporary knowledge of the early Christian baptismal process is due, in large part, to the documentary evidence that exists from this period, namely, the extant catechetical homilies of the great "mystagogues" (e.g., Cyril of Jerusalem, John Chrysostom, and Theodore of Mopsuestia for the East, and Ambrose of Milan for the West).

At the same time, however, it ought not be forgotten that the various cultural and social shifts in the Constantinian era and beyond brought with them the need for the churches themselves to respond to those changing circumstances. One of those responses was the first

25. This is the subtitle of Quasten's third volume of his monumental work, *Patrology* (Utrecht: Spectrum, 1966).
26. *The Rites of the Catholic Church,* vol. 1 (Collegeville, MN: The Liturgical Press, 1990), 1–515.
27. Evangelical Lutheran Church in America, *Welcome to Christ: Lutheran Rites for the Catechumenate* (Minneapolis: Augsburg Fortress, 1997).
28. Evangelical Lutheran Church in America, *Renewing Worship: Holy Baptism and Related Rites* (Minneapolis: Augsburg Fortress, 2002), 25–54.
29. Evangelical Lutheran Church in America, *Evangelical Lutheran Worship: Leader's Desk Edition* (Minneapolis: Augsburg Fortress, 2006), 592–95.

of several great periods of liturgical reform and renewal in the history of the church.[30] But, as recent liturgical scholarship has demonstrated, what we see in this first reform or renewal is the development of what has been called "liturgical homogeneity," wherein through a process of assimilation to the practices of the great patriarchal and pilgrimage churches of the world—for example, Rome, Jerusalem, Alexandria, Antioch, and Constantinople—and through the cross-fertilization of borrowing and exchange, distinctive local practices and theologies disappear in favor of others becoming copied, adapted, and synthesized.[31] Therefore, what we often appeal to as *the* early Christian pattern for Baptism is but the end result of a process of assimilation, adaptation, and change, wherein some of the distinctive and rich theologies and spiritualites of an earlier period either disappear or are subordinated to others.

As a result of "mass conversions" in the wake of Constantine's own "conversion,"[32] the subsequent legalization and eventual adoption of Christianity as the official religion of the Roman Empire, and the Trinitarian and christological decisions of the first ecumenical councils, this fourth- and fifth-century "homogenization" in liturgical practice is easily demonstrated. Thanks to the extant

---

30. The other periods of liturgical reform and renewal in the history of the church are, of course, Charlemagne's wholesale adoption of the Roman Rite as *the* normative rite for Western Europe in the ninth century, the sixteenth-century Protestant and Catholic Reformations and their liturgical products, and, of course, the period of ecumenical liturgical convergence following the Second Vatican Council and continuing still today among us.

31. See P. Bradshaw, "The Homogenization of Christian Liturgy—Ancient and Modern: Presidential Address," *Studia Liturgica* 26 (1996): 1–15.

32. How widespread such "mass conversion" actually was in this time period has been questioned recently by R. Stark, *The Rise of Christianity: A Sociologist Reconsiders History* (Princeton: Princeton University Press, 1996), who suggests that a major part of the increase in Christianity had to do, among other things, with the large number of women, fertility, and substantially higher birth rates among Christians in this period in distinction to their pagan neighbors. Similarly, according to Stark, Christianity's appeal to women, its high view of marriage for both partners, its prohibition of abortion and infanticide, especially of female babies, and its offer of status and protection to women, and the fact that women were highly influential in the church, were also strong contributing factors to its success in the Greco-Roman world.

catechetical homilies noted above, while some local diversity continued to exist, the following came to characterize the overall ritual pattern of Baptism throughout the Christian East:

(1) the adoption of paschal Baptism and the now forty-day season of Lent as the time of prebaptismal (daily) catechesis on Scripture, Christian life, and, especially, the Nicene Creed for the *photizomenoi* (those to be "enlightened");

(2) the use of "scrutinies" (examinations) and daily exorcisms throughout the period of final baptismal preparation;

(3) the development of specific rites called *apotaxis* (renunciation) and *syntaxis* (adherence) as demonstrating a "change of ownership" for the candidates;

(4) the development of ceremonies like the solemn *traditio* and *redditio symboli* (the presentation and "giving back" of the Nicene Creed);

(5) the reinterpretation of the once pneumatic prebaptismal anointing as a rite of exorcism, purification, and preparation for combat against Satan;

(6) the rediscovery and use of Romans 6 as the dominant paradigm for interpreting the baptismal immersion or submersion as entrance into the "tomb" with Christ;

(7) the introduction of a postbaptismal anointing associated with the gift and "seal" of the Holy Spirit; and

(8) the use of Easter week as time for "mystagogical catechesis" (an explanation of the sacramental "mysteries" the newly initiated had experienced).

Although a similar overall pattern also existed in the West, Western sources display some significant differences. Ambrose of Milan, for example, witnesses to a postbaptismal rite of footwashing (*pedilavium*) as an integral component of baptism.[33] Some sources from Rome (e.g., the *Letter of John the Deacon to Senarius*[34]) and North Africa (Augustine[35]) indicate the presence of three public scrutinies (including even physical examinations) held on the third, fourth, and fifth Sundays of Lent. And, thanks to an important fifth-century letter from Pope Innocent I to Decentius of Gubbio,[36] it is clear that at Rome itself the pattern of episcopal hand laying with prayer and second postbaptismal anointing was understood as an essential aspect and was associated explicitly with the bishop's prerogative in "giving" the Holy Spirit.

The adoption of several of these ceremonies for the preparation and Baptism of candidates was, undoubtedly, the result of the church seeking to ensure that its sacramental life would continue to have some kind of integrity when, in a changed social and cultural context, where Christianity was now favored by the emperor, authentic conversion and properly motivated desire to enter the Christian community could no longer be assumed automatically. Defective motivations for "converting" to Christianity included the desire to marry a Christian, as well as the seeking after political or economic gain in a society having become increasingly "Christianized." And, since it was thought that the forgiveness of sins that Baptism conveyed could only be obtained once, with the exception of the one-time postbaptismal "canonical penance," there was a widespread tendency to *delay* Baptism as long as possible in order to be more sure of winning ultimate salvation. Even Constantine himself was not baptized until he was on his deathbed. Because entry into the catechumenate assured one's status as a Christian, the postponement

---

33. See Edward Yarnold, *The Awe-Inspiring Rites of Initiation: The Origins of the R.C.I.A.* (Collegeville, MN: The Liturgical Press, 1994), 121–23.
34. *DBL*, 208–12.
35. Ibid, 145–47.
36. Ibid, 205–6.

of Baptism became a common practice in this period and there were those, who, like Constantine, remained catechumens for life. Indeed, as the experience of Augustine himself demonstrates,[37] it became common in some places to enroll infants in the catechumenate and then postpone their Baptism until later in life, if ever. Similarly, as the rites themselves take on either numerous ritual elements or interpretations of the rites from the context of the Greco-Roman mystery religions, which heightened dramatically the experience of those being initiated, the overall intent was surely to impress upon the catechumens and elect the seriousness of the step they were taking.[38]

It is not, however, only the baptismal candidates who seem to have regularly experienced this process. Egeria, the late fourth-century Spanish pilgrim to Jerusalem near the end of Cyril's episcopate, records in her travel diary that, along with the candidates and their sponsors, members of the faithful also filled the Church of the Holy Sepulchre in Jerusalem for the daily catechetical lectures of the bishop. "At ordinary services when the bishop sits and preaches," she writes, "the faithful utter exclamations, but when they come and hear him explaining the catechesis, their exclamations are louder . . . ; and . . . they ask questions on each point." Further, during the Easter week of mystagogy she notes that the applause of the newly baptized and faithful "is so loud that it can be heard outside the church." Because of this, she states that "all the people in these parts are able to follow the Scriptures when they are read in church."[39]

Designed, of course, with adult converts in mind, the overall ritual process of Baptism in these several sources was to be shortlived, due, according to John Baldovin, to its success.[40] In other words,

---

37. *Confessions* 1.11.
38. Yarnold, *The Awe-Inspiring Rites of Initiation*, 59–66.
39. J. Wilkinson, *Egeria's Travels* (London: SPCK, 1971), 144–46.

it eventually died out, in part at least because, apparently, it had worked and, for good or ill, the empire had become "Christian!" The North African controversy between "Pelagianism" and Augustine over the long-standing practice of infant initiation, and Augustine's theological rationale for infant initiation based on a theology of "original sin," however, will lead to its further decline, even if in the case of Rome it would still be contained in the various liturgical books. At the same time, Augustine's lengthy battle with "Donatism," over the Donatist practice of "rebaptizing" Catholics and their insistence on the moral character of the baptizer in assuring the validity of Baptism in the aftermath of the Diocletian persecution, will lead also to an "orthodox" sacramental theology based on the use of proper elements and words with Christ himself underscored as the true sacramental minister. If Augustine himself knew an initiation rite similar to those summarized above,[41] his own theological emphases, born in the heat of controversy, would set the agenda for what I refer to as a later Western-medieval "sacramental minimalism" focused on "matter" and "form," the *quamprimum* ("as soon as possible") Baptism of infants, and an objective sacramental validity ensured by an *ex opere operato* understanding.

In spite of the apparent success of this baptismal process in early Christianity, however, we should be careful not to romanticize it today. We have little to corroborate Egeria's perhaps exaggerated description of the apparently large numbers of catechumens and faithful in late fourth-century Jerusalem who gathered to hear Cyril's lectures and who greeted them with thunderous applause. Jerusalem, after all, was a major pilgrimage center, whose liturgical practices

---

40. John Baldovin, "Christian Worship to the Eve of the Reformation," in *The Making of Jewish and Christian Worship*, ed. P. Bradshaw and L. Hoffman (Notre Dame: University of Notre Dame Press, 1991), 167.

41. See William Harmless, *Augustine and the Catechumenate* (Collegeville, MN: Pueblo, 1995), 79ff.

may or may not have been typical of churches elsewhere or everywhere. In other words, while we know that such a baptismal process clearly existed in the church of this period, we do not know how many people actually went through such an extended catechumenate in preparation for Baptism or what the overall ritual shape of Baptism was really like in the various and numerous *parish* churches themselves.[42] For that matter, even Easter Baptism, notes Paul Bradshaw, appears to have been a custom that lasted for only about fifty years in some places, and there is enough evidence to suggest that, even if it remained on the books as the theoretical norm, other occasions besides Easter, such as Epiphany, the feasts of particular local martyrs, and even Christmas remained and continued in some places, even in the West, as baptismal occasions.[43] Our evidence for this "Golden Age" of Baptism, then, is pretty much limited to the practice of the large patriarchal and pilgrimage centers and to surviving texts from their illustrious bishops. Hence, we should not automatically assume that everyone everywhere was doing this anymore than we should assume that actual parish liturgical practice today can be read from liturgical manuals, the texts of our current worship books, or, from exceptional parishes and university churches.

Nevertheless, as an excellent and proven manner by which the early churches, in a changed social and cultural environment, attempted to form adult converts, in the power of the Holy Spirit, by a highly ritual-sacramentalized all-encompassing process "in the Word, prayer, worship, Christian community, and service in the world,"[44] this process still has much to commend itself for our usefulness today. It is to this, my final point, "The Implications of

---

42. Cf. Juliette Day, *Baptism in Early Byzantine Palestine 325–451*, Alcuin/GROW Liturgical Study 43 (Cambridge: Grove Books, Ltd., 1999).

43. See P. Bradshaw, "*Diem baptismo sollemniorem*': Initiation and Easter in Christian Antiquity," in *LWSS*, 137–47.

Usefulness of This Spirituality for the Church Today," that I now turn.

The Implications or Usefulness of This Spirituality for the Church Today

However one may assess the contemporary social and cultural context of the church in the United States and world today, whether "postmodern," "post-Christian," or "post-Christendom," it is abundantly clear that we find ourselves today in a world similar to that of the early churches at the beginning of the Constantinian era, with increasing numbers of unchurched, unbaptized, and uncatechized people in our midst, an abundance of competing spiritualities and self-help manuals, varieties of available gnostic and new "mystery" religions, what some have called a "crisis in morality," what others have labeled the lack of a formative and common narrative by which the world might be ordered coherently, and in which the quest for some kind of life-shaping ultimate Truth is as near and as obvious as the book rack in local grocery and drug stores. Lutheran liturgical scholar Frank Senn has written of the challenges of our age, saying that

> we need to preserve, provide, and protect the forms and content of orthodox Christian worship; we need to be sensitive to the culturally-conditioned needs, quests, and forms of expression of the generations who come to worship; and we need to be alert to, in conversation with, and wary of the "postmodern" world that is emerging. . . . Contemporary quests for wholeness, community, and transcendence should be welcomed, even as we recognize that quests for these conditions constitute a rejection of the compartmentalization, individualism, and immanentalism of the "modern" worldview. At the

44. Lutheran World Federation, *Chicago Statement on Worship and Culture: Baptism and Rites of Life Passage* (Geneva 1998), para. 2.1., n6.

same time the faith community has its own ways of addressing these issues, all of them rooted in its historic liturgical life. Only by exploring these historical liturgical traditions can we reach out to the rising generations with something that at least matches their quests.[45]

The publication of catechumenal resources, noted above, provides us Lutherans with a golden opportunity to "reach out to the rising generations with something that at least matches their quests," and, in the process, to renew parish life at all levels in exciting ways with "the heartbeat of the sacraments" at the very center. One of the explicit goals of the Inter-Lutheran-Commission on Worship (hereafter, ILCW) in the publication of the *Lutheran Book of Worship* (hereafter *LBW*) was "to restore to Holy Baptism the liturgical rank and dignity implied by Lutheran theology,"[46] and that process is certainly continued in *Evangelical Lutheran Worship*. The Lutheran catechumenal resources listed above, *Welcome to Christ, Renewing Worship* and the contents of *Evangelical Lutheran Worship* related to the catechumenante, can be a major part of that still-needed and ongoing process of restoration. Indeed, the overall importance of the modern restoration of the adult catechumenate for the faith and life of the contemporary church *cannot* be overestimated! "What the Roman documents contain," wrote Aidan Kavanagh of the Roman Catholic RCIA several years ago, "are not merely specific changes in liturgical rubrics, but a restored and unified vision of the church." *That's* what a baptismal spirituality provides, a vision of the *church*. Kavanagh continues,

One may turn an altar around and leave *reform* at that. But one cannot set an adult catechumenate in motion without becoming necessarily

45. F. C. Senn, "'Worship Alive': An Analysis and Critique of 'Alternative Worship Services,'" *Worship* 69, no. 3 (1995): 224.

46. *Lutheran Book of Worship*, Pew ed. (Minneapolis/Philadelphia: Augsburg Publishing House and Fortress Press, 1978), 8.

involved with *renewal* in the ways a local church lives its faith from top to bottom. For members of an adult catechumenate must be secured through evangelization; they must be formed to maturity in ecclesial faith through catechesis both prior to Baptism and after it; and there must be something to initiate them into that will be correlative to the expectations built up in them throughout their whole initiatory process. This last means a community of lively faith in Jesus Christ dead, risen, and present actually among his People. In this area, when one change occurs, all changes.[47]

In short, because of the need for the active involvement of the entire faith community in this process, all of our modern attempts at restoring the adult catechumenate do not so much offer a new way to do ritual as much as they offer a new way to *be* and *do* the church. Indeed, as several of our Roman Catholic colleagues, based on their experience with the RCIA, can testify, in those places where the adult catechumenate leading to full Christian initiation in water, chrism, and eucharistic table has been restored, and along with it the immense variety of lay ministries needed (e.g., catechesists, sponsors, and the role of the entire faith community in general) to lead and assist in such a process of conversion, parishes themselves have experienced a renewal in faith and life, the recovery of the dignity of their Baptism, and a renewed sense of their own identity as church, as the body of Christ on mission in the world. That possibility awaits us as Lutherans as well if we "replunge ourselves" into the great tradition, and if, in the words of George Lindbeck, "rather than present *experience* being allowed to hold sway over the inherited tradition," we let "the inherited *tradition* shape and govern present experience."[48]

Even if rooted in the answers of the church in a much older historical context, the modern recovery of this patristic-based

47. A. Kavanagh, "Christian Initiation in Post-Conciliar Catholicism: A Brief Report," in *LWSS*, 8–9.
48. G. Lindbeck, cited by G. Wainwright, "Divided by a Common Language," in Wainwright, *Worship with One Accord*, 156 (emphasis added).

baptismal process cannot be written off today as mere "Golden Age Romanticism" on the part of modern "High Church" armchair liturgists who might like to dress up in ancient costumes and "play church." The increasing numbers of unbaptized and "unchurched" adults today would seem, just as it did in the context of the fourth and fifth centuries, to call the church to assist in the evangelization and formation of new Christians with authenticity and integrity. Indeed, if current estimates are correct that there are approximately one hundred million unchurched people in the United States alone today, the need for an adult catechumenal process of formation should become increasingly obvious to us. The issue is *not* only liturgy, but it is evangelism and formation in Christ and the church. And the great gift of our classic liturgical tradition is that we don't have to invent a new process for this but can receive it from our ancestors in the faith most gratefully.

There are, however, some pitfalls or concerns to be avoided in a modern recovery of this process, some of which, unfortunately, have been incorporated already into the current Lutheran adaptations. First, since this baptismal process is, historically and theologically, about the preparation of *unbaptized* adults for Baptism into Christ and the church, it is most unfortunate that, like its Roman Catholic RCIA counterpart, Lutheran adaptations of the catechumenal process also provide for the presence of those who seek to become "Lutherans" through the rite of Affirmation of Baptism.[49] It is well known that in Roman Catholic circles today the Easter Vigil, in spite of official directives to the contrary, has become the prime time not only for adult Baptism but for the *Rite of Reception into Full Communion with the Catholic Church* and confirmation for those who seek through this catechumenal process to become Roman Catholics. The Easter

49. See *Welcome to Christ: Lutheran Rites for the Catechumenate* (Minneapolis: Augsburg Fortress, 1997), 14–15, and *Renewing Worship*, 69–90.

Vigil, I fear, is rapidly becoming *not* a baptismal occasion but the great festival of Christian *disunity*, a "New Members Night" or an "Ecclesial Musical Chairs Night" wherein already baptized members of Christ's *one* body pass from one particular way of ecclesial living into another.[50] On this night *some* are joined to Christ through the paschal sacraments of Baptism and Eucharist but *several* become Roman Catholics, Lutherans, Episcopalians, and others through a combination of other rites after experiencing a similar process of formation. Let, then, the catechumenate be the catechumenate, let the dignity of Baptism be paramount, and let us find another time for the reception of those who used to be called *converts*. While the need for extended catechesis might often be similar to those who are unbaptized, the dignity of Baptism itself suggests that the two groups and occasions not be mixed. For the same reasons, I would suggest strongly that this process cannot become yet another "program" in religious education or a replacement for what we have come to call confirmation ministry, even if some aspects of this formative process might be adapted in some ways. Aidan Kavanagh said in 1987, "The RCIA is *not* directed to the already baptized as its objects. *The RCIA is directed basically to the never baptized.* . . . The never baptized are our fundamental evangelical and catechetical challenge to be faithful to God's grace in them. Hold on to that thought."[51] But because of the way in which this process has been used as a rite for "making converts," and for using the process as a parish renewal program for those already members of the church, he concluded, "In all candor, I must confess that *I give it less than a fifty percent chance of success,*

50. See my essays, "Let's Stop Making 'Converts' at Easter," *Catechumenate: A Journal of Christian Initiation* 21, no. 5 (September 1999): 10–20; and "Christian Initiation at Easter: For 'Joiners,' Not Switchers,'" in *Liturgy*, 25, no. 3 (2010): 1–4 (reprinted from *Celebrate!* 46, no. 1 [January–February 2007]: 4–7).

51. A. Kavanagh, "Critical Issues in the Growth of the RCIA in North America," *Catechumenate* 10 (1988): 13–14.

and you will recall that I have been one of its most consistent public advocates for the past fifteen years."[52] And Roman Catholic Christian initiation scholar Paul Turner addressed this problem ecumenically, saying,

> We can only hope that the need for a rite of transferring membership will become minimized. Progress in the ecumenical movement should help us move toward a single eucharistic table for all Christian families. This would reduce the need for a separate rite of "Reception of Baptized Christians into the Full Communion of the Catholic Church" and purify the purpose of confirmation. . . . Current pastoral practice sadly initiates such candidates in much the same way as catechumens. The two groups are catechized together, and pass through either the same rituals or ponderous adaptations which struggle to challenge the non-baptized without offending non-Catholic Christians. Frequently, candidates are disappointed that they cannot be baptized like catechumens, that they should not sign the book of the elect like catechumens, that they are not called to scrutinies like catechumens, that they are not anointed with the oil of catechumens like catechumens. . . . By making candidates imitate the path of catechumens we have too often made it too difficult for Christians who share one Baptism to share one eucharistic table. The ecumenical movement longs for the day when the rites which prepare baptized Christians for full communion will be ripped from our books, and the catechumenate now so freely adapted for the *baptized* may become again the proper province of the unbaptized.[53]

Second, I am also concerned that, apart from references here and there in the Lutheran adaptations to the possibility of this catechumenal process taking place at other seasons, there is a strong tendency to put what I like to call "all of our baptismal eggs into the Easter basket." I have no qualms whatsoever about giving a theological priority to Easter in terms of a baptismal theology flowing from Romans 6, a theology that emphasizes not only death, burial,

---

52. Ibid, 20; emphasis added.
53. P. Turner, *Confirmation: The Baby in Solomon's Court* (New York: Paulist Press, 1993), 129. Turner, of course, is being too nice. Too often, in fact, candidates for full communion *do* sign the book of the elect, are *scrutinized*, but probably are not anointed with the oil of catechumens.

and resurrection but also a process of life-long conversion, that daily baptismal death and resurrection as we know it from Luther's *Small Catechism*. But this does not mean, necessarily, that Easter always has a *liturgical* priority for celebrating Baptism. Several other occasions are equally suited, and have been used historically, even for the full adult catechumenal process. At the very least, the feast of the Baptism of our Lord, on the Sunday after the Epiphany, is most suitable for this and attending to this might help us recover the baptismal meaning of Advent in the life of the church, especially with the frequent appearance of John the Baptist in the Advent Gospel readings each year, and even with the use of Titus 3 in the lectionary for Christmas itself. Here, if death and resurrection is not dominant, new birth in water and the Spirit, baptismal adoption, and being equipped for mission might suggest themselves theologically. The construction even of an Epiphany Vigil with several Old Testament readings could easily be done, and a model is provided in the current *Book of Occasional Services*[54] of The Episcopal Church. Along with Epiphany, of course, Pentecost, the great Feast of the Spirit, the very culmination and fruit of Jesus' death and resurrection, is certainly suitable, again, with a traditional vigil often attached, or easily constructed, and, for that matter, the feast of All Saints in November could also be chosen. Vigils for both Pentecost and All Saints are again provided for in the 1979 *Book of Occasional Services*.[55] I have no objections to the Lutheran theological priority of Easter Baptism whatsoever, but these other feasts of the church may actually help to remind us of the other equally inviting interpretations of Baptism that form part of the rich mosaic of baptismal images in Scripture and the classic, early Christian, liturgical tradition. I think we would do well to explore them more fully both theologically and in our pastoral-

---

54. *The Book of Occasional Services* (New York: Church Hymnal Corporation, 1979), 49–50.
55. Ibid, 126–27 and 104–5.

liturgical practice. Indeed, the words of Tertullian in this context bear repeating: "If there is any difference of solemnity, it makes no difference to the grace."[56]

Third, excitement and enthusiasm about the recovery and restoration of this process *can* lead to the impression that infant Baptism in the life of the church is to be downplayed or undervalued. Again, it is Aidan Kavanagh, who, in 1977, stated "that the days of Baptism in infancy and confirmation in adolescence as our norm are numbered."[57] But, so far at least, Kavanagh's prediction was wrong. By all accounts, infant Baptism is here to stay and it should be here to stay both theologically and pastorally. Yet, this does not mean that infant Baptism itself cannot be incorporated somehow into this catechumenal process as well, just as it appears to have been done in the early centuries of the church. I have always been intrigued by the rubrics in the *Gelasian Sacramentary* and elsewhere that continue to assume that parents are to bring their elect infants to the public Lenten scrutinies, now by this late date shifted to weekdays and increased to seven in number, before Easter Baptism. Of this process, the great historian of the catechumenate Michel Dujarier writes,

> We must stress that there was a kind of "catechumenate" for infants. It is interesting to note that, even for babies, the celebration of Baptism was not limited to one single liturgical ceremony. The practice of seven scrutinies on the weekdays of Lent developed when there were many infants among the candidates. The testimony of Caesar of Arles in the sixth century is irrefutable: addressing himself to mothers bringing their babies to the scrutinies, he urged them not to miss these celebrations. This custom was undoubtedly a vestige of the tradition of baptizing infants at the same time as adults. . . . This custom also had the great advantage of having the parents of these infants participate in the preparation for baptism. Since the parents "answered" for their children,

---

56. *DBL*, 10 (emphasis added).
57. A. Kavanagh, "Christian Initiation in Post-Conciliar Roman Catholicism: A Brief Report," in *LWSS*, 1.

it was normal that they make the catechetical and liturgical journey leading to baptism.[58]

The recovery and restoration of the catechumenal process should in no way be interpreted as a preference for adult *over* infant Baptism. Far from it. Rather, including infant Baptism into this process may even afford us other opportunities for exploring how we might do prebaptismal catechesis with parents more effectively and incorporate even that process somewhat into the public liturgy of the church. To that end, Gail Ramshaw has written a delightful essay on adapting the catechumenal process to infant Baptism in a manner that goes all the way from conception and birth to the celebration of Baptism and First Eucharist.[59] Indeed, it may well be that the selection of suitable baptismal occasions according to the calendar of the liturgical year would provide several opportunities each year for some kind of adaptation of this process for the Baptism of infants and the continual "mystagogical" or catechetical formation of their parents in the gift of their own Baptisms.

Fourth, and finally, my greatest concern about the recovery and restoration of the classic early Christian baptismal process for adults has little to do with the process itself and much to do with several other things needing to be accomplished if this process is going to become little more than another "resource" for a few liturgically minded pastors and parishes. Kavanagh's comment, quoted earlier, that "there must be something to initiate [catechumens] into that will be correlative to the expectations built up in them throughout their whole initiatory process . . . [i.e.,] a community of lively faith in Jesus Christ dead, risen, and present actually among his People" must be

---

58. M. Dujarier, *A History of the Catechumenate* (New York: Saliers, 1979), 133.
59. See G. Ramshaw, "Celebrating Baptism in Stages: A Proposal," in *Alternative Futures for Worship*, vol. 5: *Baptism and Confirmation*, ed. M. Searle (Collegeville, MN: The Liturgical Press, 1987), 137–56.

taken seriously. As this process has been recovered for Lutherans, then its use necessitates that, at the very least, our parishes once and for all finally restore Sunday Eucharist to its rightful place at the heart of worship; that the season of Lent be rescued finally from its medieval passion history, the Seven Last Words of Christ, and devotional dominance in favor of baptismal preparation and renewal; and that not only the Easter Vigil but the entire paschal Triduum become the annual center of parish life; that pastors, mission developers, and parish education directors be formed so they are able to lead in this process; that not only at the national level but on the synodical and district levels there be trained—and paid—directors of liturgy to assist parishes with this process and in other liturgical manners; and that synod and district bishops and presidents and their staffs themselves be converted to see that this liturgical-sacramental process *is* the synthesis of everything the church is about in its worship, education, evangelism, stewardship, and ministry all rolled into one grand spirituality of life in Jesus Christ to the glory of God in the Holy Spirit. Until this happens, I fear that our modern adaptations of what the early church called *Baptism* will simply be one available "resource" among several others, take it or leave it, from which a selection is made in determining various evangelism, programmatic, and educational curricula.

Conclusion

While serving in a parish several years ago I had an ongoing conversation with a bishop's assistant about what the most important element of parish ministry was. I, of course, said that it was worship, while his response was that people with strong commitments to the other areas of parish life, evangelism, education, stewardship, or social ministry, might make similar and equally valid claims. Although it is still beyond my comprehension how we can even *begin* to speak of the other areas of ministry without the foundation of word and sacrament in their liturgical and life-shaping contexts, the recovery and restoration of the classic pattern of adult Baptism, in spite of some pitfalls and concerns, means that we don't have to choose among several options. All of them are included under the umbrella of word and sacrament themselves.

Finally, I want to return to Wainwright's statement, that "without the heartbeat of the sacraments at its center, a church will lack confidence about the gospel message and about its own ability to proclaim that message in evangelism, to live it out in its own internal fellowship, and to embody it in service to the needy." *That's* what early Christian baptismal spirituality has to teach us still today, the restoration of "the heartbeat of the sacraments" at the center of the church in act, in order that we might have confidence about the gospel and our ability to proclaim it effectively, to live it out in our corporate, ecclesial lives, and to embody it faithfully in lives of *martyria* and *diakonia* in the world. That is, let us embrace this willingly so that in our postmodern, post-Christian, or post-Christendom context we, like saints before us, may proclaim the very common narrative by which we live and that gives life to the world, and so offer a *solid* spirituality for those who seek a true life in the Spirit worthy of the term *spirituality*.

2

The Holy Spirit and Lutheran Liturgical-Sacramental Theology

Lutheran liturgical-sacramental theology has always rightly placed a central emphasis on the role of the Holy Spirit in the gracious and saving gifts of word and sacrament. It is "through the Word and the sacraments, as through instruments," says Article V of the *Augsburg Confession*, that "the Holy Spirit is given, and the Holy Spirit produces faith, where and when it pleases God, in those who hear the Gospel."[1] Similarly, notes Luther in his *Small Catechism*, it is the Holy Spirit who "calls, gathers, enlightens, and sanctifies the whole Christian church on earth,"[2] and Lutherans have always looked to word and sacrament as the vehicles by which the Spirit does this.

As is well known among liturgical scholars, throughout the history of Christian worship this role of the Holy Spirit has often been most expressed in the prayer of blessing or sanctification of water

1. Tappert, *The Book of Concord*, 31.
2. Ibid., 345.

in the rite of Baptism and in the anaphora, Eucharistic Prayer, or Great Thanksgiving either by an invocation (epiclesis) of the Spirit to "come" or by asking the Father to "let come," or "send" the Holy Spirit upon the baptismal waters and upon the bread and wine of the Eucharist and the assembled community itself.[3] With regard to the Eucharist, traditional scholarship has argued that such epicleses have tended to be of two general types. Either they may be "consecratory" in that they request the Spirit to make, change, show, declare, bless, or sanctify the bread and wine as Christ's Body and Blood, or they may be a "communion" type in that they ask that the assembled community itself might receive various "fruits" of holy communion by the Spirit's activity.[4] Often they are both consecratory and communion at the same time. However, as Robert Taft has demonstrated, "originally . . . the epiclesis was primarily a prayer for communion, not for consecration; it was directed at the sanctification of the communicants, not of the gifts. Or, to put it better, perhaps, it was a prayer for the sanctification of the ecclesial communion, not for the sanctification of its sacramental sign, the Holy Communion."[5]

So also, the location of such epicleses in the anaphora has varied within the different liturgical traditions of the church. In the West Syrian and Byzantine East the epiclesis was located after the Words

3. See Sebastian Brock, "The Epiklesis in the Antiochene Baptismal *Ordines*," in *Symposium Syriacum 1972*, Orientalia Christiana Analecta 197 (Rome, 1974), 183–218.

4. Gabriele Winkler has argued that there are actually more than these two types, especially when the earliest form seems to be a direct address to the Holy Spirit to come, without specifying either the eucharistic gifts or the fruits of communion reception. See Gabriele Winkler, "Nochmals zu den Anfängen der Epiklese und des Sanctus im Eucharistischen Hochgebet," *Theologisches Quartalschrift* 74, no. 3 (1994): 214–31. The best current guide to the development and theology of the epiclesis in history and in the current liturgical reforms is the doctoral dissertation of my former student, Anne McGowan, "In Search of the Spirit: The Epiclesis in Early Eucharistic Praying and Contemporary Liturgical Reforms" (PhD diss., University of Notre Dame, 2011). See Anne McGowan, *Eucharistic Epicleses, Ancient and Modern: Speaking of the Spirit in Eucharistic Praying* (Collegeville: The Liturgical Press, 2014).

5. Robert Taft, "From Logos to Spirit: On the Early History of the Epiclesis," in *Gratias Agamus: Studien zum eucharistischen Hochgebet, Für Balthasar Fischer* (Freiburg–Basel–Wien: Herder, 1992), 492–93.

of Institution and anamnesis in the prayer. In the Egyptian (or Alexandrian) Eastern tradition, two epicleses of the Spirit developed: one before and one after the Words of Institution and anamnesis. But while in the non-Roman West Spirit epicleses could and did appear in either location, in the *Roman* West, that is, in the *canon missae* as it evolved in the Roman tradition, no epiclesis of the Spirit was contained whatsoever. Even so, some form of invocation, or epiclesis-type petition, was still present in that God himself (in the *Quam oblationem*) was asked before the Institution Narrative to "bless and approve" the offering and to "let it become" Christ's Body and Blood and, at a point after the Narrative (in the *Supplices te rogamus*), the fruits of communion were also requested: "We humbly beseech you, almighty God, bid these things be borne by the hands of your angel to your altar on high, in the sight of your divine majesty, that all of us who have received the most holy body and blood of your Son by partaking at this altar may be filled with all heavenly blessing and grace."[6]

Epicleses of the Holy Spirit in Lutheran Worship in North America

The Holy Spirit has not always been very obvious in Lutheran worship but has tended to function behind the scenes, in the words of Frederick Dale Bruner and William Hordern, as "the shy member of the Trinity,"[7] always directing attention to Christ. Lutheran baptismal and eucharistic liturgies have not tended traditionally to use epicleses of the Holy Spirit in their liturgical prayers. Luther's

---

6. R. C. D. Jasper and G. J. Cuming, *Prayers of the Eucharist: Early and Reformed*, 3rd. ed., hereafter *PEER* (Collegeville, MN: The Liturgical Press, Pueblo Books, 1987), 165.
7. Frederick Dale Bruner and William Hordern, *The Holy Spirit—Shy Member of the Trinity* (Minneapolis: Augsburg Publishing House, 1984).

own reforms of the Roman Rite of Baptism in 1523 and 1526 and his similar reforms of the Mass in the same years, the *Formula Missae* and *Deutsche Messe,* did not introduce an epiclesis of the Holy Spirit either over the baptismal waters in his famous *Sindflutgebet* or in the consecration of the bread and wine. And, with the notable exception of the Paul Zellar Strodach and Luther Reed Eucharistic Prayer in the 1958 *Service Book and Hymnal,* which invoked both the Word and Holy Spirit in the West Syrian position "to bless us, thy servants, and these thy own gifts of bread and wine, so that we and all who partake thereof may be filled with heavenly benediction and grace," and so on,[8] explicit epicleses of the Holy Spirit in the trial liturgical booklets leading to the publication of *Lutheran Book of Worship* were rather new to United States Lutheranism. In *Contemporary Worship 7: Holy Baptism,* the prayer over the baptismal waters read,

> Pour out your Holy Spirit, gracious Father, to make this a water of cleansing. Wash away the sins of all those who enter it, and bring them forth as inheritors of your glorious kingdom.[9]

And the eucharistic epiclesis in the West Syrian or Syro-Byzantine position in *Contemporary Worship 2: The Holy Communion* was equally direct:

> Send the power of your Holy Spirit upon us and upon this bread and wine, that we who receive the body and blood of Christ may be his body in the world, living according to his example to bring peace and healing to all [hu]mankind.[10]

So "new," in fact, were these baptismal and eucharistic epicleses of the Holy Spirit for some contemporary Lutherans that the work of

---

8. *Service Book and Hymnal* (Minneapolis: Augsburg Publishing House, 1958), 11.

9. Inter-Lutheran Commission on Worship, *Contemporary Worship 7: Holy Baptism* (Minneapolis: Augsburg, 1974), 27.

10. Inter-Lutheran Commission on Worship, *Contemporary Worship 2: The Holy Communion* (Minneapolis: Augsburg Publishing House, 1970), 35.

the Inter-Lutheran Commission on Worship itself was criticized for having departed from traditional Lutheran doctrinal and sacramental theology. As Oliver K. Olson, one of the most outspoken critics of both *Holy Baptism* and *The Holy Communion*, wrote,

> The problem of the epiclesis confronts us in two ways. Not only is the ILCW proposing the epiclesis of the Holy Spirit in the communion order, but also an epiclesis of the baptismal water. To begin with the latter, we should be aware that the answer to the catechism question, "How can water produce such great effects," is a re-statement of the resistance of the Western church to the practice of epiclesis. Luther, in re-stating the position of Augustine that it is the Word of God that is the means of grace, not the water, can be said to speak for the Western church. . . . Restoration of the baptismal epiclesis, as planned, will produce an order at odds with Lutheran doctrine on baptism.[11]

He continued elsewhere: "The Eucharistic epiclesis as at Baptism corresponds to a Hellenistic personification of the Spirit . . ., detracts from the actual import of the celebration and . . . runs into contradiction with the apostolic Gospel."[12] Another critic argued similarly that

> repeated use of Spirit prayers displays a failure to take the Risen Lord at his Word. . . . The approach of the gracious God . . . has been liturgically blunted . . . liturgical gears have been shifted and direction reversed (man to God instead of God to man) at the crucial place in the service where God's sacramental initiative ought to be underscored. . . . The focus of the [baptismal] prayer . . . is the water rather than the initiate. . . . Is there a parallel here to the ILCW insistence upon making the bread and wine rather than the communicant the chief focus of its Eucharistic epiclesis?[13]

11. Oliver K. Olson, "Contemporary Trends in Liturgy Viewed from the Perspective of Classic Lutheran Theology," *Lutheran Quarterly* 26, no. 2 (1974): 140.
12. Ibid., 141.
13. Robert Hughes, "CW 7: A Critique," *The Mount Airy Parish Practice Notebook 10* (June 1976): 2. I owe this reference to Jeffrey Truscott, *The Reform of Baptism and Confirmation in American Lutheranism* (Lanham: The Scarecrow Press, Inc., 2003), 78.

That these critics were heard, at least in part, was reflected in the final shape of the baptismal and eucharistic epicleses in the 1978 *Lutheran Book of Worship*. The baptismal invocation now reads simply,

> Pour out your Holy Spirit, so that *those* who *are* baptized may be given new life. Wash away the sin of *all those* who *are* cleansed by this water and bring *them* forth as *inheritors* of your glorious kingdom.[14]

And the epiclesis in the first optional Eucharistic Prayer reads,

> Send now, we pray, your Holy Spirit, the spirit of our Lord and of his resurrection, that we who receive the Lord's body and blood may live to the praise of your glory and receive our inheritance with all your saints in light.
>
> Amen. Come, Holy Spirit.[15]

The second option merely recasts this as,

> Send now, we pray, your Holy Spirit, that we and all who share in this bread and cup may be united in the fellowship of the Holy Spirit, may enter the fullness of the kingdom of heaven, and may receive our inheritance with all your saints in light.
>
> Amen. Come, Holy Spirit.[16]

Eucharistic Prayer III is a modern reworking of the Strodach-Reed prayer noted above ("With your Word and Holy Spirit to bless us, your servants, and these your own gifts of bread and wine") and Eucharistic Prayer IV is based on the anaphora in the so-called *Apostolic Tradition*, the epiclesis of which is translated as, "Send your Spirit upon these gifts of your Church; gather into one all who share

---

14. *Lutheran Book of Worship*, Minister's Edition (Minneapolis: Augsburg Publishing House, 1978), 309.
15. Ibid, 223.
16. Ibid, 223.

this bread and wine; fill us with your Holy Spirit to establish our faith in truth."[17]

Apart from the possibility of using the Institution Narrative by itself after the Sanctus, the other option in *LBW* was a short pre-Institution Narrative prayer, based on a Church of Sweden model, which contains the following invocation: "Send now your Holy Spirit into our hearts, that we may receive our Lord with a living faith as he comes to us in his holy supper. Amen. Come, Lord Jesus."[18] Along similar lines, the 1982 Lutheran Church, Missouri Synod (LCMS) worship book, *Lutheran Worship* (*LW*), also included this type of "Swedish prayer" before the Lord's Prayer and Words of Institution in the two settings of Divine Service II, asking God to "send your Holy Spirit into our hearts that he may establish in us a living faith and prepare us joyfully to remember our Redeemer and receive him who comes to us in his body and blood."[19]

The state of Spirit epiclesis in baptismal and eucharistic liturgies is little different in the more recent Lutheran liturgical resources, the 2006 *Evangelical Lutheran Worship* of the Evangelical Lutheran Church in America and the 2006 *Lutheran Service Book* (*LSB*) of the Lutheran Church, Missouri Synod. The only real difference, in fact, is that *ELW* provides several more examples of basically the

17. Ibid, 226. On the *Apostolic Tradition* and its place in current scholarship and liturgical renewal see Paul F. Bradshaw, Maxwell E. Johnson, and L. Edward Phillips, *The Apostolic Tradition: A Commentary*, Hermeneia (Minneapolis: Fortress Press, 2002).

18. Ibid, 70. What is most interesting, however, is that the Swedish prayer upon which this was based says explicitly, "Send your Spirit in our hearts that he might work in us a living faith. Sanctify also through your Spirit this bread and wine, fruits of the earth and the toil of people which we bear unto you, so that we, through them, partake of the true body and blood of our Lord Jesus Christ" (text in M. Thurian and G. Wainwright, eds., *Baptism and Eucharist; Ecumenical Convergence in Celebration* [Grand Rapids: Eerdmans, 1983], 141). And the prayer continues after the Institution Narrative with an anamnesis and concluding doxology.

19. Lutheran Church, Missouri Synod, *Lutheran Worship* (St. Louis: Concordia Publishing House, 1982), 171.

same approach. In *ELW*'s baptismal rite[20] the Spirit is invoked in the following ways:

> *Thanksgiving I:* Pour out your Holy Spirit, the power of your living Word, that those who are washed in the waters of Baptism may be given new life.

> *Thanksgiving II:* Pour out your Holy Spirit; wash away sin in this cleansing water; clothe the baptized with Christ. . . .

> *Thanksgiving III:* Pour out your Holy Spirit, and breathe new life into those who are Baptized. By your Spirit adopt us all as your children.

> *Thanksgiving IV:* Pour out your Holy Spirit, so that those who are here baptized may be given new life.

> *Thanksgiving V:* Breathe your Spirit into all who are gathered here and into all creation.

And, in the now *eleven* Eucharistic Prayers in *ELW*,[21] all shaped according to the West-Syrian or Syro-Byzantine anaphoral pattern, the epicleses are formulated as such:

> *Option I (the Strodach-Reed Revision):* We ask you mercifully to accept our praise and thanksgiving and with your Word and Holy Spirit to bless us, your servants, and these your own gifts of bread and wine, so that we and all who share in the body and blood of Christ may be filled with heavenly blessing and grace. . . .

> *Option II:* The Institution Narrative alone.

> *Option III (Advent—Epiphany of Our Lord):* Holy God, we long for your Spirit. Come among us. Bless this meal. May your Word take flesh in us. Awaken your people. Fill us with your light. Bring the gift of peace on earth. Come, Holy Spirit.

> *Option IV (Ash Wednesday—Day of Pentecost):* O God of resurrection

20. *Evangelical Lutheran Worship: Leader's Desk Edition* (Minneapolis: Augsburg Fortress, 2006), 586–89.
21. Ibid, 194–205.

and new life: Pour out your Holy Spirit on us and on these gifts of bread and wine. Bless this feast. Grace our table with your presence. Come, Holy Spirit.

Option V: Pour out upon us the Spirit of your love, O Lord, and the unite the wills of all who share this heavenly food. . . .

Option VI: Send now, we pray, your Holy Spirit, the spirit of our Lord and of his resurrection, that we who share the Lord's body and blood may live to the praise of your glory and receive our inheritance with all your saints in light. Amen. Come, Holy Spirit.

Option VII: Send upon us and this meal, your Holy Spirit, whose breath revives us for life, whose fire rouses us to love. Enfold in your arms all who share this holy food. Nurture in us the fruits of the Spirit, that we may be a living tree, sharing your bounty with all the world. Amen. Come, Holy Spirit.

Option VIII: Send your Holy Spirit, our advocate, to fill the hearts of all who share this bread and cup with courage and wisdom to pursue love and justice in all the world. Come, Spirit of freedom! And let the church say, Amen. Amen.

Option IX: We pray for the gift of your Spirit; in our gathering; within this meal; among your people; throughout the world.

Option X: O God, you are Breath; send your Spirit on this meal.

Option XI: Send your Spirit upon these gifts of your Church; gather into one all who share this bread and wine; fill us with your Holy Spirit to establish our faith in truth.

The baptismal texts in *LSB* can be dispensed with rather quickly here. No epiclesis of the Holy Spirit appears in the baptismal rites, though in the second option, based directly on Luther's 1523 *Betbüchlein,* a version of his *Sintflutgebet* is employed, which does ask that those to be baptized would be blessed "with true faith by the Holy Spirit."[22]

---

22. Lutheran Church, Missouri Synod, *Lutheran Service Book, Agenda* (St. Louis: Concordia Concordia Publishing House, 2006), 14.

With regard to a Spirit epiclesis in the Eucharist, however, *LSB* is even less explicit than was *LW*:

> *Divine Service, Settings 1–2:* Gathered in his name and the remembrance of Jesus, we beg You, O Lord, to forgive, renew, and strengthen us with Your Word and Holy Spirit.[23]

> *Divine Service, Setting 4 (Pentecost only):* Pour out your Holy Spirit upon your gathered people, that, faithfully eating and drinking the body and blood of Your Son, we may go forth to proclaim his salvation to the ends of the earth.[24]

The Spirit epicleses in the prayers from all of the modern Lutheran books above, with some exceptions here and there, are ambiguous both liturgically and theologically. In many it is not clear what role, if any, the epiclesis actually plays in the particular sacramental event in question or even upon what or whom the Holy Spirit is being invoked, though it would seem that in the majority of cases the baptismal epiclesis is for the baptized, not the water, and in the various eucharistic prayers, for the communicants and the fruits of communion, not the bread and wine. Now I suppose that one could argue that, with phrases like *Come, Holy Spirit*, without specifying any place, person, or thing, Lutherans are in touch with a very archaic epicletic theology such as we see in the classic New Testament invocation *Maran atha!* or in the baptismal and eucharistic epicleses in the third-century Syrian Acts of the Apostles. But I would be very surprised to discover that the work of Sebastian Brock and Gabriele Winkler on the early Syrian epicleses played much role in the formulation of these texts.[25] Nevertheless, there is something rather primitive about the formulation of these various texts—either

---

23. Lutheran Church, Missouri Synod, *Lutheran Service Book, Altar Edition* (St. Louis: Concordia Publishing House, 2006), 165.
24. Ibid., 268.
25. See above, nn.3–4.

as invoking the Holy Spirit for the baptized or for the communicants—corresponding to Taft's comment above that "originally . . . the epiclesis was primarily a prayer for communion, not for consecration." At the same time, in light of contemporary ecumenical liturgical scholarship, one must ask whether Lutheran theology and liturgy might not be in a position today to embrace a more explicitly consecratory form of epiclesis as well.

Rethinking Spirit Epicleses In a Lutheran Context

We have seen above the claim of Oliver K. Olson that Luther's liturgical reform testified to "the resistance of the Western church to the practice of epiclesis. Luther, in re-stating the position of Augustine that it is the Word of God that is the means of grace, not the water can be said to speak for the Western church." But, of course, such a statement is not borne out by any evidence whatsoever and Olson's position is very misleading and ultimately deceptive. Only if one takes the Roman *canon missae* as the sole witness to eucharistic praying in the West could one perhaps make the claim that the West resists a *Spirit* epiclesis in the Eucharistic Liturgy. But even so, as we have seen, the Roman Canon itself has two paragraphs, which are clearly petitionary, invocative, and, hence, epicletic in nature, and, of course, some of the numerous non-Roman Western Gallican and Mozarabic Eucharistic prayers do, in fact, have explicit epicleses of the Holy Spirit![26] Hence, even with this, a thesis of the West being against any kind of epiclesis is simply wrong. One prayer from the Roman tradition is hardly the totality of the *West* and even *that* prayer has what might be called an epicletic structure. And, with regard to baptismal liturgy, Spirit epicleses on the baptismal waters are as old as Tertullian's *De Baptismo*[27] and should be obvious from

---

26. Compare *PEER*, 153.

the multiple liturgical witnesses of both East and West through the Middle Ages and into the present.[28] No, Luther in not providing Spirit epicleses in his baptismal and eucharistic reforms did *not* simply restate some kind of Western resistance, since there was no obvious Western resistance whatsoever to begin with in this context!

Several years ago, Bryan Spinks published a significant essay in *Lutheran Quarterly* entitled "Berakah, Anaphoral Theory, and Luther."[29] One part of this study was a critique of the over-reliance on and dominance of the West Syrian or Syro-Byzantine pattern of Eucharistic praying in contemporary ecumenical liturgical reform and renewal. As he rightly noted, this particular anaphoral structure has been viewed "not only [as] the perfect and only paradigm for authentic Eucharistic prayers, but also that [it] can be traced back directly to the Jewish euchology used by Jesus at the Last Supper, and implied by him in the words 'Do this in remembrance of me.'"[30] I shall come back to this below.

Another part of Spinks's short study had to do precisely with the question of the epiclesis for Lutheran liturgy. For although, as noted, Luther's liturgical reforms of the Roman Rite did not introduce an epiclesis of the Holy Spirit, Luther did relate the Holy Spirit theologically to Baptism and Eucharist. In his 1526 *Sermon against the Fanatics*, he wrote, "For as soon as Christ says 'This is My Body,' it is his body through the word and power of the Holy Spirit."[31] Regarding this, Spinks argued that "an epiklesis may not be so difficult for Lutheran theology as some have maintained."[32] Similarly, Regin Prenter, in his classic study of the role of the Holy Spirit in

---

27. Tertullian, *De Baptismo* ,4
28. Confer the blessing of water in the *Gelasian Sacramentary* in *DBL*, 233–34.
29. Bryan D. Spinks, "Berakah, Anaphoral Theory, and Luther," *Lutheran Quarterly* 3, no. 3 (Autumn 1989): 267–80.
30. Ibid., 279.
31. As cited in ibid., 277.
32. Ibid., 277.

Luther's theology, writes that "the Holy Spirit makes the crucified and risen Christ such a present and redeeming reality to us that faith in Christ and conformity to Christ spring directly from this reality."[33]According to Prenter, it is the Holy Spirit who, for Luther, "takes the crucified and risen Christ out of the remoteness of history and heavenly glory and places him as a living and redeeming reality in the midst of our life with its suffering, inner conflict, and death."[34] Indeed, if in Lutheran theology it is the Holy Spirit who does all this, then, grounded as Lutheran theology is in word and sacrament as the very "means of grace" by which the Spirit works, it would seem that the church's liturgical rites cry out for such an explicit liturgical textual acknowledgement of the Spirit's role and work.

In relationship to the Lutheran epicletic texts we looked at above, it is certainly clear that Lutheran liturgy in the United States has witnessed a more explicit recovery of the role and work of the Holy Spirit in its baptismal and eucharistic rites. But must Lutheran liturgy be characterized by epiclectic texts that remain somewhat theologically and liturgically ambiguous? If, in the words of Prenter, it is "the Holy Spirit [who] makes the crucified and risen Christ . . . a present and redeeming reality to us," then why not say that liturgically by petitioning the Spirit to do that sacramentally?

Other Lutherans throughout history have not been as reluctant as have the framers of *LBW*, *ELW*, and *LSB* to embrace a more consecratory-type epiclesis within, at least, the Eucharistic Liturgy. Taking its structural cue from the *Quam oblationem* of the Roman *canon missae*, for example, the Pfalz-Neuburg Church Order of 1543 contained the following consecratory petition immediately before the Institution Narrative:

33. Regin Prenter, *Spiritus Creator* (Philadelphia: Fortress Press, 1953), 52–53.
34. Ibid., 53–54.

O Lord Jesus Christ, thou only true Son of the living God, who hast given thy body unto bitter death for us all, and hast shed thy blood for the forgiveness of our sins, and hast bidden all thy disciples to eat that same thy body and to drink thy blood whereby to remember thy death; we bring before thy divine Majesty these thy gifts of bread and wine and beseech thee to hallow and bless the same by thy divine grace, goodness and power and ordain (*schaffen*) that this bread and wine may be (*sei*) thy body and blood, even unto eternal life to all who eat and drink thereof.[35]

Influenced by this, the *Kassel Agenda* of 1896 contained a similar petition but addressed God the Father, rather than directly petitioning Christ:

Almighty God, heavenly Father, who hast delivered Thy Son, our Lord Jesus Christ, and hast ordained that His body and blood be our food unto eternal life, we bring these Thy gifts before Thy divine Majesty, Thy own from Thy own, and pray Thee to hallow and bless them through Thy divine mercy and power, that this bread and this cup may be the body and blood of our Lord Jesus Christ for all who eat and drink of the same, and that Thou wouldst let them be blessings unto eternal life for them.[36]

And, of course, one cannot but note here in these Lutheran texts a parallel to what Thomas Cranmer did in the 1549 *Book of Common Prayer*, where he revised the Roman Canon's *Quam oblationem* to say,

Hear us, O merciful Father, we beseech Thee and with Thy Holy Spirit and word vouchsafe to ble✝ss and sanc✝tify these Thy gifts and creatures of bread and wine, that they may be unto us the body and blood of thy most dearly beloved Son Jesus Christ.[37]

Prior to the wider "recovery" of the Eucharistic Prayer among North American Lutherans from the 1958 *Service Book and Hymnal* (the

---

35. Luther Reed, *The Lutheran Liturgy* (Philadelphia: Fortress Press, 1947), 753.
36. Text cited in Peter Brunner, *Worship in the Name of the Jesus*, trans. M. H. Bertram (St. Louis: Concordia Publishing House, 1968), 301.
37. *PEER*, 239.

Zeller Strodach-Reed prayer) and into the 1978 *LBW* and 2006 *ELW*, all of which follow the West Syrian or Syro-Byzantine anaphoral pattern, what Lutheran attempts at eucharistic praying there were placed an epiclesis of various constructions *before* the Institution Narrative. In the 1879 *Agenda* of the Lutheran Church in Bavaria, used also by the former Joint Synod of Ohio, in fact, there was both a pre- and post-Institution epiclesis, both of which were clearly "communion" in nature:

> (*Before the Institution Narrative*): Sanctify us, therefore, we beseech Thee, in our bodies and souls, by Thy Holy Spirit, and thus fit and prepare us to come to Thy Supper, to the glory of Thy grace, and to our own eternal good.

> (*After the Institution Narrative*): O Thou everlasting Son of the Father, sanctify us by Thy Holy Spirit, and make us worthy partakers of Thy sacred Body and Blood, that we may be cleansed from sin and made one with all the members of Thy Church in heaven and one earth.[38]

It is here in particular where I find Spinks's critique of the over-reliance on and dominance of the West Syrian or Syro-Byzantine pattern of eucharistic praying in contemporary ecumenical liturgical reform and renewal so compelling and important. For, with the exception of the Eucharistic Prayers, in addition to the *canon missae,* in the *Missale Romanum* of Paul VI and Eucharistic Prayer C in the 1979 Episcopal *Book of Common Prayer*, one looks in vain for contemporary Eucharistic Prayers in North America that follow an alternative anaphoral pattern. But, of course, there are even *classic* alternatives, most notably that reflecting what has come to be called the Alexandrian or Egyptian anaphoral structure. While the current texts of that tradition, reflected in the Greek and Coptic Anaphoras of Saint Mark,[39] contain double epicleses (one before and one after the

---

38. Reed, *The Lutheran Liturgy*, 755–56.

Institution Narrative), many scholars agree that the original Egyptian epiclesis, based on the "full is heaven and earth" in the *Sanctus*, was a short invocation of the Holy Spirit to "fill" the eucharistic gifts immediately before the Institution Narrative, which is attached by the word *hoti* ("for" or "because"). As this tradition developed, however, the anaphora came to include either a single expanded epiclesis prior to the Institution Narrative or, through Syrian influence, the addition of a second epiclesis following the Institution Narrative and anamnesis, with the explicit consecratory focus now located in the second.[40] It is this second epiclesis in the location of the single epiclesis in the West Syrian or Syro-Byzantine anaphora that Hans Leitzmann referred to as a "Fremdkorper,"[41] a "foreign body" in the prayer. Two fourth-century Egyptian or Alexandrian anaphoral fragments—*the Deir Balyzeh Papyrus* and *the Louvain Coptic Papyrus*—provide examples of the single expanded epiclesis of the Holy Spirit before the Institution Narrative.

> *The Deir Balyzeh Papyrus:* Fill also with the glory from (you), an vouchsafe to send down your Holy Spirit upon these creatures (and) make the bread the body of our (Lord and) Savior Jesus Christ, and the cup the blood . . . of our Lord and Savior.[42]

The Louvain Coptic Papyrus even weaves an anamnesis into this pre-Institution position:

39. For an English text, see *PEER*, 59–66.

40. Compare R.–G. Coquin, "L'Anaphore alexandrine de saint Marc,' *Le Muséon* 82 (1969): 329ff; C. H. Roberts and B. Capelle, *An Early Euchologium: The Deir-Balyzeh Papyrus Enlarged and Re-edited* (Louvain: Bureaux du Muséon, 1949), 52; J. van Haelst, "Une nouvelle reconstitution du papyrus liturgique de Deir Balyzeh," *Ephemerides Theologicae Lovanienses* 45 (1969): 210; A. Baumstark, "Die Anaphora von Thmuis und ihre Überarbeitung durch den hl. Serapion," *Römische Quartalschrift* 18 (1904): 132–34; and Maxwell E. Johnson, *The Prayers of Serapion of Thmuis: A Liturgical, Literary, and Liturgical Analysis,* Orientalia Christiana Analecta 249 (Rome: Pontificio Istituto Orientale, 1995), 270–71.

41. Hans Leitzmann, *Mass and Lord's Supper: A Study in the History of the Liturgy* (Leiden: Brill, 1979), 63.

42. *PEER*, 80.

Heaven and earth are full of that glory wherewith you glorified us through your only-begotten Son Jesus Christ, the first-born of all creation, sitting at the right hand of your majesty in heaven, who will come to judge the living and the dead. We make the remembrance of his death, offering to you your creatures, this bread and cup. We pray and beseech you to send out over them your Holy Spirit, the Paraclete, from heaven . . . to make (?) the bread the body of Christ and the cup the blood of Christ of the new covenant.[43]

One is struck here by how closely parallel the epicleses in the Pfalz-Neuburg Church Order of 1543 and *Kassel Agenda* of 1896 are especially to the formulation of the *Louvain Coptic Papyrus*, including both anamnetic and offering language, even without any possible access to such a text at the time of their compilation. Indeed, the Egyptian anaphoral structure as a pattern for Lutheran eucharistic praying has been appealed to before. In 1947, for example, Arthur Carl Piepkorn composed a Eucharistic Prayer with the following petition before the Institution Narrative:

Send down upon us the grace of Thy Holy Spirit, and through Thy Holy Word vouchsafe to bless and sanctify these thy gifts and creatures of bread and wine, that they may be unto us the Body and the Blood of the same Thy most dearly beloved Son, our Lord Jesus Christ, Who, the same night.[44]

But the real proponent of what we might call the "Egyptian connection" was Peter Brunner in his classic study *Worship in the Name of Jesus*, first appearing in German in 1954, but not in English until fourteen years later in 1968.[45] For Brunner, while clearly respecting the Syro-Byzantine anaphoral pattern, especially because of its creedal and overall historical plan of salvation structure, the

---

43. Ibid, 81.

44. A. C. Piepkorn, "The Eucharistic Prayer," *Una Sancta* 7, no. 3 (1947): 10–12.

45. Peter Brunner, *Worship in the Name of Jesus*, trans., M. H. Bertram (St. Louis: Concordia Publishing House, 1968).

ideal place for a *Western* epiclesis is before the Words of Christ. Why? According to him,

> in the Son's assumption of the flesh we behold the word of the Holy Spirit (Luke 1:35; Matt. 1:18). The *unio hypostatica* between the deity and the humanity of Christ does not take place without the Spirit's coming to the creature, without His singling out the creatural for a union with the divine; without his hallowing it and consummating the union. In Holy Communion, the *unio sacramentalis* between the earthly bread and Christ's sacrificial body, glorified in eschatological consummation and in divine-pneumatic derestriction, is involved; the sacramental union between the creatural wine of this earth and Jesus' covenantal blood, shed on the cross and eternally present in eschatological freedom before God's throne (Heb. 12:24), is involved. Nor is the bond of this union effected without the particular cooperation of the Holy Spirit, who, from His inner-trinitarian origin, is the binding bond, and who in His work in the plan of salvation again and again proves Himself the bond which assembles, joins, and unites. Therefore it is most appropriate to ascribe the work of uniting the food with the body and blood of Jesus in Holy Communion to the ministry of the Holy Spirit.[46]

Further,

> we recognize . . . that the words of institution spoken in Christ's stead are, by the power of Christ, the means of consecration in Holy Communion, in the entire act commanded by Christ. The work of the Spirit on bread and wine takes place simultaneously with this event, in which bread and wine, by virtue of Christ's institution, become bearers of His body and blood. Here the work of the Spirit enters the work of Christ, ministering and mediating. May this simultaneousness and this cooperation of the Spirit's work, dependent on Christ's institution, be expressed by the position of the epiclesis in the liturgy? The simultaneousness cannot be expressed. Our language is bound to the before and the after. The liturgical language, too, must express simultaneous events in a succession of sentences. Only the proximity of the epiclesis to the words of institution can intimate that both the

46. Ibid, 304–5.

implored work of the Spirit and the real presence of Christ take place in one pneumatic "now."[47]

As such, Brunner concludes, "since the work of the Spirit does not complete the work of Christ in the consecration but only accompanies it cooperatively, an epiclesis petitioning for consecration must stand, in our Western tradition, before the words of institution, if it is to be used in any form whatsoever."[48] And Brunner himself provided the following as an appropriate epicletic text:

> Assembled in His name and in His memory, we pray Thee for His saving presence in this sacred Meal. We place this bread and this wine, Thy gifts, before Thy countenance, heavenly Father, and pray Thee to consecrate and to bless them through the power of the Holy Spirit, that this bread be the body of our Lord Jesus Christ and this wine be His blood, as we now administer His own Testament according to His command.[49]

While Brunner's approach may not be above critique, especially today in light of scholarship on the earliest anaphoral texts,[50] he did provide a way for Lutheran eucharistic worship both to respect its

---

47. Ibid., 306. Note the similarities between Brunner's theological approach and that of Cyprian Vagaggini, who was himself responsible for the three additional Eucharistic Prayers of the *Missale Romanum* of Pope Paul VI: "The action of Christ and the action of the Holy Spirit are not two diverse actions, but a single action of Christ in the Holy Spirit or through the Holy Spirit. Theoretically speaking, therefore, it is possible to emphasize quite well that which is, so to speak, the role of the Holy Spirit in the Mass without thereby abandoning the idea that Christ, our High Priest, now in heaven at the right of the Father, is the principal minister of the Eucharistic sacrifice" (Cyprian Vagaggini, *The Theological Dimensions of the Liturgy* [Collegeville, MN: The Liturgical Press 1976], 263).

48. Ibid., 307.

49. Ibid., 310.

50. Compare Bryan Spinks, *Addai and Mari—The Anaphora of the Apostles: A Text for Students*, Grove Liturgical Study 24 (Cambridge: Grove Books, Ltd., 1980); Gabriele Winkler, "A New Witness to the Missing Institution Narrative," in *Studia Liturgica Diversa: Essays in Honor of Paul F. Bradshaw*, ed. L. E. Phillips and M. E. Johnson (Portland: The Pastoral Press, 2004), 117–28; and Robert Taft, "Mass without Consecration? The Historic Agreement on the Eucharist between the Catholic Church and the Assyrian Church of the East Promulgated 26 October 2001," *Worship* 77, no. 6 (2003): 482–509.

Augustinian-Western heritage of the central importance of the word in sacramental theology, so strongly emphasized by critics of North American Lutheran liturgical materials like Oliver K. Olson, and to consider an alternative pattern by which Lutherans might embrace other eucharistic prayer structures from the wider liturgical tradition, including that of the West as well as patterns in its own limited tradition. Indeed, if, as Luther said, "as soon as Christ says 'This is My Body,' it is his body through the word and power of the Holy Spirit," the Lutheran position for a Spirit-epiclesis may well be, as Brunner claims, *before* and not after the Institution Narrative. In this way the power of the Holy Spirit through which Christ speaks the word and by which the bread and wine are his Body and Blood is given clear liturgical acknowledgement and expression. But such invocation—though *not* the Holy Spirit, of course—is subordinated and, hence, bound to the *Verba Christi* themselves, which remain the vehicle of the Holy Spirit's work of uniting and joining together both bread and cup with Christ's body and blood and the communicants themselves with Christ and one another through them.

Apart from Piepkorn's 1947 version of a Lutheran Eucharistic prayer with a pre-Institution epiclesis, the only other North American Lutheran attempt at a Eucharistic prayer with a similar pattern was that of Robert Jenson in a 1974 volume of *Lutheran Quarterly*, the entire issue of which was dedicated to providing a commentary and critique of then current experimental Lutheran liturgical resources.[51] Such an attempt must have died the death of neglect among those eventually producing *LBW*, though Jenson's first model, of the Syro-Byzantine type, became Eucharistic Prayer 2 in *LBW*. What I have always found rather fascinating, however, is the fact that then as now the liturgical tradition of the Church of

---

51. Robert Jenson, "Liturgy of the Spirit," *Lutheran Quarterly* 26, no. 2 (1974): 189–203.

Sweden has a euchological heritage that appears to be quite consistent with what we have seen in the Pfalz-Neuburg Church Order of 1543, the *Kassel Agenda* of 1896, the 1879 *Agenda* of the Lutheran Church in Bavaria, and in the work of Brunner and others. While, unlike its North American counterpart, the Eucharistic Prayers of the Lutheran Church of Sweden[52] are not limited to *one* anaphoral structure, five of its seven alternative texts have a pre-Institution epiclesis, some of which (like Prayer G) are clearly "consecratory" in content, and two of which even have offering language (Prayers A and D) akin to the prayers for the Preparation of the Gifts in the Missal of Paul VI:

> *Eucharistic Prayer A:* Let Your Holy Spirit come into our hearts to enlighten us with a living faith. Sanctify by your Spirit this bread and wine, which earth has given and human hands have made. Here we offer them to you, that through them we may partake of the true body and blood of our Lord Jesus Christ.

> *Eucharistic Prayer D:* Send your holy Spirit into our hearts that he may in us kindle a living faith. By your Holy Spirit, bless these gifts of bread and wine and make them holy, fruits of the world and work of human hands that we offer to you. We thank you that through them you give us a sharing in the body and blood of Christ, who. . . . *After the Institution Narrative and Anamnesis:* Unite us all, by the power of the Holy Spirit, into one body, and make us a perfect and living sacrifice through Christ. Through him and with him and in him, all glory and honour belong to you, God, the Father Almighty in the unity of the Holy Spirit, forever and ever.

> *Eucharistic Prayer E:* Send your Holy Spirit and bless these gifts of bread and wine and make them holy. We thank you that through them you give us a share in the body and blood of Christ. *Eucharistic Prayer F:* Send your Spirit on us and on these gifts that we may come to share in the heavenly bread and the cup of salvation that is the body

---

52. *Den Svenska Kyrkohandboken, I* (Stockholm: Verbum Förlag, 1987). See also http://www.svenskakyrkan.se/omoss/liturgy-and-worship.

and blood of Christ. *Eucharistic Prayer G:* Send your Spirit on us and on these gifts of bread and wine that they may be for us the body and blood of Christ.

The only other place in contemporary liturgical materials I am aware of, where a similar anaphoral structure is present, is in the 2000 *Common Worship* of the Church of England, where out of its own eight Eucharistic Prayers in what is called "Use One," a total of *four* fall in this category (Prayers A, B, C, and E).[53] What is intriguing about these Church of Sweden and Church of England Eucharistic Prayers, together with the theological position of Brunner and the small but significant Lutheran heritage in this context, is how close all of this is to the often-maligned structure of the Eucharistic Prayers of the Missal of Paul VI, where the emphasis on a pre-Institution epiclesis is so strong that it influenced how texts like the anaphora from *Apostolic Tradition* 4 and the anaphora called "Egyptian Basil" were used to compose Eucharistic Prayers 2 and 4, respectively. One may certainly critique the changing of the structure of *classic* liturgical texts like these in order to conform to a particular structure and theology (which, by the way, all of our liturgical traditions have done in one way or another), but I suspect that the reason why this structure of the Roman Eucharistic Prayers has often been criticized is because it does not correspond to the contemporary hegemony of the Syro-Byzantine anaphoral pattern, which is, of course, viewed as "the perfect and only paradigm for authentic Eucharistic prayers . . . traced back directly to the Jewish euchology used by Jesus at the Last Supper, and implied by him in the words 'Do this in remembrance of me.'"[54] And yet this structure, with some obvious affinity to the early Alexandrian liturgical tradition, is itself also clearly a legitimate and

---

53. *Common Worship: Services and Prayers for the Church of England* (London: Church House Publishing, 2000), 184–93, 196–97.
54. Spinks, "Berakah, Anaphoral Theory, and Luther," 279.

self-consciously *Western* liturgical structure with a clearly legitimate and orthodox theology of the Holy Spirit, which should be ecumenically fruitful in the West for Lutherans, Anglicans, and Roman Catholics. How surprising and lamentable, especially in light of developments in *Common Worship* and in contemporary Swedish Eucharistic euchology, that not even *one* example of such a prayer exists in something like *ELW*.

The Ritualization of the Gift of the Holy Spirit in Baptism and Rites of Confirmation

The epiclesis in Lutheran baptismal and Eucharistic worship, while probably the most obvious place, is not the only place to look for the question of the relationship between the Holy Spirit and Lutheran worship. The postbaptismal rites in *LBW*, *ELW*, and *LSB* provide a fascinating look at what we might call a contemporary migration of the Spirit among Lutherans. Before the process of producing those worship books began, however, almost all Lutheran baptismal rites concluded with a handlaying blessing prayer, based on the traditional Western postbaptismal anointing prayer, first attested by Ambrose of Milan and revised by Luther in his 1526 *Taufbüchlein* to accompany the giving of the garment: "The almighty God and Father of our Lord Jesus Christ, who hath regenerated thee through water and the Holy Ghost and hath forgiven thee all thy sin, strengthen thee with his grace to life everlasting. Amen. Peace be with thee. *Answer.* Amen."[55]

---

55. Martin Luther, *The Order of Baptism Newly Revised, 1526*, in *Luther's Works*, vol. 53, ed. U. Leupold (Philadelphia: Fortress Press, 1965), 109.

Often defended by appeal to Luther's 1523 *Taufbüchlein*,[56] the rite called *Holy Baptism* in the *LBW* restored for the majority of Lutherans in North America many of the traditional rites and ceremonies of the classic Western baptismal rite omitted in the later stages of liturgical revision during the Protestant Reformation. But what is by far the most notable distinction between this rite and Luther's 1523 rite was the addition of the following postbaptismal rite, at the very place where Luther had originally retained the traditional Western postbaptismal prayer and anointing:

The minister lays both hands on the head of each of the baptized and prays for the Holy Spirit:

> P. God, the Father of our Lord Jesus Christ, we give you thanks for freeing your sons and daughters from the power of sin and for raising them up to a new life through this holy sacrament. Pour your Holy Spirit upon <u>name</u>: the spirit of wisdom and understanding, the spirit of counsel and might, the spirit of knowledge and the fear of the Lord, the spirit of joy in your presence.

> C. Amen.

The minister marks the sign of the cross on the forehead of each of the baptized. Oil prepared for this purpose may be used. As the sign of the cross is made, the minister says:

> P. <u>Name</u>, child of God, you have been sealed by the Holy Spirit and marked with the cross of Christ forever.

The sponsor or the baptized responds: "Amen."[57]

---

56. For a comprehensive and detailed account of the modern development and revision of the rites of Christian initiation in North American Lutheranism, see Jeffrey Truscott, *The Reform of Baptism and Confirmation in American Lutheranism*, foreword by Maxwell E. Johnson (Lanham: Scarecrow Press, 2003).
57. *LBW*, Minister's Edition, 311.

Here in the *LBW* baptismal rite the traditional Roman *confirmation* prayer for the sevenfold gift of the Spirit and the chrismation from the *Gelasian Sacramentary*, reformulated—as in the current Roman Rite of Confirmation itself, in language more akin to the single postbaptismal chrismation of the Byzantine rite—to refer to being "sealed by the Holy Spirit," is rather pronounced. Similarly the rite appears to express an explicit conferral of the Holy Spirit in asking for a postbaptismal "pouring of the Holy Spirit" upon the newly baptized. The language of the formula for the signing and optional anointing in the *LBW* is rather unclear and suggests various possible interpretations. Because it refers to the sealing of the Holy Spirit in the perfect tense (i.e., "you have been sealed . . ."), for example, it is not certain whether it is Baptism or the hand-laying prayer that, supposedly, has constituted this "sealing."

Since Lutheran theology has always been adamant in its assertion that Baptism in the Trinitarian name, with or without additional rites and gestures, constitutes *full* Christian initiation in water *and* the Holy Spirit, *the* theological question, then, is what *LBW* intended by a postbaptismal rite such as this. In fact, it is precisely this postbaptismal rite that was cited as problematic for the official adoption of the *LBW* baptismal rite within the LCMS. In the December, 1977, LCMS "Report and Recommendations of the Special Hymnal Review Committee" the following critical note appeared in relationship to this unit: "Both the rubric and the prayer imply that the Spirit comes after (apart from?) the new life through this sacrament. One wonders why the traditional prayer with its clear connection of water and the Spirit was dropped for this doubtful one."[58] Questioning also even an *optional* postbaptismal anointing, the final rite prepared and accepted by the LCMS, appearing, of

---

58. Lutheran Church, Missouri Synod, "Report and Recommendations of the Special Hymnal Review Committee," December 1977, 27.

course, in *LW*, contained a postbaptismal section which consisted of Luther's own 1526 revision of the anointing prayer with hand laying, followed by the giving of the baptismal garment and lighted candle. What *LW* did, therefore, was to restore partially the postbaptismal rites and formulas of Luther's 1523 *Taufbüchlein*, without, however, the anointing. Only then does the baptismal group assemble before the altar for a concluding prayer and welcome.[59]

It is instructive at this point to look at what happened to this rite in *ELW*:

> *The ministers and the baptismal group may move to a place that is visible to the assembly.*
>
> *The presiding minister continues:*
>
>> Let us pray:
>>
>> We give you thanks, O God,
>> That through water and the Holy Spirit
>> You give your daughters and sons new birth,
>> cleanse them from sin,
>> and raise them to eternal life.
>
> *The presiding minister lays both hands on the head of each of the newly baptized persons while praying for each:*
>
>> Sustain <u>name</u> with the gift of your Holy Spirit:
>>
>> the spirit of wisdom and understanding,
>> the spirit of counsel and might,
>> the spirit of knowledge and the fear of the Lord,

---

59. *LW*, 203–4.

the spirit of joy in your presence,
both now and forever.

C. Amen.

*The presiding minister marks the sign of the cross on the forehead of
each of the baptized. Oil prepared for this purpose may be used. As
the sign of the cross is made, the minister says:*

Name, child of God, you have been sealed by the Holy
Spirit and marked with the cross of Christ forever.

C. Amen.[60]

What is most interesting about the *ELW* version of the hand-
laying prayer is how clearly distinct it is from that which appeared at
this place in *LBW*. While the *LBW* prayer made no reference to John
3:5 or Titus 3:5 and, in asking for a postbaptismal "pouring of the
Holy Spirit" upon the newly baptized, could certainly be interpreted
as asking for an explicit postbaptismal conferral of the Holy Spirit, the
version of the prayer in *ELW* is perfectly clear. That is, Baptism and
Holy Spirit go together and the prayer not only acknowledges that,
but asks simply that the newly baptized might now be "sustained"
with that gift *already* received. Similarly, because the formula for
consignation or anointing still refers to the sealing of the Holy Spirit
in the perfect tense (i.e., "You have been sealed . . ."), the particular
wording of the hand-laying prayer in *ELW* now makes it clear that
what has constituted this "sealing" of the Holy Spirit is *baptism* itself.
Hence, this unit, together with the giving of the garment and candle,
is best interpreted as constituting what the current Roman Catholic
initiation rites call "explanatory rites," or what the ELCA statement

---

60. *ELW*, 590–91.

on the practice of word and sacrament, *The Use of the Means of Grace*, calls "symbolic acts,"[61] that is, acts or rites that merely explain, underscore, or symbolically express further what the church believes happens and is given in Baptism itself.

One might conclude reasonably that with the particular revision of the *LBW* hand-laying prayer in *ELW* the theological concerns expressed by the LCMS would have been now adequately addressed. Instead, the LCMS has again produced its own liturgical resources, with the *LSB* and *Agenda* also appearing in 2006. Since the LCMS and the ELCA had been involved together both with *Welcome to Christ,* a series of study and ritual books for the adult catechumemate,[62] and with the 1999 African-American Lutheran liturgical resource, *This Far by Faith*, in which the baptismal rite, while containing some culturally specific adaptations, was essentially that of *LBW*, this development is to be viewed as most unfortunate.[63] And while the baptismal rite in the *Agenda*, now with prebaptismal exorcism, Luther's Flood Prayer, optional anointing, garment, and candle, more closely resembles Luther's 1523 *Taufbüchlein* than did *LW*, it is to be lamented especially now that the two major Lutheran bodies in the United States cannot even share the same baptismal rite!

Some mention must be made here also of the question of confirmation in Lutheran worship, especially because of its traditional associations both with Baptism and with the Holy Spirit. *ELW*, in a rite entitled "Affirmation of Baptism," provides several different options for use: (1) confirmation; (2) the beginning of one's participation in a community of faith, that is, reception into

61. *The Use of the Means of Grace: A Statement on the Practice of Word and Sacrament* (Minneapolis: Augsburg Fortress, 1997), 33.

62. *Welcome to Christ: A Lutheran Catechetical Guide* (Minneapolis: Augsburg, 1997); *Welcome to Christ: A Lutheran Introduction to the Catechumenate* (Minneapolis: Augsburg, 1997); and *Welcome to Christ: Lutheran Rites for the Catechumenate* (Minneapolis: Augsburg, 1997).

63. *This Far by Faith* (Minneapolis: Augsburg Fortress, 1999), 64–68.

membership; (3) renewed participation in a faith community; and (4) at a time of a significant life passage.[64] In all of these options the rite contains a presentation of the candidate(s), the renunciation of evil and the profession of faith from the baptismal rite, followed by prayers of intercession, a short address to those making affirmation and their response, and a blessing with a laying on of hands consisting of a version of the postbaptismal handlaying prayer, with the phrase "sustain <u>name</u> with the gift of your Holy Spirit" replaced by "stir up in ___ <u>name</u> the gift of your Holy Spirit." The following prayer with hand laying, reserved to confirmation alone in *LBW*, is provided in *ELW* as an option to the above prayer:

> Father in heaven, for Jesus' sake, stir up in <u>name</u> the gift of your Holy Spirit; confirm *his/her* faith, guide *his/her* life, empower *him/her* in *his/her* serving, give *him/her* patience in suffering, and bring *him/her* to everlasting life.[65]

Lutherans and Episcopalians alike have viewed such "affirmation of baptism" rites as repeatable rites adaptable to a variety of circumstances marking significant transition moments in life. And they do this "by connecting these significant transitions with the baptismal understanding of our dying and rising with Christ. These rites mark moments when the faith given in Baptism finds new expression, and the spiritual gifts given in Baptism are stirred up to meet new challenges."[66] As such, "confirmation" is only one of many possible applications.

Theologically speaking, confirmation in the *ELW* is not understood to be part of the rites of Christian initiation per se but as a rite in which, after a period of catechetical instruction, the "confirmands" publicly affirm God's past baptismal action on their

---

64. *ELW*, 234.
65. *ELW*, 236.
66. *LBW*, Minister's Edition, 9.

behalf. Among Lutherans, even the term *confirmation* itself, then, tends to be interpreted not in a liturgical or ritual manner but, consistent with classic Lutheran theology, in catechetical ways. That is, confirmation is seen less as a particular *rite* than it is, as current ELCA policy states, "a pastoral and educational *ministry* of the church that helps the baptized through Word and Sacrament to identify more deeply with the Christian community and participate more fully in its mission,"[67] or, as the introduction to the rite in *LBW* said, "Confirmation marks the completion of the congregation's program of confirmation ministry, a period of instruction in the Christian faith as confessed in the teachings of the Lutheran Church."[68] Seen in this way, the *ELW* rite of "confirmation," while including hand laying and prayer for the stirring up of the gift of the Holy Spirit, is to be interpreted not as an initiatory rite *completing* Baptism at all, "for Baptism is already complete through God's work of joining us to Christ and his body, the Church."[69]

If the confirmation rite of *ELW* is viewed in this way as a public celebration of mature ratification or present owning of one's previous Baptism and marking the completion of the church's ministry *to* those being "confirmed," one must note, by way of contrast, the unique confirmation rite of *LW*. The LCMS, as noted above, rejected the baptismal rite of *LBW* partly because its postbaptismal rites supposedly separated the gift of the Holy Spirit from the water bath of Baptism itself. How surprising then that the confirmation rite of *LW* had what could have clearly been interpreted as an explicit conferral of the Holy Spirit to those being confirmed! What was referred to as the "blessing" in this rite reads, " __Name, God, the Father of our Lord Jesus Christ, *give* you his Holy Spirit, the Spirit of

---

67. ELCA, *The Confirmation Ministry Task Force Report* (September 1993), 1.
68. *LBW*, Minister's Edition, 324.
69. ELCA, *The Confirmation Ministry Task Force Report*, 4.

wisdom and knowledge, of grace and prayer, of power and strength, of sanctification and the fear of God."[70]

This apparent inconsistency between the baptismal and confirmation rites in *LW* presents a serious theological problem about the gift of the Holy Spirit in Baptism and in the life of the baptized. And, when this confirmation conferral of the Holy Spirit is related to the specific questions addressed to those being confirmed—inexplicably called *catechumens*—even greater problems arise. For, not only do these "catechumens" acknowledge the gifts they received in Baptism by reciting a renunciation of evil and a profession of faith, they also are asked specific questions about their acceptance of doctrine (biblical interpretation and Lutheran confessional doctrine) and their desire for church membership (both in the Evangelical Lutheran Church and this particular congregation) and, subsequently, are invited and welcomed to "share . . . in all the gifts our Lord has for his Church and to live them out continually in his worship and service."[71] In other words, the confirmation rite in *LW* can be interpreted not so much as a rite of baptismal *affirmation* but as a rite of *reception* or initiation *into* the LCMS and one of its congregations. And, when combined with the explicit language about the gift of the Holy Spirit in this context, one could legitimately wonder, indeed, whether this rite was not the *real* rite of initiation itself with the gift of the Holy Spirit related explicitly to *Lutheran* Church membership.

How refreshing, then, that the compilers of confirmation rite in the 2006 *LSB* and *Agenda* have faced this problem squarely. While it remains unfortunate that the term *catechumen* is still applied to the baptized in this rite, the confirmation blessing with the laying on of

---

70. *LW*, 206–7; emphasis added.
71. Ibid., 206–7.

hands and signing of the forehead is now the following adaptation of the classic Western postbaptismal anointing prayer: " _Name, the almighty God and Father of our Lord Jesus Christ, who has given you the new birth of water and the Holy Spirit and has forgiven you all your sins, strengthen you with His grace to life everlasting. Amen."[72] While one might certainly critique the use of this particular prayer for a confirmation formula, including the specific use of *strengthen*, this prayer is clearly much more in line with classic Lutheran theology of confirmation and, thankfully, has avoided the theological ambiguity of *"give* you His Holy Spirit." But again, with the changes to the *LBW* rite of Baptism represented by *ELW*, one wonders what objections there could possibly be on the part of the LCMS to either "Baptism" or "Affirmation of Baptism" in *ELW*.

Conclusion

From the 1960s until the present, Lutheran worship, like most other contemporary forms of Christian worship, is characterized by an increasing emphasis upon and recovery of the role of the Holy Spirit, at least, in its baptismal and eucharistic worship. But, again, like most other contemporary forms of Christian worship, this emphasis and recovery has been one that has had a decidedly Eastern Christian, most notably Byzantine, flavor. The current Roman rite of confirmation, for example, especially in the RCIA, where the confirmation chrismation with the formular, "_Name, be sealed with the gift of the Holy Spirit," has simply replaced the traditional Western postbaptismal anointing, has created an unprecedented liturgical and theological connection between Western confirmation

72. LCMS, *Agenda*, 30.

and Byzantine postbaptismal chrismation. As is well known, Aidan Kavanagh referred to this as the "Byzantinization of western confirmation."[73] But modern Protestant rites have done essentially the same thing. For, by omitting the traditional Western postbaptismal anointing prayer from the rites altogether, and by similarly placing a version of this Eastern formula for the "seal of the Holy Spirit" in its place, Lutheran baptismal rites might surely be subject to the same critique. Further, as we have seen, the charge of "Byzantinization" may also be a fitting way to characterize how and where the Holy Spirit has been recovered in the Eucharistic Prayer. And here Bryan Spinks's critique of the over-reliance on and dominance of the West Syrian or Syro-Byzantine pattern of eucharistic praying in contemporary ecumenical liturgical reform and renewal is especially appropriate with regard to the Eucharistic Prayers in *LBW* and *ELW*, where all eucharistic epicleses appear in the West Syrian or Syro-Byzantine postanamnesis location.

While I have nothing but respect for the Byzantine Rite, Lutherans need not borrow Byzantine liturgical patterns outright in order to give liturgical expression to the role of the Holy Spirit in its worship. Critiques like those of Spinks remind us that there are other liturgical alternatives. Even from within the liturgical traditions of Western Christianity, as I have attempted to demonstrate above, there are alternatives for contemporary consideration or usage. Spinks is correct to assert that "an epiklesis may not be so difficult for Lutheran theology as some have maintained," but prior to *LBW* and *ELW* there was developing a strong theological position in favor of a pre-Institution Narrative location for such a Spirit invocation, a location obviously characteristic of Swedish Lutheran Eucharistic praying as well. Similarly, while I have nothing against being "sealed with the

---

73. Aidan Kavanagh, *Confirmation: Origins and Reform* (New York: Pueblo Books, 1988), 92ff.

Holy Spirit" in Lutheran baptismal rites, I too lament the loss of the classic Western-Ambrosian-Roman postbaptismal anointing prayer, a prayer that unmistakably relates Baptism and Holy Spirit, indeed the entire Trinitarian act of Baptism, so clearly and closely together: "The Almighty God, the Father of our Lord Jesus Christ, who has made you to be regenerated *of water and the Holy Spirit* [John 3.5], and has given you remission of all your sins, himself anoints you with the chrism of salvation in Christ Jesus unto eternal life. R. Amen."

3

The Real and Multiple Presences of Christ in Contemporary Lutheran Liturgical and Sacramental Praxis

To accomplish so great a work, Christ is always present in His Church, especially in her liturgical celebrations. He is present in the sacrifice of the Mass, not only in the person of His minister, "the same now offering, through the ministry of priests, who formerly offered himself on the cross," but especially under the Eucharistic species. By His power He is present in the sacraments, so that when a man baptizes it is really Christ Himself who baptizes. He is present in His word, since it is He Himself who speaks when the holy scriptures are read in the Church. He is present, lastly, when the Church prays and sings, for He promised: "Where two or three are gathered together in my name, there am I in the midst of them" (Matt. 18:20).

—*Constitution on the Sacred Liturgy*, paragraph 7.[1]

1. A. Flannery, ed., *Vatican Council II*, vol. 1 (Collegeville, MN: The Liturgical Press, 1975), 4–5.

What would a contemporary Lutheran, or, more specifically, an Evangelical Lutheran Church in America (ELCA), liturgical-sacramental practice and theology look like that took seriously the multiple presences of Christ underscored by the above paragraph 7 of Vatican II's *Constitution on the Sacred Liturgy* (*CSL 7*)? In attempting to answer such a question, I simply must acknowledge that there is a certain artificial quality about this exercise from the very beginning. To take what is a *Roman Catholic* "recovery" of the multiple presences of Christ in the church and then apply that "recovery" to a Lutheran—or Anglican or other Protestant—liturgical-sacramental context seems to me, at first sight anyway, to move in a backward direction. That is, the emphases of *CSL* 7 on the multiple real presences of Christ in the church within its liturgical celebrations—the ministers, the eucharistic elements, the sacraments in general, his word, and the community itself at prayer—sound to Lutheran ears, at least, somewhat like a Roman Catholic vindication of what the Lutheran Reformers themselves argued within the overall context of the sixteenth century. That is, the Lutheran Confessions, for example, couldn't be clearer in their assertion that what have been called, traditionally, the "means of grace" include, rather broadly, the spoken word, Baptism, Eucharist, the power of the keys (confession and absolution), and the "mutual conversation and consolation of brethren,"[2] while being unconcerned with the precise enumeration of what may or may not be called specific "sacraments."[3] Similarly, at least Lutherans would want to point out that with regard to the presence of Christ in the "ministers," the Confessions again not only equate the "office" of ministry *with* word and sacrament as the very means by which the church is called into being by the

---

2. See *The Smalcald Articles* IV–VIII in Tappert, *The Book of Concord*, 310–13.
3. See *The Apology of the Augsburg Confession*, Article XIII.17, in Tappert, *The Book of Concord*, 213.

Holy Spirit in the first place,[4] but have no qualms in asserting that the ordained "do not represent their own persons but the person of Christ" (*repraesentat Christi personam*) and that "when they offer the Word of Christ or the sacraments, they do so in Christ's place and stead" (*Christi vice et loco porrigunt*).[5] As such, ordination itself can appropriately even be called a "sacrament" by Lutherans,[6] if for no other reason, it appears, than that the ordained, "representing" the person of Christ in and to the church through the actual *doing* of the ministry of word and sacrament, become themselves concrete, embodied, or "sacramental" signs of Christ's continued presence. At the same time, a *Lutheran* reading of *CSL* 7, especially with regard to the presence of Christ in the community itself, would want to underscore that the ecclesiology of the Lutheran Confessions is, precisely, an ecclesiology of the liturgical assembly, which asserts that "the church is the assembly of saints [or believers] in which the Gospel is taught purely and the sacraments are administered rightly."[7] And—might I be so bold as to point out?—it was Luther himself, who, while limiting the number of sacraments to three, based on the defining criteria he *inherited* from the Western medieval tradition, nevertheless stated, in words that sound downright prophetic vis-à-vis modern Roman Catholic sacramental theology as expressed by theologians such as Edward Schillebeeckx, OP,[8] and Karl Rahner, SJ,[9] that "if I were to speak according to the usage of the Scriptures, I should have only one *single* sacrament [Christ, 1 Tim. 3:16], but with three sacramental signs."[10]

---

4. See ibid., Article V, p. 31.
5. Ibid., Articles VII and VIII.28, p. 173.
6. Ibid., Article XIII.11–12, p. 212.
7. Ibid., Article VII, p.32. On this, see chapter 9 below, 221–39.
8. Edward Schillebeeckx, *Christ the Sacrament of the Encounter with God* (New York: Sheed & Ward, 1963).
9. Karl Rahner, *The Church and the Sacraments*, Quaestiones Disputatae 9 (London: Search Press, Ltd., 1963).

Hence, when Lutherans read *CSL* 7, or read in the 1993 *Directory for Ecumenism* that "Baptism constitutes the *sacramental* bond of unity existing among all who through it are reborn,"[11] or hear Pope John Paul II say in his 1995 encyclical *Ut Unum Sint* that that "in the fellowship of prayer *Christ is truly present*; he prays 'in us,' 'with us,' and 'for us,'"[12] they recognize a common theological bond, heritage, and participation in the presence of Christ himself. And, they would underscore strongly the following statement about the very *sacramentality* of the word itself offered ecumenically by Karl Rahner and Heinrich Fries some years ago:

> *Pulpit fellowship* is already being practiced in many cases; and it no longer presents a disquieting exception, even to Catholic Christians. But one really should think about this more than ever, *since it is precisely a pulpit fellowship which presupposes a community of faith.* Consider the reality of salvation of the Word of God; consider Christ's presence in its various forms, including the form of proclamation; finally consider the theological conformity of Word *and* Sacrament—sacrament as visible Word (*verbum visibile*), the Word as audible sacrament (*sacramentum audible*).[13]

Because there is so much in common between *CSL* 7 and the classic Lutheran confessional, liturgical, and theological tradition, *the* question is *not* really how the *Roman Catholic* recovery of the multiple presences of Christ might shape *Lutheran* liturgical-sacramental practice and theology (even if Lutherans are most grateful for this recovery in Roman Catholic thought and practice). Rather, the question is, what does a Lutheran liturgical-sacramental practice and

---

10. M. Luther, *The Babylonian Captivity of the Church*, in *Luther's Works*, vol. 36, p. 18 (emphasis added).
11. *Directory for Ecumenism*, para. 129, in *Origins* 23, no. 9 (July 29, 1993).
12. *Ut Unum Sint* 22 in *Origins* 25, no. 4 (June 8, 1995).
13. *Unity of the Churches: An Actual Possibility* (New York/Philadelphia: Paulist Press and Fortress Press, 1985), 125 (emphasis added).

theology look like when, in an ecumenical context, it takes its own classic tradition seriously? With regard to this, I will divide my comments into two major sections: (1) What, in fact, has been and is happening toward a richer liturgical-sacramental life among especially ELCA Lutherans; and (2) what factors still need serious attention?

Developments toward a Richer Liturgical-Sacramental Life among Lutherans

The general answer to the question of what a *Lutheran* liturgical-sacramental life looks like that takes the multiple presences of Christ seriously is rather simple. Given the commonality in texts, rites, and rubrics in the worship books of Lutherans and Roman Catholics today, though now somewhat challenged by the unfortunate 2011 translation of the *Roman Missal*, it looks very much like post-Vatican II Roman Catholic worship is also supposed to look: in other words, where the word of God is proclaimed clearly, audibly, intelligibly, and with dignity by carefully prepared readers; where ministers, presiding and otherwise, know their particular roles in the assembly and carry them out in a manner befitting the worship of the Trinitarian God; where bread that looks, smells, feels, and tastes like (and, of course, *is*) real bread is broken and shared and where wine, rich and good wine, is shared in common; where the other sacraments or "sacramental rites" are seen as corporate and communal events with the rich and abundant use of the sacramental signs of water and oil and the healing and benedictory gestures of hand laying and touch; where the Liturgy of the Hours is the church being itself in its constant, prayerful, eschatological, intercessory, and expectant vigil; where the Paschal Triduum, especially the Great Vigil of Easter, prepared for by a renewing, baptismal in orientation, forty-day Lent and an ensuing fifty-day period of paschal joy, are seen as the pulsating center and heartbeat not only of the liturgical year but of life in Christ; and where the community itself, both in assembling to do *leitourgia* and in scattering for its missions of *martyria* and *diakonia* knows itself—"fully, actively, and consciously"—as that body of Christ it receives and celebrates so that it may itself be broken for the life of the world. Indeed, within these general themes, there are several positive developments to note and to celebrate among contemporary Lutherans.

First, as the overall intent of the 1978 *Lutheran Book of Worship* (*LBW*) made clear and the 2006 *Evangelical Lutheran Worship* (*ELW*) continues to make clear, the place, dignity, and full celebration of Baptism, including infant Baptism, within the public liturgical assembly of the church is emphasized, as is the use of full immersion as the preferred mode of baptism, as well as the use of postbaptismal hand laying and anointing to signify the baptismal gift of the "seal" of the Holy Spirit. Here as well, architectural shifts geared toward providing baptismal pools and fonts enabling immersion are to be noted. Similarly, as we saw already above in chapter 1, the renewing and formative power of the Rites of Christian Initiation of Adults within Roman Catholic circles has led to new and recent adaptations of the catechumenal process in Lutheran circles—including Missouri Synod and Evangelical Lutheran Church in Canada (ELCiC) cooperation—with the development of several catechumenal and liturgical resources under the general title of *Welcome to Christ,* part of which, such as the "Welcome to Baptism," appears now in *ELW*.[14]

---

14. Evangelical Lutheran Church in America, *Evangelical Lutheran Worship: Leader's Desk Edition* (Minneapolis: Augsburg Fortress, 2006), 592–95; *Welcome to Christ: A Lutheran Catechetical Guide* (Minneapolis: Augsburg Fortress, 1997); *Welcome to Christ: A Lutheran Introduction to the Catechumenate* (Minneapolis 1997); and *Welcome to Christ: Lutheran Rites for the Catechumenate* (Minneapolis 1997). For a fuller discussion see the first chapter in this volume, "Baptismal Spirituality in the Early Church and Its Implications for the Church Today," 32.

And, along with this, of course, comes the continual need and opportunity for the development and training of parish catechists and sponsors, and the reorganization and renewal of parish life in general centered around sacramental-liturgical formation and catechesis. While still in its infancy among Lutherans, such holds great promise for the future in the changing cultural context of a "post-Christendom" world.

With further regard to issues concerning Christian initiation, it should also be noted here that, like the unbroken initiatory tradition of the Eastern Orthodox churches, and like The Episcopal Church, the express wishes of the Roman Catholic Federation of Diocesan Liturgical Commissions (FDLC) in one of its 1992 resolutions,[15] and its Canadian Lutheran (ELCiC) neighbors to the north,[16] the ELCA has also moved decisively toward instituting the communion of *all* the baptized, including the first communion of newly baptized infants within the baptismal Eucharist. The ELCA's 1997 statement on sacramental practices, *The Use of the Means of Grace: A Statement on the Practice of Word and Sacrament,* says clearly that "infants and children may be communed for the first time during the service in which they are baptized."[17] Such is surely a harbinger of things to come within the ELCA.

---

15. "It is the position of the delegates . . . that the Board of Directors of the [FDLC] and the Bishops' Committee on the Liturgy urge the National Conference of Catholic Bishops to take the initiative to propose to the Apostolic See a discussion on the restoration of the ancient practice of celebrating confirmation and communion at the time of baptism, including the Baptism of children who have not yet reached catechetical age, so that through the connection of these three sacraments, the unity of the Paschal Mystery would be better signified and the Eucharist would again assume its proper significance as the culmination of Christian initiation." *FDLC Newsletter* 22, no. 4 (December 1995): 45.

16. Evangelical Lutheran church in Canada, *Statement on Sacramental Practices* (Winnipeg, 1991), 5.8, 6.9.

17. Evangelical Lutheran Church in America, *The Use of the Means of Grace: A Statement on the Practice of Word and Sacrament* (Minneapolis: Augsburg Fortress Press, 1997), 3.37D, p. 42.

Second, in spite of still some resistance related to ungrounded Lutheran fears of "becoming *too* Roman Catholic" in liturgical-sacramental practice, there is no question but that the recovery of the Lutheran confessional norm of the centrality of Sunday and feast-day Eucharist is gradually happening within the ELCA. Thanks, at least, in part, to the influence of Gordon Lathrop's book, *Holy Things: A Liturgical Theology*,[18] Lutherans are increasingly coming to understand that the very *ordo* or overall pattern of Christian liturgy is constituted by the *Sunday* assembly of the *baptized*, who *gather*, hear the *word*, share the *Meal*, and are *sent* on mission in the world. Indeed, while details of this approach are not above criticism here and there,[19] based on the resurrection appearances of Jesus in the New Testament (cf. especially the Emmaus account in Luke 24), the mid second-century description of Justin Martyr in his *First Apology* 61 and 65, and the liturgical ecclesiology of the Lutheran Confessions, such an ordo is clearly the conceptual framework behind not only *The Use of the Means of Grace* but also *ELW* itself. Within the not-so-distant past the norm for those churches now comprising the ELCA was usually a celebration on the first Sunday of the month, and, within the first half of this century, the norm in those churches was the continuation of the late medieval practice of communion reception only four times a year. To have moved, then, from this to a situation where now almost a majority of ELCA congregations now celebrate Eucharist at, at least, *one* of their Sunday liturgies each week is highly significant.

Hand in hand with this recovery of eucharistic frequency it is also important to note that the style of eucharistic liturgy, due in no small part to the ecumenical nature and influence of the liturgical movement, has also changed dramatically, so dramatically, in fact,

---

18. Gordon Lathrop, *Holy Things: A Liturgical Theology* (Minneapolis: Fortress Press, 1993).

19. See below, chapter 5, "What Is Normative in Contemporary Lutheran Worship? Word and Sacrament as Nonnegotiable," 113-33.

that contemporary eucharistic celebrations among Lutherans, Roman Catholics, Episcopalians, and others often look, sound, and are, essentially, the same. It is for this reason that I often challenge my Notre Dame Roman Catholic undergraduate students to experience liturgy at some of the local Lutheran and Episcopalian parishes in the South Bend–Mishawaka area and tell me what they perceive that the real differences are in relationship to the experience of their own parishes (with the general exception that people might regularly sing better in these other places). And, the late Professor James White liked to say of his own United Methodist parish, Broadway United Methodist Church in South Bend, that the primary difference, compared with Roman Catholic practice, is that Broadway uses real bread while Roman Catholics use real wine.[20] (Another major difference, of course, is that one might actually encounter an ordained *woman* presider, vested in alb, stole, and chasuble, in these churches.) Lectors, communion ministers, and lay assistant ministers, who often fulfill liturgical roles traditionally assigned to deacons in some traditions, are frequently employed in contemporary Lutheran practice. Because of *Evangelical Lutheran Worship*, ELCA Lutherans now have at least *eleven* full Eucharistic Prayers available for their use, a highly significant development when one considers that the use of *any* Eucharistic Prayer—beyond Preface, Sanctus, and Institution Narrative—has been an issue of some argument and debate within Lutheran circles in the past thirty years or so, as was noted and discussed in the previous chapter.

At the same time, the recovery of the centrality of the Eucharist has led to a concern for the inclusion of those unable to attend the Sunday assembly, due to illness, hospitalization, and other factors. Here is to be noted the increasingly frequent Lutheran practice of

20. J. F. White, "Roman Catholic and Protestant Worship in Relationship," in *Christian Worship in North America: A Retrospective: 1955–1995* (Collegeville, MN: Liturgical Press, 1997), 3.

lay ministers, who are dismissed from the Sunday assembly in order to bring communion to the sick and homebound from the Sunday liturgy itself, again along the lines of Justin Martyr's own mid second-century description of this practice and some sixteenth-century Lutheran *Church Order* practices.[21] Using a relatively new-for-Lutherans rite of "Sending of Holy Communion,"[22] in which the already "consecrated" eucharistic gifts are shared in the context of the reading of the word and prayer, has not only fostered some kind of recovery of the propriety of eucharistic reservation for the communion of the sick but has actually led in some places to the practice of ongoing eucharistic reservation itself. In South Bend–Mishawaka, for example, at least *three* of the seven ELCA parishes regularly reserve the Eucharist—both bread and wine—in a visible aumbry somewhere within their liturgical spaces. One of these parishes does so even on the former high altar in the very center of its worship space, and another of them, for good or ill, not only regularly uses this reserved Eucharist for distribution to the assembly on Sundays in addition to the newly consecrated bread and wine, but, in clear imitation of current Roman Catholic practice, actually distributes communion to the assembly on Good Friday from what has been solemnly reserved in a special place at the conclusion of the Holy Thursday Liturgy the evening before.[23]

Third, an ELCA Lutheran focus on the multiple presences of Christ in the Liturgy would not limit the signification of that "presence" either to the particular gender of ministers, presiding and otherwise, nor to being in a situation of "full communion" with a specific ecclesial tradition. With regard to the reading and

21. On this, see F. Senn, *Christian Liturgy: Catholic and Evangelical* (Minneapolis: Fortress Press, 1997), 353.
22. *Evangelical Lutheran Worship: Pastoral Care* (Minneapolis: Augsburg Fortress, 2008), 81–92.
23. On this, see the next chapter in this study, chapter 4, "Eucharistic Reservation and Lutheranism: An Extension of Sunday Worship?" 85–111.

proclamation of the word of God itself, ELCA Lutherans have not only recently adopted and adapted the *Revised Common Lectionary* but now use regularly the New Revised Standard Version of the Bible as that translation has come to be offered, finally, in actual, large, and dignified *Lectionary* and *Gospel* books designed for Lutheran liturgical use. Given the fact that both male and female together reflect the very "image of God," according to Gen. 1:26–27, and given Saint Paul's radical *baptismal* reversal of ethnicity, social status, and gender in terms of the identity of the church itself in Christ, according to Gal. 3:28 (i.e., in Christ Jesus "there is no longer Jew nor Greek . . . slave nor free . . . *male nor female*" [emphasis added]), ELCA Lutherans—as several other churches today—have been able to receive gratefully the gift of women's ordination to the office of ministry in the church and have accepted women pastors among those who "do not represent their own persons but the person of Christ" and who, "when they offer the Word of Christ or the sacraments, they do so in Christ's place and stead."

Ecumenically speaking, ELCA Lutherans also hold that since "admission to the [Eucharist] is by invitation of the Lord presented through the Church to those who are baptized,"[24] eucharistic hospitality toward members of other Christian traditions is practiced. To that end, "all baptized persons are welcomed to Communion when they are visiting in the congregations of [the ELCA],"[25] and "when a wedding or a funeral occurs during [the Eucharist], communion is offered to all baptized persons."[26] Eucharistic hospitality to individuals, however, should *not* be taken as a substitute for the pursuit of full communion between different churches, a goal toward which the ELCA is also oriented and firmly committed.

24. *The Use of the Means of Grace*, 49A, p. 52.
25. Ibid., 49, p. 52.
26. Ibid., 49B, p. 52.

At the same time, the practice of eucharistic hospitality and the goal of full communion between currently separated churches are related. Viewed as constituting a *source* for and means *toward* full communion, rather than simply the *expression* or *summit* of Christian unity, as is expressed by the Roman Catholic and Orthodox churches, the ELCA and The Episcopal Church recognizing substantial agreement between themselves on various issues of doctrine and practice, were involved together since the early 1980s in an officially recognized "Interim Eucharistic Sharing," which led toward the eventual establishment of full communion in *Called to Common Mission* in 2001. But with regard to Lutheran-Roman Catholic eucharistic sharing, echoing the above-quoted statement of Roman Catholic theologians Karl Rahner and Heinrich Fries that "a pulpit fellowship . . . presupposes a community of faith," that Christ is "present" in "the form of proclamation," and that there is a "theological conformity of word *and* sacrament—sacrament as visible word (*verbum visibile*), the word as audible sacrament (*sacramentum audible*)," and pointing to *CSL* 7, as well as to other recent Vatican statements on the sharing of the real presence of Christ in word, Baptism, assembly, and prayer in common, ELCA Lutherans might wonder how seriously such "modes" of Christ's *real* presence are actually taken in and by the Roman Catholic Church. Indeed, if Christ is *present* in such multiple ways, then he is really present. And if his real presence in word is acknowledged to exist in other communions to such an extent that the ELCA and the American Roman Catholic Bishops could actually produce a (now already out of print) *Lutheran-Catholic Service of the Word* for common use, then what *does* the "theological conformity of Word *and* Sacrament" actually imply? If divided Christians can already share *some* "modes" of that real presence *officially*, why not the *eucharistic* mode as well?

Similarly, with the Lutheran World Federation and Vatican *Joint Declaration on the Doctrine of Justification*, signifying, finally, a rather explicit and substantial *unity in faith* between Lutherans and Roman Catholics, one can only hope that some form of Eucharistic Hospitality or "Interim Eucharistic Sharing" might eventually result. To that end, it is significant that Walter Cardinal Kasper, President Emeritus of the Pontifical Council for Promoting Christian Unity, expressed his great regret that shared communion between Roman Catholics and Protestants did not become a reality during his time as president.[27] But in the meantime, because ELCA Lutherans see a theological consistency flowing from the conformity of audible word and visible word (sacrament), welcoming all the baptized to Christ's inclusive, egalitarian, and community-building table companionship naturally follows. Both word and sacrament, in Lutheran thought at least, function together under the category of the proclamation of the gospel, one audible, the other visible.

Fourth, and finally for this section, other liturgical sacramental practices recovered among contemporary ELCA Lutherans in the years since Vatican II should at least be briefly noted as they relate to this question of "multiple presences." Within *ELW* and *LBW*, ELCA Lutherans have for their use a style of the Liturgy of the Hours clearly rooted in the "cathedral" rather than "monastic" tradition, at least with regard to Evening Prayer and its *Lucernarium* and Psalm 141. Regular provisions for private confession and absolution as well as corporate confession and absolution have been made in the current worship books. There has even been a recovery of the practice of the laying on of hands and "anointing of the sick," with forms provided for individual use in ministering to the sick and for public celebrations within the context of the eucharistic liturgy or Liturgy of

27. ENI Press Release, Stuttgart, Germany, July 22, 2010.

the Word,[28] a practice that several congregations employ on a fairly regular basis. And, of course, at least in principle, the importance of preaching the word of God has remained a constant and abiding emphasis. All in all, with regard then to the multiple presences of Christ in word, Meal, assembly, ministers, sacraments, and prayer, the liturgical practice and theology of the ELCA, at least according to its liturgical books and statements, has been one of recovering its classic liturgical-sacramental heritage within a contemporary ecumenical context. As such, an ELCA liturgical-sacramental practice that takes the multiple presences of Christ seriously looks a lot like the vision of Vatican II and the worship books of its own tradition.

Issues Still Needing Serious Attention

All things liturgical and sacramental within the ELCA, however, do not reflect this common ecumenical vision, and I certainly do not want to give the deceptive impression that they do. In fact, there are several issues that still need serious attention in the ELCA if liturgical renewal is to go forward from this point. Let me simply list here—without too much additional comment—what I see some of these issues to be:

(1) In spite of frequent attempts and some notable examples to the contrary, the Eucharist itself remains in far too many places but an "occasional service," either still monthly, bimonthly, or, even in those places having at least one Eucharist each Sunday, only after others have been dismissed from the principal Sunday assembly;

---

28. See *Evangelical Lutheran Worship: Leader's Desk Edition* (Minneapolis: Augsburg Fortress, 2006), 660–65; and *Evangelical Lutheran Worship: Pastoral Care*, 163–68.

(2) in spite of a clear preference for the use of full sacramental signs in the celebration of Liturgy,[29] minimalistic use of water in Baptism (administered in some places even by only a finger dipped in the font and on the head of the candidate), mass-produced communion wafers instead of real bread, and what I refer to as (often even prefilled), individualized, "shot glasses" for the reception of the Eucharistic Wine, has continued in far too many places. But the concern of the Lutheran Reformers for communion under both elements was the sacramental significance of sharing the *cup*, not merely the reception of wine;

(3) in spite of the eleven Eucharistic Prayers currently available for use, a bare-bones *Verba* (Institution Narrative) alone often constitutes the normative pattern of eucharistic consecration—occasionally without even dialogue, Preface and Sanctus—in still far too many places on "Communion" Sundays;

(5) apart from some notable exceptions and the willingness of many parishes to embrace it, the Paschal Triduum has yet to be even *experienced* by many Lutheran congregations and clergy, much less instituted as the annual center of parish life gathered around the Light of Christ risen from death, the watery stories of salvation history, the font, and the table of the Lord, after a Lent oriented toward baptismal renewal and affirmation;

(6) occasional proposals to move or do away with the Advent season altogether, or the creation of new liturgical seasons such as "Prepent," as a time of preparation for Pentecost, in the name of an ambiguous "inculturation" in the modern world, find some sympathetic response and reveal a church rather unsure of the

---

29. See *The Use of the Means of Grace*, 25 and 26, 31–32; and 44A, 48.

theological meaning and overall purpose of the liturgical year itself[30];

(7) even the theological and normative priority of Sunday itself as *the* day of resurrection, day of encounter with the crucified and risen Lord, and the day for the Christian assembly around word and table, as expressed in *The Use of the Means of Grace*,[31] is met with some incredulity and resistance;

(8) often with synodical and national support, "contemporary" and nonsacramental forms of "worship," in the name of an ambiguous "hospitality" for "seekers," based on what some have called "entertainment evangelism," is permitted to substitute for or provide an alternative to "traditional" Sunday worship (i.e., the classic Sunday worship of the one, holy, catholic, and apostolic church centered in word *and* table);

(9) contemporary or locally created "Statements of Faith" are permitted to modify or even replace the classic Nicene and Apostles' Creeds themselves and so call into serious question the precise relationship of some local Lutheran congregations to the historic faith of the church altogether;

(10) the medieval and Thomistic emphasis on the *one* office of ordained ministry (that of presbyter or priest) is maintained with a tenacity approaching a *status confessionis*, in spite of the fact that the contemporary Roman Catholic and Anglican emphasis on the "threefold" office and "ordination" of bishops, presbyters,

---

30. See S. K. Wendorf, "Let's Move Advent," in *Lutheran Partners* (November/December 1991) and the numerous favorable letters her plea engendered in *Lutheran Partners* (March/April 1992). For my response to this, see my "Let's Keep Advent Right Where It Is," *Lutheran Forum* 28, no. 4 (November, 1994): 45–47. On the season of "Prepent" see my comments in chapter 5 below, 113–17.
31. *The Use of the Means of Grace*, 6, 13.

and deacons has moved beyond this context and owes more to a recovery of a patristic understanding of "orders" *within* the church, including the laity as an "order(!)" itself, than it does to the priestly ordination theology of Western Scholasticism[32]; and, finally,

(11) in spite of the traditional Lutheran emphasis on the importance of the oral proclamation of the word in the assembly, far too often, in my experience, the overall performance and quality of proclaiming the Sunday readings, on the part of lectors and presiders alike, pales in comparison with the dignity, care, and attention to oral proclamation that I often experience within post-Vatican II Roman Catholic practice.

There is still much to do for the renewal of liturgical-sacramental practice in the ELCA, even if it is moving, generally, in what I consider to be the right direction. Issues of ecclesiology and ministry, and the recovery of a rich and full liturgical-sacramental practice that corresponds to and expresses its theological understanding, still

---

32. Until this becomes clear, I fear that Lutherans, Roman Catholics, and Anglicans will continue to talk right past each other on questions of ministry and ordination. Interestingly enough, even Thomas Aquinas held that bishops weren't "ordained," since ordination was to priesthood itself. Because the permanent diaconate no longer existed in Thomas' time, deacons were "ordained" only as a transitional step toward presbyteral ordination. Bishops—as priests already—could only be "consecrated." It is within *contemporary* Roman Catholic and Anglican practice, due in large part to that patristic recovery noted above, that bishops and permanent deacons now are also "ordained" to particular "offices" of ministry within the one "priesthood" of Christ and the church. It appears here that Lutherans remain more in debt to *medieval* theology and practice with an emphasis on "one ordained office" than do modern Roman Catholics and Anglicans. At the same time, I've often wondered what Lutherans think they are doing at the "installation" of newly elected bishops when the presiding minister "may" lay "a" hand on them during the "blessing." If this isn't liturgically an "ordination" to an office—*ut legem credendi statuat lex supplicandi*—I do not know what it is. Of course, there is only *one* priesthood, *one* "office" of word and sacrament, *one* ministry, *one* church, and, for that matter, even and only one *Sacrament*, namely, Christ himself in the power of the Holy Spirit. But how that "oneness" is "ordered" in the life of the church does not imply only "one" *presbyteral* way as the once-for-all, dominically mandated, ecclesial norm for this ordering. If anything, that "oneness" was signified traditionally by the *episkope* of one *bishop* and not by the presbyteral college.

loom large for the future, as the ELCA seeks to find its ecclesial and ecumenical place in the first decades of the twenty-first century.

Conclusion

In spite of the several issues that remain in all of the major liturgical traditions today, what has been accomplished already over the past now fifty-plus years since the Roman Catholic *Constitution on the Sacred Liturgy* in 1963 should also give us both a sense of hope and a renewed call toward the continued implementation of that common ecumenical liturgical-sacramental vision centered in the multiple and real presences of Christ among us. Never can we allow the occasional calls within some Roman Catholic circles for the "undoing" of contemporary liturgical reform, the "reform of the reform," or for a "restorationist-revisionistic" reinterpretation of that reform, based on an incomplete late medieval ecclesiology and sacramental theology, or for Lutherans, a sixteenth-century fundamentalist repristination, to deter or detract us from that continued implementation. For at stake in all this is not really the liturgy itself but the very identity and life of the people of God for whom the liturgy exists to serve in the first place. And it serves them in forming them to be what they celebrate, to become what they receive, in lives broken and shared for the sake of the world that others too may come to the fullness of life in the real presence of the crucified, yet living, Christ, who is known not only in the apostolic teaching and *koinonia*, in the breaking of bread and the prayers (see Acts 2:42), but is known and revealed especially there. We have come a long way but there is still a long ways to go.

4

———

Eucharistic Reservation and Lutheranism

An Extension of Sunday Worship?

In ecumenical conversations Roman Catholics frequently ask Lutherans, "If you Lutherans actually believe in the real presence of Christ in the Eucharist as you say you do, how come you do not normally reserve the Eucharist in your churches?" This is, of course, a most legitimate question for Lutherans to be asked by Roman Catholics and other Christians who regularly do practice forms of eucharistic reservation. But there is rather interesting assumption behind this question, namely, that the practice of eucharistic reservation in one Christian tradition can or should be some kind of litmus test for determining whether another Christian tradition "really" holds to a theology of real presence. Is this necessarily the case? What *is* the precise relationship between eucharistic reservation and real presence? This particular chapter will deal with these questions from a Lutheran theological perspective in light of the early history of the practice of reservation and Communion, related doctrinal and dogmatic issues, and current Lutheran liturgical-pastoral practice. In spite of their long history of not doing so, might there be ways today in which Lutheranism could embrace some form of eucharistic reservation without compromising its confessional position?

A Variety of "Lutheran" Practices

As noted in the previous chapter, the congregational practices I want to consider here all come from four Evangelical Lutheran Church in America (ELCA) congregations in the South Bend, Indiana, area, all of which celebrate the Eucharist at every Sunday Liturgy and on major festival days.[1] The first congregation, Transfiguration Lutheran Church, has three Sunday Eucharists, one on Saturday evening and two on Sunday morning. Real bread is used for the celebrations. All of the bread and wine needed for all three celebrations is placed on the credence table before the Saturday evening Liturgy and, hence, whatever remains of those elements after the first or second Liturgies is simply used again (= "reconsecrated") at the next Liturgy. At the end of all three Liturgies any remaining bread and wine is scattered or poured on the ground outside. The theological rationale for both practices (using what remains at the next Liturgy and eventually disposing of them on the ground) is that Lutherans believe that after the Liturgy the bread and wine, which *were* the Body and Blood of Christ, are no longer that Body and Blood but revert back to common food and drink.

A similar practice and theological rationale is present at the second imaginary congregation, Faith Lutheran Church. At Faith, however,

---

1. The names of the congregations have been changed. Also, while I have indicated that these are all ELCA congregations, I suspect that a similar variety of practices could be found also in congregations of the Lutheran Church, Missouri Synod.

any "hosts" remaining after its two Sunday celebrations are simply stored with unconsecrated ones and any wine remaining in the flagon is poured back into the bottle in preparation for the next Sunday's celebrations. At both Transfiguration and Faith, distribution of Communion to the sick and homebound requires the presence of the pastor who will use an occasional service called "Holy Communion in Special Circumstances," a service that includes a short Eucharistic Prayer containing the Words of Institution, or the Words of Institution alone.[2]

The third congregation, Saint Paul's Lutheran Church, practices a different custom from either that of Transfiguration or Faith. At Saint Paul's, any of the elements remaining after each of its two Sunday Eucharists are reverently consumed by the pastor and assisting ministers, a portion is sent with lay Communion ministers to the sick and homebound who will use a service called "Sending of Holy Communion,"[3] and another portion is reserved for the future Communion of the sick in what is essentially a "tabernacle" on the back wall (former) altar in the very center of the church. Until only recently this tabernacle was kept in the sacristy. At Saint Paul's the obvious theological rationale is that there is a permanence to the real presence of Christ "in, with, and under" the bread and wine, a presence that does not somehow cease after the celebration of the Eucharistic Liturgy itself.

The practice of the fourth congregation, Christus Rex, is similar to that of Saint Paul's but actually goes one or two steps further. That is, Christus Rex regularly sends lay Communion ministers out to the sick and homebound from its single Sunday celebration and reserves both elements in an "aumbry" within a side wall of the sanctuary. But, in obvious imitation of Roman Catholic practice,

2. *Evangelical Lutheran Worship: Pastoral Care* (Minneapolis: Augsburg Fortress 2008), 93–103.
3. Ibid., 81–92.

Christus Rex celebrates a "Mass of the presanctified" on Good Friday wherein elements consecrated at the Maundy Thursday Eucharist are distributed to the congregation. And further, in equally obvious imitation of an unfortunately common Roman Catholic practice—a practice, in fact, that Roman Catholic liturgists consider to be liturgically scandalous![4]—Christus Rex *regularly* distributes Holy Communion at the time of distribution not only from what has just been consecrated at the Sunday liturgy but from the *reserved* sacrament as well! Indeed, there is no question but that approximately half of the relatively small congregation at Christus Rex receives holy Communion from the *reserved* sacrament each week.

While it is certainly true that no liturgical or extraliturgical "cult" of the Blessed Sacrament exists at Saint Paul's or at Christus Rex, the mere fact that the Eucharist is reserved in these congregations under both elements indicates that within the ELCA—even within the same city—there is no consistency whatsoever in eucharistic practice, especially with regard to the question of what to do with elements remaining after the liturgy itself. Nevertheless, if I were to speculate on which of these four congregations best reflects the most common practice in the ELCA I would have to say that is probably that of both Transfiguration and Faith, where what has been consecrated is either reused or used to the feed the birds. The question, therefore, naturally arises: Which of these imaginary congregations is most "Lutheran" in its eucharistic practice and theological interpretation?

That is not an easy question to answer for the simple reason that, while strongly affirming the real presence of Christ in the Eucharist, at times even in language that approximates the Roman Catholic doctrine of "transubstantiation,"[5] the Lutheran Confessions do not deal *in detail* with the *duration* of Christ's eucharistic presence. What

---

4. See below, n43.

they do say on this issue, however, if limited, is rather significant. In relationship to Corpus Christi processions, for example, Article XXII of the *Augsburg Confession* states, "Because the division of the sacrament [= the withdrawal of the cup] is contrary to the institution of Christ, the customary carrying about of the sacrament in processions is also omitted by us."[6] If this article might be interpreted as but critiquing a "misuse" or "abuse" of the sacrament, the *Formula of Concord, Solid Declaration* (1580) is much stronger in its approach. In its rejection of the specific doctrine of transubstantiation, Article VII states,

> They assert that under the species of the bread, which they allege has lost its natural substance and is no longer bread, the body of Christ is present even apart from the action of the sacrament (when, for instance, the bread is locked up in the tabernacle or is carried about as a spectacle and for adoration). For nothing can be a sacrament apart from God's command and the ordained use for which it is instituted in the Word of God.[7]

Such statements would seem to support the practice of either Transfiguration or Faith. Without the sacramental "action," the "ordained use" of the Eucharist, frequently interpreted as the reception or *sumptio* of the Body and Blood of Christ in Communion (often times called "receptionism"), the Eucharist is not the Eucharist and the Body and Blood of Christ are not present.

But is it really that simple? Herman Sasse, in his now classic study of Luther's eucharistic theology, *This Is My Body*, wrote that

Luther and the early Lutheran Church avoided forming any theory

---

5. Article X of the Augsburg Confession, for example, states that "the true body and blood of Christ are really present in the Supper of our Lord under the *form* of bread and wine." Tappert, *The Book of Concord*, 34 (emphasis added).

6. Ibid., 51. Unfortunately, Philipp Melanchthon does not deal with this particular issue further in his *Apology*.

7. Ibid., 588.

about the "moment" when the Real Presence begins and the "moment" when it ceases. Some later orthodox theologians advanced the theory that Christ's body and blood are present only at the "moment" when they are being received. This is frequently regarded, within and without the Lutheran Church, as the genuinely Lutheran doctrine. . . . [But] as far as Luther himself is concerned, there cannot be the slightest doubt that he never did limit the Real Presence to the instant of distribution and reception. He never abandoned the view that by the words of consecration bread and wine "become" the body and blood of Christ. Otherwise neither the elevation, which was in use at Wittenberg up to 1542, nor the adoration of Christ, who is present in the elements, could have been justified. He always regarded it as Zwinglianism to neglect the difference between a consecrated and an unconsecrated host, and it has always been the custom of the Lutheran Church to consecrate the new supply of bread or wine or both if more is needed than originally was provided for. The rule that Luther, like Melanchthon and the Lutheran Confessions, followed was that that there is no sacrament, and consequently no presence of the body and blood of Christ, "apart from the use instituted by Christ" or "apart from the action divinely instituted." Since the word "usu" is explained by "actio" it cannot mean the same as "sumptio." If it has sometimes been understood in this way, it must be said that neither Luther nor the Formula of Concord . . . identified the "sumptio" (eating and drinking) with the use or action of the sacrament.[8]

In a related footnote Sasse adds,

Luther demanded the dismissal of a pastor who had given to a communicant an unconsecrated host instead of a consecrated one, which had been dropped. This unfortunate man was imprisoned. Luther does not approve of such punishment, but he thinks him unfit for the

8. Herman Sasse, *This Is My Body: Luther's Contention for the Real Presence of Christ in the Sacrament* (Minneapolis: Augsburg Publishing House, 1959), 173–74. In this context one might nuance Sasse's remarks to say that it is only until recently among Lutherans that consecrating new elements was the custom. In the current ELCA statement on sacramental practices, *The Use of the Means of Grace* (ELCA, 1997), 50, for example, the following appears: "In the rare event that more of either element is needed during distribution, it is not necessary to repeat the words of institution." But no clear rationale is given for what amounts to a departure from Lutheran tradition in this context. Sasse (and probably Luther himself) would have found this statement as undoubtedly indicative of a Zwinglian approach to the Eucharist in modern American Lutheranism.

Lutheran ministry: "He should go to his Zwinglians" (Letter of Jan. 11, 1546; WA Br 11, No. 4186). In 1543 Luther and Bugenhagen gave their opinion in a controversy about the question whether consecrated hosts could be preserved together with unconsecrated ones for another consecration. Luther criticizes this. Nothing of the consecrated elements should be saved, but must be consumed. In this connection he gives a clear definition of the sacramental "time" or "action": "sic ergo definiemus tempus vel actionem sacramentalem, ut incipiat ab initio orationis dominicae et duret, donec omnes communicaverint, calicem ebiberunt, particulas comederint, populus dimissus et ab altari descessum sit" (WA Br 10, No. 3894, lines 27ff.). In a Table Talk of 1540 Luther goes so far as to allow the blessed sacrament to be carried to another altar (in the same church) or even, as was still customary in some churches, to be brought to the sick in their home (WA TR 5, No. 5314), provided this could be regarded as part of the "action." This was tolerated as an exception. However, a reservation of the sacrament was not allowed. The remnants of the elements should be either consumed or burned.[9]

On the basis of the above two quotations from Sasse, it would seem, then, that all four of our ELCA congregations are, in various ways, at odds with the Lutheran sacramental tradition. Both Transfiguration and Faith are at odds in their practice of mixing unconsecrated bread and wine with consecrated bread and wine, either from one service to the next or in preparation for the following week's Liturgies. Certainly Transfiguration is at odds by scattering the remaining bread and pouring out the remaining wine on the ground rather than consuming both reverently. But Saint Paul's and Christus Rex are also at odds with that tradition in their own ways. Consistent with Luther's permitted exception of allowing the Eucharist to be

---

9. Sasse, *This Is My Body*, 174. The Latin phrase quoted above can be translated as the following: "In this way, therefore, let us define sacramental 'time' or 'action': that it might begin at the prayer of the Lord [*orationis dominicae*] and remain until all will have communed, the chalice will have been drunk, the particles [of bread] will have been eaten, and the people dismissed and left the altar." It is difficult to know here if *orationis dominicae* means the "Lord's Prayer" (= Our Father) or is a reference to the institution narrative. Since this definition was given in 1543, it is possible that the reference is to the "Our Father" in the *Deutsche Messe* that actually precedes the institution narrative. But such an interpretation is not likely.

taken to the sick as an "extension of the action," both Saint Paul's and Christus Rex do send lay Communion ministers out from the liturgy to the sick and homebound. It would seem, however, that they both depart from the Lutheran tradition in their practices of eucharistic reservation. Here, especially, it would appear that it is the practice of Christus Rex that represents the most radical departure in regularly distributing Communion from the reserved sacrament during Sunday Liturgies and in adopting the "Mass of the presanctified" for Good Friday.

If it is true, however, that all of these congregations seem to depart in some way from the Lutheran tradition, the reason for that must certainly be that the tradition itself is not all that clear. As we noted in Sasse above, "Luther and the early Lutheran Church avoided forming any theory about the 'moment' when the Real Presence begins and the 'moment' when it ceases." Consequently, even today the avoidance of forming any such theory gets expressed in various ways. On the one hand, *The Use of the Means of Grace* can direct that "any food that remains is best consumed by the presiding and assisting minister and by others present following the service."[10] On the other hand, regarding the Communion of the sick and homebound the same document says, "*Occasional Services* provides an order for the Distribution of Communion to Those in Special Circumstances. As an extension of the Sunday worship, the servers of Communion take the elements to those unable to attend."[11] And, when one reads the rubrics of this particular service in the 1982 *Occasional Services*, it becomes clear that "extension of the Sunday worship" is interpreted as an *immediate* extension of the distribution of Communion from the Sunday worship:

10. Evangelical Lutheran Church in America, *The Use of the Means of Grace: A Statement on the Practice of Word and Sacrament* (1997), 50.
11. Ibid., 51.

To underscore the significance of bringing the congregational Eucharist to those unable to participate in the assembly, the Communion should be carried to the absent *without delay* following the congregational celebration. Sufficient ministers should be appointed so that all the absent may receive Communion *within a few hours* of the congregation's service that day.[12]

But in the current book of occasional services, namely, *Evangelical Lutheran Worship: Pastoral Care*, the directions indicate only that "sending of Holy Communion *best underscores* the participation of the person visited within the larger assembly when it is used *soon after* the congregational service, normally within a few hours on the same day."[13] The use of "best underscores" in the current book does not equal the same sort of expectation for "without delay" indicated in the 1982 version of this rite. Consequently, one starts asking theologically, just how long *does* the presence of Christ remain in the bread and wine as this extension of the Sunday worship? A few hours? A few days? And if the Body and Blood of Christ remain in the elements for the purposes of communing the sick and homebound on *Sundays* does that presence disappear if the Communion minister does not arrive at the place of the sick or homebound until Monday or Tuesday? Is the real presence of the Body and Blood of Christ in the bread and wine a permanent presence that remains as long as the bread and wine themselves remain as recognizable food and drink? To ask such questions, naturally, is to ask the question of the theological and liturgical propriety of eucharistic reservation itself, and it is important here to look at this in the context of its early historical development rather than from the ideological and polemical stances of a later period.

---

12. *Lutheran Book of Worship: Occasional Services* (Minneapolis: Augsburg Fortress, 1982), 79 (emphasis added).
13. *Evangelical Lutheran Worship: Pastoral Care*, 89 (emphasis added).

Eucharistic Reservation and Communion
in Historical Perspective

Lutherans (and, undoubtedly, many Roman Catholics), both at the time of the *Formula of Concord* and today, tend to forget that the reservation of the Eucharist and Communion from the reserved Eucharist antedate the thirteenth-century doctrine of transubstantiation by *centuries*. Similarly, the practice of eucharistic reservation is no more intrinsically connected to the doctrine of transubstantiation than transubstantiation is itself intrinsically connected to the doctrine of the real presence! Even the Council of Trent said only that transubstantiation was the "most apt" and "most appropriate" way to refer to the change of the bread and wine into the Body and Blood of Christ![14] And certainly the long standing traditions of the Eastern Orthodox Churches remind us that it is possible and traditional to acknowledge the real presence of Christ in the Eucharist, to reserve the Eucharist, to celebrate Liturgies of the "Presanctified" (at least in Lent), and to commune the sick from the reserved sacrament without any recourse to the Western medieval doctrine of transubstantiation and without any concomitant cult of the Blessed Sacrament (e.g., Corpus Christi processions, Benedictions, etc.).

Thanks to the work of Nathan Mitchell and others,[15] the history of this topic is now easily narrated. Our earliest reference to the distribution and reception of Communion *outside* of the Liturgy

14. H. J. Schroeder, *The Canons and Decrees of the Council of Trent* (St. Louis: B. Herder, 1941), Session XIII.4.
15. See Nathan Mitchell, *Cult and Controversy: The Worship of the Eucharist Outside Mass* (New York/Collegeville, MN: Pueblo, 1982), 10–19. In addition to Mitchell, the following historical survey is based on Robert Taft, "The Frequency of the Eucharist throughout History," in *Beyond East and West: Problems in Liturgical Understanding* (Rome: Pontifical Oriental Institute, 1997), 87–110; Edward Foley, *From Age to Age* (Chicago: Liturgy Training Publications, 1991), and, of course, the classic study of O. Nussbaum, *Die Aufbewahrung der Eucharistie*, Theophaneia 29 (Bonn: Hanstein, 1979).

appears already in the middle of the second century (ca. 150 C.E.).
in Justin Martyr's *First Apology*, 65. Herein Justin indicates that, at
the conclusion of the Liturgy, "deacons" carried the Eucharist to
those who were absent from the community's celebration, a practice
seemingly consistent with the distribution to the sick and
homebound as the "extension of the Sunday worship" in the ELCA
today. A short time later in North Africa Tertullian witnesses to the
fact that the faithful regularly took the Eucharist home with them
from the Sunday celebration for the reception of Communion during
the week (at least on the "station" or fasting days of Wednesdays and
Fridays).[16] In the middle of the third century, Cyprian of Carthage
also refers to this practice and informs us that the consecrated bread
was kept in little boxes called *arcae* (or chrismals).[17] These *arcae* were
either worn around the neck of believers or kept in their homes.

If Tertullian and Cyprian seem to refer only to the reservation and
reception of the Body of Christ in this context, rubrics preserved in
the so-called *Apostolic Tradition*, traditionally but no longer ascribed
to Hippolytus of Rome (ca. 215 C.E.),[18] not only corroborate the
practice of home reservation and Communion, but make it clear that
the ritual of Communion included reception from the cup as well:

> For blessing [the cup] in the name of God, you received [it] as the
> antitype of the blood of Christ. Therefore refrain from pouring out
> [any], so that an alien spirit may not lick it up. You will be guilty of
> blood, as one who scorned the price with which he has been bought.[19]

It is quite possible, then, notes Mitchell, that early Christian domestic
rituals of Communion from the reserved Eucharist included "blessing

---

16. See *ad uxorem* 2:5, 2ff., and *De oratione* 19.4.
17. Cyprian, *De Lapsis* 26. See also Foley, *From Age to Age*, 38.
18. *Apostolic Tradition*, chs. 36–38.
19. *Apostolic Tradition*, ch. 38; ET by Paul F. Bradshaw, Maxwell E. Johnson, and L. Edward
    Phillips, *The Apostolic Tradition: A Commentary*, Hermeneia (Minneapolis: Fortress Press, 2002),
    184.

the cup" by means of dropping a small portion of the bread into it, in other words, a "consecration by contact." Such a method of consecrating the wine, in fact, has continued to the present day in the "Liturgy of the presanctified" and distribution of Communion to the sick within various rites of the Christian East.[20]

That the practice of domestic eucharistic reservation and reception continued into the late fourth century is clearly attested by Basil of Caesarea (379), who, in reference to desert monastics and others, writes,

> All the solitaries in the deserts, where there is no priest, keep the Communion by them and partake of it by themselves. At Alexandria too, and in Egypt, each one of the laity, for the most part, keeps the Communion at home, and whenever he wishes partakes of it himself. For after the priest has completed the sacrifice and distributed it, he who then received it in entirety . . . must believe that he duly takes and receives it from the hand that first gave it. For even in the church, when the priest distributes each portion, he who receives takes it into his complete control, and lifts it to his mouth with his own hand. It comes to the same thing, whether one or many portions at a time are received from the priest.[21]

In light of the contemporary ELCA practice of carrying Communion to the sick and homebound as an "extension of the Sunday worship," it is interesting that Mitchell would comment on the words of Basil, noting that "quite clearly, Basil regards Communion at home as simply *an extension of the public liturgy in church*; postponing the consumption of some of the bread until a later time is quite inconsequential, since one still 'takes and receives it from the hand that first gave it.'"[22]

---

20. See the important study by my former student, Stefanos Alexopoulos, *Presanctified Liturgy in the Byzantine Rite: A Comparative Analysis of Its Origins, Evolution, and Structural Components*, Liturgia Condenda Series (Leuven: Peeters, 2009).
21. Basil, *Letter 23*, as quoted in Mitchell, *Cult and Controversy*, 17–18
22. Ibid., 18 (emphasis added).

Nevertheless, if still in the fourth-century eucharistic reservation at home and domestic rituals of Communion reception on days when the Eucharistic Liturgy itself was not celebrated in church were rather common and approved, the custom of taking the Eucharist home came to be discouraged for a variety of reasons. Jerome, for example, expressed his strong disapproval regarding those banned from receiving Communion publicly in church, who yet received privately in their homes.[23] Similarly, the Council of Saragossa (ca. 379–381), perhaps out of fear of the Eucharist falling into the hands of heretics (i.e., the Priscillianists), decreed that "if anyone is found guilty of not consuming *in church* the Eucharist he has received, let him be anathema."[24] At the same time, it *is* documented that the practice of home reservation and Communion did continue in some places until the seventh and eighth centuries.

If home reservation and Communion would cease for a variety of reasons, however, the reservation of the Eucharist in churches, especially for the Communion of the sick and for public distribution of Communion on fasting days, certainly continued. Canon XIII of the Council of Nicea refers to the necessity of viaticum being given to the dying, but it is the late fourth-century *Apostolic Constitutions* (ca. 381) that contains our first clear reference to the reservation of the Eucharist in the church (i.e., in the sacristy).[25] For several centuries the reserved Eucharist was frequently kept inside an *arca*, chrismal, or pyx within a sacristy cupboard, and it is quite possible in some places, as a letter of Chrysostom indicates, that the wine was also reserved.[26] There is no reason to think that these practices were new developments in the fourth century but rather a continuation of what

---

23. See ibid., 17.
24. See ibid., 18–19.
25. *Apostolic Constitutions* 8.13.17. See also Foley, *Cult and Controversy*, 60.
26. John Chrysostom, *Ep. Ad Innoc.* 3.

had already been evolving previously. A *Life of St. Basil*, attributed to Amphilochius of Iconium, indicates that Basil had commissioned a golden dove into which he had placed a portion of the Eucharist. This was then suspended over the altar "as a figure of the sacred dove that appeared at the Jordan over the Lord during his baptism."[27]

What is most interesting to note in this overall context, however, is the close relationship that seems to develop in some quarters between the practice of eucharistic reservation and christological orthodoxy. This becomes the case especially within the context of the fifth-century Nestorian controversy.[28] Whatever the eucharistic theology and practice of Nestorius himself might have been in Constantinople, the followers of Cyril of Alexandria apparently interpreted the strict christological diophysitism of Nestorius and his followers as leading to a eucharistic practice that held that there could be no complete or permanent union between the divine Logos and the bread and wine. Hence, in words that sound surprisingly "Lutheran," according to some interpretations, the Body and Blood of Christ were present in Holy Communion but only *temporarily* and limited to the day of the Eucharistic Liturgy itself. What remained of the eucharistic elements until the next day was no longer considered to be Christ's Body or Blood. Already Cyril of Alexandria had attacked this approach, saying,

> I hear that some people say that the mystical blessing is no longer active to effect sanctification when the Eucharist is left over to the next day. Those who reason this way are insane. For Christ does not become different, and His Holy Body does not undergo any change. On the contrary, the effectiveness of the blessing and the life-creating grace in It remains unchanged.[29]

27. Text as quoted by Mitchell, *Cult and Controversy*, 60.
28. See N. D. Uspensky, *Evening Worship in the Orthodox Church* (Crestwood, NY: St. Vladimir's Seminary Press, 1985), 154–56.
29. Cyril of Alexandria, *A Letter to Calosirius*, as translated in Uspensky, *Evening Worship in the Orthodox Church*, 154.

Further, for Cyril the very question of the life-giving nature of the Eucharist was at stake in this controversy. That is, for him Nestorius had so separated the divine and human natures in Christ from each other that in the Eucharist itself only the "human" body and blood of Christ could be received.[30] Cyril writes,

> Not as common flesh do we receive it, not at all, nor as a man sanctified and associated with Word according to the unity of dignity, or as having had a divine indwelling, but as truly the life-giving and very flesh of the Word himself. For He is life according to His nature as God, and when He became united to His flesh, He made it life-giving.[31]

What Nestorius and his followers might have actually held and taught about the Eucharist, however, is difficult to uncover and one must always be cautious of discerning a position based on the critique of opponents. The fact that the ancient Assyrian Church of the East did not historically—and still does not (!)—reserve the Eucharist nor celebrate the Liturgy of the presanctified is what undoubtedly has led others to make certain assertions about eucharistic theology in that tradition. For example, according to N. Uspensky and other Orthodox theologians, eucharistic reservation and the Liturgy of the presanctified in the Byzantine tradition signify the victory of Orthodox Christology over Nestorianism in that both practices presumably safeguard the unity of the Person of Christ in the Eucharist as the God-Man whose Body and Blood are life-giving.[32] The only problem is that they do not produce any hard evidence

---

30. On this, see the classic article by Henry Chadwick, "Eucharist and Christology in the Nestorian Controversy," *Journal of Theological Studies*, new series 2 (1951): 145–64. Unfortunately, Chadwick does not deal with the question of reservation.

31. Cyril of Alexandria, *Letter* 17.3. English translation in Daniel Sheerin, *The Eucharist*, Message of the Fathers of the Church, vol. 7 (Wilmington/Collegeville, MN: Michael Glazier, 1986), 276–77. See also W. H. C. Frend, *The Rise of the Monophysite Movement: Chapters in the History of the Church in the Fifth and Sixth Centuries* (Cambridge: University of Cambridge Press, 1972), 124–25.

32. Uspensky, *Evening Worship in the Orthodox Church*, 155. See also n38 below.

to support such a claim and, in spite of Cyril of Alexandria's own critiques of the East Syrian approach, the Coptic Orthodox Church also does not regularly reserve the Eucharist.

What is most likely the case is that the practice of the ancient Assyrian Church of the East regarding eucharistic reservation is nothing other than a continuation of early Christian liturgical diversity and the survival of one ancient practice. That is, some early Christian communities clearly reserved the Eucharist and regularly communed the sick from the reserved sacrament. Others did not do so but simply carried the Eucharist to the sick on the same day as the celebration. In fact, it may well be that Justin Martyr's own description of deacons carrying Communion to the absent in his *First Apology* is quite consistent with the practice of the Assyrian Church of the East, and that Justin's own quite likely Syrian community at Rome did not practice reservation. Only later within the developing homogeneity of liturgical practice across ecclesial boundaries and within the context of a developing christological orthodoxy, would certain practices come to be criticized and even condemned in light of those developments. Indeed, it would be preposterous to assume that prior to the Council of Ephesus (431 C.E.) East Syrian Christians regularly reserved the Eucharist and then stopped reserving in response to the christological position of the other churches that had now become recognized as the orthodox position. Does it not make more sense to see nonreservation as one ancient practice that became reinterpreted later on, reinterpreted not by those who followed the practice, but by those who sought to critique and condemn that practice in terms of their own christological position? Even today, according to Mar Bawai Soro, Western California Bishop of the Assyrian Church of the East,

> The Church of the East holds that once the Eucharistic elements are consecrated, they become really, truly and permanently, the Body and

Blood of Christ. This theological statement can clearly be seen in Church of the East's liturgical-Eucharistic texts, the writings of the Fathers, and in canonical legislation. Church of the East official texts do not dispute or contradict the common orthodox, catholic faith of the real and permanent presence of Christ in the Holy Qurbana. Now, concerning the practice of Eucharistic preservation and the Presanctified: At present, we certainly do not preserve the Eucharist, nor am I aware of any such practice in the past. Yet, as recently as the early 1990's, the Holy Synod (not the Patriarch) allowed priests to take the consecrated Holy Qurbana to the sick out in hospitals and homes. Sometimes, it may be through the overnight that the patient receives the Eucharist. But there is still definitively no practice of preserving the Qurbana in our churches.[33]

Hence, in spite of the approaches of Uspensky and others, there is no necessary correlation whatsoever between eucharistic reservation and the theology of Christ's real presence in the Eucharist itself. Those who reserve and those who do not reserve might both assert Christ's real and permanent presence!

Further developments regarding eucharistic reservation and even the developing cult of the reserved Eucharist in the medieval West and at the time of the Protestant Reformation are more widely known than are the practices from the patristic period. Hence, these developments need not be treated in detail here. At the risk of oversimplification, however, it is important to note that the very criticisms of the Lutheran Confessions against late medieval Roman practice (e.g., reservation of the Host and Corpus Christi processions) are those that arose because the cult of the Blessed Sacrament outside Mass—including an emphasis on the elevation of the Host in Mass—had come to be in practice the practical surrogate for the reception of Communion itself. That is, the desire to see and adore the Host ("spiritual" and "ocular" Communion) became, in the words of Joseph Jungmann, the "be all and end all" of eucharistic devotion

33. Email correspondence with Robert Taft, May 20, 2002.

and the Host itself became the supreme relic among many lesser relics.[34] And yet, it was only *after* the Protestant Reformation, and in response to what was perceived to be a denial of the real presence on the part of the Reformers, that, increasingly, the Eucharist became reserved in tabernacles placed in the center of the main altar of Roman Catholic churches. Hence, for Roman Catholics the reservation or nonreservation of the Eucharist became most closely associated with the affirmation or denial of Christ's real presence.[35]

Mitchell summarizes the development of the Eucharist outside the Eucharistic Liturgy per se as the story of a significant shift from "Eucharist as Meal" to "Eucharist as Food," increasingly separated from the context of the "Meal" itself.[36] If this is so, then the concern of the Lutheran Reformers for *usus* and *actio* and their suspicion of the external eucharistic cult associated with the reserved sacrament—"nothing can be a sacrament apart from God's command and the ordained use for which it is instituted in the Word of God"—might surely be viewed as nothing other than a concern for restoring the very Meal character of the Eucharist itself. In other words, without questioning the meaning of the "Eucharist as Food," and while strongly affirming the real presence of Christ in, with, and under the "Food," the Lutheran Reformers were adamant that such "Food" was not an object to be adored *outside* of the overall liturgical *actio* but a Gift to be received within that *actio* ("Eucharist as Meal") itself. If this seems so obvious to us now, it was surely not so obvious in a late medieval context where Communion was received by the laity at most four times a year, and, at the least, by law, once during

---

34. Joseph A. Jungmann, *The Mass of the Roman Rite*, vol. 1 (New York: Benziger Bros., 1951), 120ff. See also Robert Cabié, *History of the Mass* (Washington, DC: The Pastoral Press, 1992), 75–84.

35. See Theodore Klauser, *A Short History of the Western Liturgy* (New York: Oxford University Press, 1979), 135–40.

36. See Mitchell, *Cult and Controversy*, 19–29.

Easter as decreed by Lateran IV (1215). What David Holeton has written with regard to the cessation of infant Communion in the medieval West is certainly related to our topic here as well:

> A Christian society that has degenerated to such a state that it becomes necessary to legislate that Christians need receive the Eucharist once a year is fertile for most everything to take place in the context of Baptism and the eucharist. The whole vision of what the Eucharist was, and what its relationship was to the community, had . . . changed.[37]

Eucharistic Reservation and Lutheranism Today

In light of the previous section, it would seem that the variety of Lutheran practices represented by our four contemporary ELCA congregations, with some exceptions, might all be considered somehow consistent not only with Lutheran sacramental theology and practice but with the variety of sacramental practices known throughout the history of the church. That is, the practice of nonreservation of the Eucharist represented by Transfiguration and Faith is surely consistent with the emphasis in both Luther and the Lutheran Confessions as well as with the continuing practice of the ancient Assyrian Church of the East. Indeed, with the concerns expressed both by Luther and the *Formula of Concord* against reservation and about the proper *usus* and *actio* of the sacrament within the context of the Eucharistic Liturgy itself, one wonders if the early Lutheran movement did not somehow accidentally restore that ancient eucharistic practice still characteristic of the Assyrian Church of the East. Here it is interesting to note that certain polemical Eastern Orthodox theologians, who have condemned

---

37. D. Holeton, "The Communion of Infants and Young Children: A Sacrament of Community," in *And Do Not Hinder Them: An Ecumenical Plea for the Admission of Children to the Eucharist*, ed. G. Müller–Fahrenholz, Faith and Order Paper 109 (Geneva 1982), 63.

Nestorian eucharistic practices, have seen in those practices the origins of Protestant "receptionism."[38]

What is very significant, however, is that the lack of reserving the Eucharist in the Assyrian Church of the East has *not* been a factor in the very recent determination of pastoral guidelines for Communion reception between the Assyrian Church of the East and the Chaldean Church, the latter of which is the closely related Eastern Catholic Church in communion with Rome. Beginning in 1994 with a *Common Christological Declaration between the Catholic Church and the Assyrian Church of the East*, continued ecumenical dialogue and convergence led in 2001 to a document entitled *Guidelines for Admission to the Eucharist between the Chaldean Church and the Assyrian Church of the East*. While these guidelines are ecumenically significant for a variety of reasons, it is clear that eucharistic reservation was and is not a related issue in this context. That is, even without the practice of eucharistic reservation, the *Guidelines* state clearly that "the Assyrian Church of the East has . . . preserved a full eucharistic faith in the presence of our Lord under the species of bread and wine."[39] In other words, as this development surely confirms, the reservation of the Eucharist can *not* be a litmus test for determining the orthodoxy of a particular church's theology of the real presence of Christ in the Eucharist. Consequently, in dialogue between Roman Catholics and Lutherans on the question of the real presence the issue of reservation might appear to be similarly moot.

At the same time, the apparent careless disregard for the elements remaining after the Eucharistic Liturgy at Transfiguration and Faith must also be addressed. That is, reverent disposal is one thing.

---

38. Cf. George Bebis, "Symbolai eis ten peri tou Nestoriou Ereunan (ex Apopseos Orthodoxou)," (PhD diss., University of Athens 1964), 320–22; and Chrestos Androutsos, *Symbolike*, 2nd ed., (Athens, 1930), 285–89ff. and 339ff. I owe these references to Father Stefanos Alexopoulos.

39. Pontifical Council for Promoting Christian Unity, *Guidelines for Admission to the Eucharist between the Chaldean Church and the Assyrian Church of the East* (Rome, 2001), para. 3.

Reusing and mixing consecrated and unconsecrated elements, or using what remains to feed the birds and squirrels is another, and it belies an un-Lutheran notion of "receptionism" that cannot be supported theologically. The words of the so-called *Apostolic Tradition* 38 seem to be a rather strong indictment of this: "Refrain from puring out [any], so that an alien spirit may not lick it up. You will be guilty of blood, as one who scorned the price with which he has been bought." The Lutheran Reformers may well have considered various extraliturgical practices associated with the Eucharist (e.g., processions and the like) to be abuses, but they did not teach a "receptionism." Hence, if the remaining eucharistic elements are to be reverently consumed or burned in the Lutheran tradition it is because they *are* consecrated and cannot be returned simply to common use, mixed for reuse, or merely scattered on the ground. Indeed, to paraphrase an early Christian document, the *Didache*, "One does not give what is holy to dogs" (or to birds and squirrels).

What then of the practice of eucharistic reservation at both St. Paul's and Christus Rex? While there may be an accidental parallel in the practice of nonreservation and belief in the real presence within both the Assyrian Church of the East and the Lutheran churches, this parallel certainly fails when it is remembered that Lutherans chose deliberately in the sixteenth century to stop reserving the Eucharist in their churches. With regard to specific Lutheran–Catholic dialogue and sacramental praxis today, then, the question of reservation is not really so moot at all since the cessation of reservation among Lutherans was a decision consciously directed against Roman Catholic praxis.

But must this still be the case in light of modern ecumenical convergence? That is, can there be a place in Lutheranism for a eucharistic reservation that does not compromise the Lutheran Confessional focus on sacramental *usus* or *actio*? One might surely think so, and congregations like St. Paul's and Christus Rex have obviously concluded that eucharistic reservation is an appropriate Lutheran option today.

In an article on eucharistic reservation in contemporary Roman Catholicism, Jesuit liturgist Peter Fink has written that,

> The food of the Eucharist is reserved after the eucharistic celebration primarily to extend the nourishment and the grace of Christ's table to those unable to participate in the liturgy itself, particularly the sick and the dying. This is clearly stated in the 1967 instruction *Eucharisticum mysterium*: "the primary and original purpose of the reserving of the sacred species in church outside Mass is the administration of the Viaticum" (E.M. III, I, A.).[40]

Of course, even the Council of Trent had made essentially the same point, saying,

> The custom of reserving the Holy Eucharist in a sacred place is so ancient that even the period of the Nicene Council recognized that usage. Moreover, the practice of carrying the Sacred Eucharist to the sick and of carefully reserving it for this purpose in churches, besides being exceedingly reasonable and appropriate, is also found enjoined in numerous councils and is a very ancient observance of the Catholic Church. Wherefore, this holy council decrees that this salutary and necessary custom be by all means retained.[41]

Similarly, the significant 1982 ecumenical convergence statement of the Faith and Order Commission of the World Council of Churches, *Baptism, Eucharist, Ministry,* suggests

> that, on the one hand, it be remembered, especially in sermons and instruction, that the primary intention of reserving the elements is their distribution among the sick and those who are absent, and on the other hand, it be recognized that the best way of showing respect for the

---

40. Peter Fink, "Eucharist, Reservation of," in *The New Dictionary of Sacramental Worship*, ed. Peter Fink (Collegeville, MN: Michael Glazier, 1990), 428.
41. Session XIII, VI, in Schroeder, *The Canons and Decrees of the Council of Trent.*

elements served in the eucharistic celebration is by their consumption, without excluding their use for communion of the sick.[42]

Closely related is the classic statement often attributed to early liturgical movement Belgian pioneer Lambert Beauduin that "the Eucharist is adored *because* it is reserved. It is not reserved in order to be adored." Clearly, the primary motive is for the Communion of the sick and dying. Any other acts of devotion or adoration of the presence of Christ associated with reservation are secondary in nature.

Together with the service called "Sending of Holy Communion," which no longer limits its use explicitly to "without delay" or "within a few hours," and in light of a renewed Roman Catholic emphasis on eucharistic reservation as an extension of "the nourishment and the grace of Christ's table to those unable to participate in the liturgy itself, particularly the sick and the dying," it should be possible for Lutheranism to reevaluate and, in some contexts, at least, to embrace a limited practice of eucharistic reservation today. With the relatively rare exception of congregations like Saint Paul's and Christus Rex, the fact that Lutherans have not traditionally reserved the Eucharist has tended to put Lutheranism at odds with what early on became the practice of the *dominant* ecclesial traditions of Christianity in both East and West. Further, reservation of the Eucharist and Communion from the reserved Eucharist, as we saw above in no less than Basil of Caesarea, can be viewed simply as the extension of the distribution of holy Communion from the Sunday Eucharist *throughout the week*. In this way Lutherans and Lutheran theology could embrace a practice of eucharistic reservation in ways that do not violate the Lutheran confessional stance about "action" and "use." That is, the reservation of the Eucharist for the purposes of the reception of Communion by

---

42. "Eucharist," III., 32, in World Council of Churches, *Baptism, Eucharist, Ministry* (Geneva, 1982).

the "absent" *is* nothing other than the extension of the eucharistic *actio* of the Sunday Liturgy itself. Surely such an understanding of reservation for the purposes of Communion reception on the part of the sick, homebound, and dying can be seen today as part of "God's command and the ordained use for which it is instituted in the Word of God." At the time of the Lutheran Reformation this focus may well have been obscured by a nonreception piety and a reservation practice viewed primarily for purposes of adoration. But that is hardly a danger today when both Lutherans and Roman Catholics place a similar emphasis on the reception of Communion in the Eucharistic Liturgy and where both now send out Communion ministers from the Sunday assembly to the sick and dying.

This does not mean, however, that either St. Paul's or Christus Rex are completely off the hook in their reservation and Communion practices. The previous reservation practice of St. Paul's, with their "tabernacle" kept in the sacristy, was certainly much more consistent with the ancient Christian practice of reserving the Eucharist for the sick, homebound, and dying in sacristy aumbries. In fact, it is hard not to interpret the moving of this tabernacle from the sacristy to the former main altar in the church as anything other than an attempt at imitation of (post-Trent) Roman Catholic and Anglo-Catholic practice. Certainly Christus Rex needs to address its practice of communing the assembly from the reserved Eucharist at the Sunday Liturgy. What Robert Taft has said about Roman Catholic practice applies doubly to congregations standing in the Lutheran tradition of the *usus* and *actio* of the Meal. Taft writes,

> It is clear that there has to be a better way of narrowing the gap between theory and execution. When one can still now, already generations after Benedict XIV (*Certiores effecti* § 3) and Pius XII (*Mediator Dei* § 118), go to Sunday Mass in a Roman Catholic parish church almost anywhere—even one whose pastor has an advanced degree in liturgical

studies, pastoral theology, or some allied area—and be subjected to communion from the tabernacle, that monstrous travesty of any true eucharistic symbolism whereby in a single moment common gifts are offered, blessed, distributed, shared—then there must indeed be a better way.[43]

One has to wonder, similarly, why it is that Christus Rex has also embraced the Roman Catholic "Mass of the presanctified" for Good Friday. Indeed, the reception of Communion from the reserved sacrament on Good Friday is itself a rather late development in the history of the Good Friday Liturgy. The core of the ancient Good Friday Liturgy, preserved in the current *Evangelical Lutheran Worship*—and in the Ambrosian Rite of the Roman Catholic Archdiocese of Milan, Italy—is the Passion of St. John 18–19, the Solemn Intercessions, and the meditation, veneration, or adoration of the Cross. *In other words, a Communion rite is not an essential part of the Good Friday Liturgy and it is difficult to understand why Lutheran congregations would want to embrace something that is so foreign to their tradition.* If Lutherans are to embrace the practice of eucharistic reservation, therefore, they need not directly imitate Roman Catholic reservation practices and especially they do not need to imitate "that monstrous travesty of any true eucharistic symbolism" by distributing Communion from the reserved Eucharist at the Sunday Liturgy.

Conclusion

In ecumenical dialogue and conversation, Roman Catholics are absolutely correct in pressing Lutherans on the question of belief in the real presence of Christ in the Eucharist in relationship to the

---

43. Robert Taft, "A Generation of Liturgy in the Academy," *Worship* 75, no. 1 (2001): 58. See also his more recent critique, "Communion' from the Tabernacle—A Liturgico-Theological Oxymoron," *Worship* 88, no. 1 (January 2014): 2–22.

reservation of the Eucharist. But, as I have attempted to demonstrate in this chapter, there is no necessary correlation between a firm belief in the real presence of Christ in the Eucharistic Liturgy and Meal and the practice of eucharistic reservation. That is, as the practice of the ancient Assyrian Church of the East indicates clearly, not all churches who hold a high doctrine of Christ's real presence have reserved the Eucharist historically. Further, lack of reserving the Eucharist in the Assyrian Church of the East has *not* been a factor in entering recently into a situation of shared Eucharist with the Chaldean Church. Perhaps, the traditional Lutheran practice of nonreservation could be viewed in the same ecumenical light today.

At the same time, however, I have suggested that Lutherans *could* reserve the Eucharist as but "an extension of the public liturgy in church" (Basil of Caesarea), an understanding toward which the occasional service called "Sending of Holy Communion," already begins to point indirectly. Such a view of reservation, I have argued, does not conflict with the classic Lutheran emphasis of *usus* or *actio*. Indeed, if as the "extension of the Sunday worship" the Eucharist can be carried to the sick, homebound, and dying within "a few hours" on Sunday afternoons, then certainly the distribution of the Sunday Eucharist can be extended in this way for a "few days" during the week. For, whether "a few hours" or "a few days," the presence of Christ obviously remains somehow beyond the strict confines of the eucharistic celebration *in* church.

Finally, there may yet be another reason why modern Lutheranism might want to reconsider embracing the practice of eucharistic reservation. It is certainly true, as both traditional Lutheran, Assyrian Church of the East, and even Coptic Orthodox practice demonstrates, that belief in the real presence of Christ in the Eucharist does not lead necessarily to eucharistic reservation and, hence, reservation itself cannot be considered a necessity for Lutherans.

But it is equally true that in those churches that do reserve the Eucharist there is little question about their belief in the real presence of Christ! It can not be forgotten that in the medieval West, where Communion reception was but an occasional act, it was precisely the practice of reservation along with associated devotional activity that not only preserved the Eucharist as central in the life of the church, but also safeguarded belief in the real presence. If at the time of the Lutheran Reformation the issue was the restoration of the Meal character of the Eucharist, perhaps in our own day and age it is the theology of and belief in the real presence itself. Indeed, were Lutherans to begin reserving the Eucharist as the "extension of the Sunday worship," consistent with the practices of some in early Christianity, it might put to rest once and for all the erroneous notion that Lutheran theology of the real presence is some form of "receptionism." Ironically, Lutheran reservation of the Eucharist today may be one of the best ways to preserve what Lutheranism actually believes, teaches, and confesses about what it understands the Eucharist to be liturgically, doctrinally, and theologically.

5

What Is Normative in Contemporary Lutheran Worship?

Word and Sacrament as Nonnegotiable

Within a few days of each other three pieces came across my desk that gave me pause and led me to reflect on the state of liturgical-sacramental life within the Evangelical Lutheran Church in America (ELCA). Two were written by parish pastors, and the third by a now-former synod bishop. In the first, Pastor #1, in a short column in *The Lutheran*,[1] as part of his attempt to give a greater emphasis to Pentecost as one of the three great but neglected festival days on the liturgical calendar, described his own practice of creating an actual season of preparation for Pentecost in his parish, which he calls "*Prepent*." This season of preparation begins on the Sunday before Pentecost ("Prepent Sunday"), that is, the Seventh Sunday of

---

1. "The Neglected Festival," *The Lutheran* (June 2001). While this appeared in 2001, the recent March, 2014, edition of *The Lutheran*, 42, provides an update: "Soon it will time to 'Prepent,'" indicating that this practice remains alive and well some thirteen years later.

Easter, and includes even a color change for paraments and vestments from the white of Easter to the red of Pentecost. In the second, Pastor #2, in a short article in *Lutheran Partners*, questioned not only the dominance of "forgiveness of sins" language within traditional Lutheran liturgical-sacramental formulations, but critiqued the way in which the sacraments of Baptism and Eucharist themselves have, apparently, come to overshadow, in an *ex opere operato* fashion(!), the primacy of both the word and the doctrine of justification by faith in contemporary Lutheranism.[2] In the third, the former synod bishop not only stated the goal of congregational worship as being "always that the Word of God can be spoken and received and that worshipers are enabled to express their prayers and praise," but argued as well that "each of us Christians must come to worship discussions with the attitude that worship is not only for me, it is also always for the sake of others." Consequently,

> One person would prefer familiar hymns and liturgy from the *Lutheran Book of Worship* every Sunday. Another would feel most comfortable with an informal service that varied each week and incorporated Christian rock music. I think our faith convictions invite the traditionalist to participate willingly in the informal worship for the sake of the need of others. These convictions invite the one who prefers rock music to participate willingly in the traditional service for the sake of the needs of others.[3]

From these three pieces I learned a great deal about what happens liturgically and how liturgy is actually perceived in some places within the ELCA today. From Pastor #1 it is clear to me that the liturgical year, in which Pentecost is a *plural* title (*Pentecostê*) referring already, by definition, to a "season" of fifty days of paschal rejoicing

---

2. "Communicating God's Forgiveness," *Lutheran Partners* 17, no. 3 (2001).

3. This former bishop's name and the publication in which his comments appeared will not be revealed in this chapter.

(i.e., one Great Sunday that lasts for seven weeks plus one day), which begins *on* Easter and concludes on the *Day* of Pentecost as its culmination, fulfillment, or "seal," is for him but a "worship resource" to be adapted and adjusted to local circumstances. In other words, although Pentecost is not a *Day* but *already* a season itself called the *Easter Season*, with its own preparatory *season* called "Lent," a time of the year that together stretches "from ashes to fire,"[4] it has become clear to me that such an understanding is far from common. From Pastor #2 I learned, much to my surprise, I might add, that it is quite possible to be an ELCA Lutheran and not really be a "sacramental-liturgical" Christian, something I find absolutely surprising in light of Luther's own comments on the *centrality* of Baptism and Lord's Supper both in the life of the church and of individual Christians:

> In Baptism . . . every Christian has enough to study and to practice all his life. He always has enough to do to believe firmly what Baptism promises and brings—victory over death and the devil, forgiveness of sin, God's grace, the entire Christ, and the Holy Spirit with his gifts. . . . No greater jewel . . . can adorn our body and soul than Baptism, for through it we obtain perfect holiness and salvation, which no other kind of life and no work on earth can acquire.[5]

But what I learned from the former bishop is, by far, the most enlightening. That is, according to him, both the "liturgy" of *Lutheran Book of Worship* (*LBW*) and so-called "informal worship" are but personal or pastoral-parish "preferences" and "choices" to be made on or for a given Sunday from a wide variety of available—and optional—"worship resources." For the sake of congregational unity, those of us who are more "liturgical" than others are to participate

---

4. *From Ashes to Fire: Services of Worship for the Seasons of Lent and Easter*, Supplemental Worship Resources 6 (Nashville: Abingdon Press, 1979).
5. Martin Luther, *The Large Catechism*, in *The Book of Concord: The Confessions of the Evangelical Lutheran Church*, ed. Theodore Tappert (Philadelphia: Fortress Press, 1959), 442.

"willingly" in those "informal" services and those of us less liturgical are to participate willingly in "traditionalist" worship.

Although the former bishop, admittedly, does not say this directly, and his concern is with an attitude of tolerance in congregations for diverse liturgical "styles," one other implication seems clear from his approach. That is, for the ELCA and its pastors and congregations there is no such thing as an "official" or "normative" Lutheran (ELCA) Liturgy. Whether that of the "authorized" *Service Book and Hymnal* of 1958, the *LBW* of 1978, and, presumably, *Evangelical Lutheran Worship* (*ELW*) of 2006, none has any real ecclesiastical "authority" in determining the shape of liturgical-sacramental practice in ELCA congregations. Unlike the mandated use of the Episcopal *Book of Common Prayer* in Episcopal congregations or the *Roman Missal* in Roman Catholic parishes, individual ELCA congregations and pastors, in voting to purchase and use the *LBW*, *ELW*, or other "resources," are actually free to pick and choose that which "works" or that which they "prefer" to use to "create" worship "experiences" for their communities.

None of the above approaches to liturgy and sacraments in the ELCA, of course, is all that surprising to anyone conscious of what actually happens in Lutheran congregations regarding worship. Individual Lutheran pastors and congregations have often done, and will continue to do, what they choose to do, sometimes in concord with "authorized" worship books of the church and sometimes in spite of those books. And, of course, no pastor or congregation will ever be put under synodical discipline or censure for a refusal to conform to some "official" standard of liturgical-sacramental practice as expressed in a worship book, a groundless fear often expressed especially by those critical of full communion with The Episcopal Church as expressed in *Called to Common Mission*.

116

If, however, the feasts and seasons of the liturgical year, including, presumably, the Sunday and festival lectionary, and even the "authorized" worship books of the ELCA, are but *options* for use from within an increasing array of "worship resources," including those now published by the "official" ELCA publishing house, then the following questions might surely be raised. What *is* liturgy for Lutherans and is there anything specific that can be called "*Lutheran liturgy?*" If so, are there criteria by which one can determine whether *a* particular liturgy is "Lutheran" or not? Is there, then, anything normatively authoritative for Christian worship among Lutherans, or is liturgy itself merely relative, a matter of personal pastoral preference or congregational choice?

Attempts at an Answer

An increasingly popular answer to these questions is that provided by Lutheran liturgiologist Gordon Lathrop in his compelling studies, *Holy Things: A Liturgical Theology*[6](Minneapolis: Augsburg Fortress Press, 1993). and *What Are the Essentials of Christian Worship?*,[7] an approach to which I have referred several times in my own publications elsewhere.[8] As is well known, Lathrop has suggested that what is essential, and therefore, central and "normative," for Christian worship is what he calls a liturgical *ordo* or overall "pattern" for the scheduled ritual of Christian worship, which is both ecumenical

6. Gordon Lathrop, *Holy Things: A Liturgical Theology*
7. Gordon Lathrop, *What Are The Essentials of Christian Worship?* (Minneapolis: Augsburg Fortress, 1994).
8. See Maxwell E. Johnson, "Can We Avoid Relativism in Worship? Liturgical Norms in the Light of Contemporary Liturgical Scholarship," *Worship* 74, no. 2 (March 2000): 135–54; Johnson, "Liturgy and Ecumenism: Gifts, Challenges, and Hopes for a Renewed Vision," *Worship* 80, no. 1 (January 2006): 2–29; and Johnson, "The Loss of a Common Language; The End of Ecumenical-Liturgical Convergence?," *Studia Liturgica* 37 (2007): 55–72.

and transcultural. This *ordo*, in part, is based on the postresurrection appearances of Jesus in the New Testament (especially the Emmaus account in Luke 24), the description of baptismal and Sunday worship provided by Justin Martyr in his *First Apology*, as well as traditional confessional documents (e.g., the *Augsburg Confession* V) and current ecumenical convergence in liturgical practice and interpretation within a variety of churches. "So these are the essentials of Christian worship," he writes:

> A community *gathers in prayer* around the scriptures *read* and *proclaimed*. This community of the word then tastes the meaning of that word by keeping the meal of Christ, *giving thanks* over bread and cup and *eating* and *drinking*. It is this word-table community, the body of Christ, which gathers other people to its number, continually *teaching* both itself and these newcomers the mercy and mystery of God and *washing* them in the name of that God. All of these essential things urge the community toward the world—toward prayer for the world, sharing with the hungry of the world, caring for the world, giving witness to the world. . . . Around these central things, which will be most evident in Sunday and festival worship, other gatherings of Christians may also take place.[9]

Other elements characteristic of the liturgical assembly, according to him, flow from this central core as well. He continues,

> The very centrality of bath, word, and table, and the very reasons for their centrality . . . do begin to give us some characteristics of the mode of our celebration. These characteristics . . . are corollaries which ought not be easily ignored. A list of such characteristics should include *ritual focus*, a *music which serves*, the importance of *Sunday* and other festivals, a *participating community*, *many ministries*, and a *recognized presider* who is in communion with the churches.[10]

---

9. Lathrop, *What Are The Essentials of Christian Worship?* 22.
10. Ibid, 23.

Lathrop's ingenious suggestion of an *ordo*, or authoritative liturgical pattern, has been decidedly influential in contemporary Lutheran and ecumenical conversations about Christian worship as well as providing an interpretative structural model of "gathering, word, Meal, and sending" for the ritual action that takes place within the Sunday Eucharist. Such, of course, has been incorporated directly into explaining the ritual structure of the Eucharist in the *With One Voice* (*WOV*) supplement to *LBW* and, now, in the 2006 *ELW* resulting from the ELCA's multiyear process called *Renewing Worship*.

As others have pointed out, however, an *ordo* or pattern apart from its concrete doctrinal, cultural, and textual expressions in actual liturgies simply does not exist in any independent or pure form. That is, an *ordo* or pattern is something deduced or abstracted from already existing liturgies and these already existing liturgies themselves concretize precisely the doctrinal, cultural, and textual expressions of the church's faith that the liturgy exists to serve and by which the faith and life of the worshiping community is nurtured and formed. In other words, there is no *ordo* apart from the ways in which this *ordo* of gathering, word, Meal, and sending is actually expressed, performed, or "done" in those liturgical assemblies called church. John Baldovin has written that in order to fully understand a particular liturgy in addition to the core, this *ordo* or pattern, one must also know the *code* (the specific *form* expressing the core) and the *culture* and both code and culture are often lacking in the sources from which the ordo is deduced. Unfortunately, we lack both *code* and *culture* in the context of Justin Martyr.[11] That is, the

---

11. John Baldovin, "The Church in Christ, Christ in the Church," in *The Many Presences of Christ*, ed. T. Fitzgerald and D. Lysik (Chicago: Liturgy Training Publications, 1999), 25–27. A further critique of Lathrop's approach is offered by Michael Aune, "Liturgy and Theology: Rethinking the Relationship: Parts 1 and 2"; part 1 appears in *Worship* 81, no. 1 (January 2007): 46–68; and part 2 in *Worship* 81, no. 2 (March 2007): 141–69.

deducing of an *ordo*, in large part, is a logical construct, an abstraction made on the basis of very minimal descriptions of the patterns of Christian liturgy in the early period. Even Justin Martyr in his *First Apology*, it must be noted, is not necessarily giving us an *ordo* for Christian liturgy for all times and all places but a brief outline for the Roman Emperor, Antoninus Pius, of what, perhaps, *one* Christian community at Rome was doing in its baptismal and Sunday worship in the middle of the second century. Hence, to abstract some kind of transcultural, timeless, and ecumenical *ordo* for Christian liturgy from such brief descriptions, in which all the precise details the historian would actually need or want are lacking, may indeed be rather risky business if the overall attempt is to find a normative pattern for what the church *should* do in its liturgical assemblies as a result.

The great value of Lathrop's deduction of this liturgical *ordo*, of course, is that, ideally, it should promote the kind of tolerance for a diversity of liturgical styles to which the former bishop's comments call us. That is to say, if, ultimately, we are talking about a ritual pattern or structure of Christian liturgy as normative (gathering, word, Meal, and sending), then the *style* of that liturgy, whether "high church" or "low church" (whatever those words mean), whether rock 'n' roll, classic hymnody and *ELW* or other musical settings, mariachi, gospel music, flamenco, folk, polka, Gregorian chant, baroque polyphony, "formal," "informal," or even spoken, should not really matter. What should matter is that the liturgical *ordo* itself be done faithfully in our worship!

But the minute we start talking about *ordo* we have to ask, which concrete expression(s) of that *ordo* do we mean? Are we talking about the "authorized" and concrete *Lutheran* expression of this *ordo* in, at least, the liturgical texts, lectionary readings, and prayers of *LBW*, *WOV*, *This Far by Faith*, *El Libro de Liturgia y Cántico*, and now

ELW? Are we talking about a tolerance for diversity in expressing that *ordo* that, in classic Christian (and Lutheran) usage bearing precisely the doctrinal, cultural, and textual developments of history, includes what used to be called commonly the "Ordinary of the Mass," the *Kyrie, Gloria in Excelsis, Credo, Sanctus,* and *Agnus Dei*? Or, are we talking about some kind of generic or timeless, even Platonic, pure or ideal *ordo* whose very concrete expression a pastor or parish worship committee creates anew each week, sometimes bearing no discernible relationship whatsoever to the Lutheran liturgical tradition—or, still too frequently, even to the Meal dimension of the *ordo*—itself?

I suspect that part of the confusion often generated over liturgical topics stems from a widespread misconception of what is that to which the word *liturgy* actually refers, a misconception reinforced by those who make distinctions between *the* "liturgy" and a "worship service" as though they are somehow distinct realities. "Liturgy" is not that "formal" aspect of the service apart from the sermon, the "everything else" we do in the front part of the *book* before or after the sermon. *The* liturgy is not that "formal" setting for "worship" identified exclusively or explicitly with the musical settings of a *book*. To juxtapose "liturgy from the *Lutheran Book of Worship*" to "an informal service that varied each week," while understandable in context as a comparison of worship *styles*, is a misleading juxtaposition and creates greater confusion about the meaning of the liturgy itself. *Both* "styles" of worship are "liturgy" because, of course, liturgy, *leitourgia*, is what the Christian community *does* and celebrates in union with Christ *the* Liturgist (Heb. 8:6) when it gathers to hear his word proclaimed, share in his Supper, and "offer . . . prayers and praise" in order to be equipped by word and sacrament for life and mission in the world as his body in that ritually enacted dialogue of divine word and grateful response. Or, better, in the words of Nathan Mitchell,

> Liturgy is God's work for us, not our work for God. Only God can show us how to worship God—fittingly, beautifully. Liturgy is not something beautiful we do for God, but something beautiful God does for us and among us. Public worship is neither our work nor our possession; as the Rule of St Benedict reminds us, it is *opus Dei*, God's work.[12]

A "service" of hymn singing, Scripture reading, sermon, and prayer, or morning and evening prayer, or the celebration of Baptism, etc., are *liturgies*, albeit different types of liturgical expression from the "liturgy" of word and Eucharistic Meal. The question is never "shall we do the liturgy or not?" since whatever we do in our congregational worship *is* the *liturgy* of this particular assembly at this point in time and place.

But even more than this needs to be said. What we do or don't do in our liturgies forms the community in one way or another. Hence, a community that celebrates and receives Christ's Body and Blood in the Lord's Supper every Sunday, attends to the rubrical options and varieties already present in the "authorized" liturgical book(s), faithfully proclaims the lectionary readings, and tenaciously keeps the feasts and seasons of the liturgical year week after week, year after year, will be a different sort of community than one that is continually experimenting with "worship alternatives" and searching for something "better" to meet the so-called needs of worshipers and potential seekers alike. And I dare say that the first type of community will, undoubtedly, be more "orthodox," more "Lutheran," in its doctrinal-theological outlook. Why? Because the issue is not simply liturgical style. The liturgy is not only about expressing our prayer and praise to God or hearing the word of God. Rather, as the very

---

12. Nathan Mitchell, "The Amen Corner: Being Good and Being Beautiful," *Worship* 74, no. 6 (November 2000): 557.

corporate expression of the self-identity and worldview of the worshiping community, the body of Christ in this time and place, expressed concretely in its liturgical texts and liturgical actions, the purpose of liturgy is not to permeate our lives with ritual but to permeate them with Christ for the very building up of his body, the church, and for the salvation and life of the world.[13] The underlying issue in the so-called Worship Wars in contemporary Lutheranism, Roman Catholicism, and much of Protestantism today is, I would submit, fundamentally *doctrinal* in its implications and not so apparently harmless as being about mere styles of worship at all. And this is why the question is of such great importance in terms of Christian, and specifically in this case, "Lutheran" identity. Let me explain further.

Is There a Lutheran *Lex Orandi, Lex Credendi*?

An ancient Christian principle attributed to Prosper of Aquitaine in the context of the Semi-Pelagian controversy, *Ut legem credendi statuat lex supplicandi* (often abbreviated as *lex orandi, lex credendi*), states that the "rule of praying establishes the rule of believing." That is, the faith of the church is both constituted and expressed by the prayer of the church.[14] On the one hand, of course, this means that the liturgy itself is the great "school for prayer." Indeed, it is the very structure and contents of the great prayers of the church enshrined especially *in* the liturgical rites, after all, that provide a model for

---

13. See Robert Taft, "What Does Liturgy Do? Toward a Soteriology of Liturgical Celebration: Some Theses," *Worship* 66, no. 3 (1992): 194–211.

14. See my recent study of this issue in the patristic period, *Praying and Believing in Early Christianity: The Interplay between Christian Worship and Doctrine* (Collegeville, MN: Michael Glazier, 2013), and my essay "Liturgy and Theology," in *Liturgy in Dialogue: Essays in Memory of Ronald Jasper*, ed. Bryan D. Spinks and Paul F. Bradshaw (Collegeville, MN: The Liturgical Press, Pueblo, 1993), 202–25.

what Christian prayer is. And that Christian prayer, so proclaims the liturgy week after week, is Trinitarian in structure and focus. Note, for example, the concluding formula for the Prayer of the Day: "Through your Son Jesus Christ our Lord who lives and reigns with you and the Holy Spirit, one God, both now and forever." Or, note the concluding doxology at the end of the Great Thanksgiving: "Through him, with him, in him, in the unity of the Holy Spirit, all honor and glory is yours, almighty Father, now and forever. Amen." Not simply a deduced *ordo* or pattern but the classic way that *ordo* has been and is expressed in the church's liturgy gives us the language and structure for prayer itself.

On the other hand, the liturgy is not only the school for prayer but also the "school for faith." Long before there was an Apostles' or Nicene Creed, or an explicit doctrine of the Trinity, for example, it was through a Prayer of Thanksgiving over the baptismal waters, through the candidate's threefold profession of faith in the Father, Son, and Holy Spirit in the context of Baptism itself, and through the Great *Eucharistia* over the bread and cup of the Lord's Supper, consisting of *praise* to God for the work of creation and redemption, *thanksgiving* for the life, death, resurrection, and ascension of Christ, and *invocation* of the Holy Spirit, that the church professed its faith in the Trinity by means of *doxology* and *praise*. While not etymologically related, a common modern misconception even among liturgiologists (!), *orthodoxy* and *doxology*, right thinking doctrinally and right liturgical expression, do go together. Whether one accepts the theological priority of the *lex orandi* over the *lex credendi* (the traditional Catholic approach) or the other way around (the traditional Protestant approach) matters very little in this context. For, in either case what is done, sung, or said liturgically and what is held, thought, or confessed doctrinally are inseparable. How and what the church *prays* shapes and *is*, in a real sense, how and what the church *believes*. Why else would the Lutheran and Protestant Reformers have made attempts at liturgical reformation itself? Even at the congregational level, to change what is done in worship carries with it the enormous responsibility of needing to be aware that such changes may well engender potential changes in the congregation's own self-understanding and faith. If I how I pray, sing, and celebrate liturgically is changed, how I believe might also be changed for good or, and this is the danger, for ill.

The "authorized" liturgy of the ELCA in *ELW* and other worship books, authorized at least by the ELCA's predecessor bodies, bears the doctrinal weight and concrete expression of what is recognized by the churches to be a faithful representation of the Lutheran theological-doctrinal tradition in union with the catholic-ecumenical liturgical traditions of the church. As Philip Pfatteicher writes in reference to *LBW* in his book on *Liturgical Spirituality*, "The liturgy of the church provides a framework within which the deepest mysteries of Christianity await discovery. With the Holy Communion and the Daily Prayer of the church, one has all one needs to know about Christianity. All the essentials are there to be pondered, explored, and acted upon."[15] Can the same be said for other "worship resources" existing in abundance for congregational use today? Perhaps so and perhaps not, but that is precisely the kind of question that must be asked.

Questions, therefore, about liturgy go far beyond mere tolerance for a diversity of worship styles in particular congregations. They are, at heart, I am convinced, theological-doctrinal questions and, unfortunately, the appeal to a liturgical *ordo*, pattern, or structure does not get us too far with this question unless we attend also

15. Philip H. Pfatteicher, *Liturgical Spirituality* (Valley Forge: Trinity Press International, 1997), 22.

to the particular ways in which this *ordo* is incarnated within the particular liturgies *and* in the particular churches from where it is deduced. Here is where I think the notion of an authoritative *ordo* is lacking. Certainly Arians and orthodox in the context of the Nicene controversy both followed the same basic *ordo*. But only one of these traditions was recognized as orthodox and the other as heterodox, not because of the *ordo* itself, but because of their theology of the person of Christ read, in part, out of the liturgical prayers used in that *ordo* (e.g., prayer *to* the Father *through* Christ the mediator *in* the Holy Spirit). And the aftermath of that controversy did not only result in a new creedal formula (the Nicene Creed) but contributed to the ways in which references to the Nicene *homoousios* abound within Eastern Christian liturgy today. Similarly, both orthodox and semi-Arians followed the same *ordo* in the late fourth century. But it is, again, in the liturgy where the Orthodox coordinate form of the doxology, ascribing equal praise to the Trinity, "Glory be *to* the Father, *with* the Son, and *with* the Holy Spirit," replaced the uncoordinate form of "*to* the Father, *through* the Son, *in* the Holy Spirit" because of its potential semi-Arian interpretations. When ancient local Councils of the church called for specific written liturgical texts to be used in North African churches it did so *not* because the *ordo* wasn't being followed but in order to ensure the doctrinal orthodoxy of the prayers being offered within that *ordo*. And, when Prosper of Aquitaine coined the phrase *ut legem credendi statuat lex supplicandi*, against the semi-Pelagians, he was referring specifically to the *text* of a liturgical prayer of intercession, which underscored the absolute necessity of divine grace for the accomplishment of any human action.[16] Indeed, because liturgy shapes believing, a faith formed

16. See Paul de Clerk, "'Lex orandi—Lex credendi,' Sens original et avatars historique d'un adage équivoque," *Questions Liturgiques* 59 (1978): 193–212, and my essay, "Liturgy and Theology," 222–25.

regularly not by variety but precisely by constant repetition, the liturgy is too important to be reduced to a matter of personal taste and preference regarding style. Put somewhat crassly, if we want Lutheran believers we form and inform our congregations with Lutheran liturgy. For the bottom line is that whatever we do in terms of parish liturgy we are also doing in terms of parish formation.

This brings me, more directly, to the question of authorization and what constitutes an official liturgy of a church. It is interesting to compare what is said for congregations regarding worship materials in the current ELCA constitution with the constitutions of the former Lutheran bodies making up the ELCA. While the former constitutions were clear in that only authorized or appropriate worship books were to be used (*LBW*, *SBH*, and, presumably, worship books of other predecessor bodies) in congregations, the ELCA constitution is completely nondirective when it comes to worship, saying only that the church is to "worship God in proclamation of the Word and administration of the sacraments and through lives of prayer, praise, thanksgiving, witness, and service,"[17] and to "provide services of worship at which the Word of God is preached and the sacraments are administered,"[18] without specifying any worship books whatsoever. With such lack of guidance one can only conclude that *LBW* or *ELW* are now only possible worship "resources" among potentially several others. Such would appear also to be the former bishop's position in his comments. If so, does this mean, given the ELCA's full communion with The Episcopal Church, that liturgical texts, including the four Eucharistic Prayers, from the *Book of Common Prayer*, are also suitable for ELCA usage? If so, given the ecumenical nature of the church, what about optional offertory and postcommunion prayers from other sources, or

---

17. *Model Constitution for Congregations of the Evangelical Lutheran Church in America 2007*, C4.02.a.
18. ibid, C4.03.a.

additional Eucharistic Prefaces and the solemn seasonal blessings from the *Roman Missal*? Or what about liturgical texts from Eastern Christian liturgies or from the more recent Presbyterian *Book of Common Worship*, especially given the situation of full communion between the ELCA and various Reformed churches in the United States? And, if all of these are suitable for ELCA liturgical usage, as I would argue they are, then what about resources from so-called nonliturgical or, more accurately, "free churches" as well? On the one hand, the answer is very simple. In all cases, what determines suitability for use, apart from other possible considerations, must be, again, *theology* and consistency with the Lutheran doctrinal tradition. Does the particular text in question reflect a theological position or orientation, which is consonant with the Lutheran doctrinal confession and the Lutheran liturgical tradition? If so, one would imagine that it is suitable.

On the other hand, however, if there is no *official* ELCA Lutheran liturgy, apart from multiple resources, it becomes next to impossible to appeal to the structure or texts of the liturgy in any kind of authoritative way to determine if another "resource" is, in fact, consistent with the Lutheran liturgical tradition. Those texts, after all, are not *official*. Within an ecumenical context as well, especially within dialogues between ELCA Lutherans, Anglicans, Roman Catholics, and Eastern Orthodox, who all share, supposedly, a relatively common liturgical-sacramental tradition, this can become especially complex. In such a situation may an ELCA Lutheran actually make an authoritative appeal, for example, to either the rite for "Holy Baptism" in *ELW*, including the postbaptismal rite of pneumatic handlaying and optional chrismation/sealing, or to *ELW*'s "The Holy Communion," as demonstrating what the ELCA actually believes, teaches, confesses, and celebrates in Baptism or Lord's

Supper? Or, must such an appeal always employ some disclaimer about the fact these rites are only reflective of "some" ELCA Lutheran liturgical practices?

It would appear quite difficult to assert that *ELW* is the *official* worship book of the ELCA. And, as such, if there is no authoritative standard of Lutheran liturgy, then, newly and locally created rites for Baptism or Lord's Supper, alternative but equally permissible services of worship, the creation of new seasons like "Prepent," or the moving of Advent to a "more appropriate" location in late November,[19] or, for that matter, of finding or creating another, more relevant alternative to the calendar of feasts and seasons and even alternative lectionaries, is precisely what is to be expected. Liturgy becomes—as it has become in many places—simply the local creation of pastors and congregations.

But must the situation remain here? I think not. Although there is at present no officially authorized Lutheran liturgical book for the ELCA, there *is* an officially authorized, approved, and authoritative Lutheran statement on the practice of word and sacrament called *The Use of the Means of Grace,*[20] which has vast liturgical implications. Note the following examples:

Baptism:

Principle 25: We seek to celebrate Baptism in such a way that

---

19. See Susan K. Wendorf, "Let's Move Advent," *Lutheran Partners* (1991). See also my response, "Let's Keep Advent Right Where It Is" in *Worship: Rites, Feasts, and Reflections* (Portland: The Pastoral Press, 2004), 237–42.

20. Evangelical Lutheran Church in America, *The Use of the Means of Grace: A Statement on the Practice of Word and Sacrament* (Minneapolis: Augsburg Fortress, 1997). All of the following principles are taken from this document. The appeal to this document as an authoritative text for what is normative in Lutheran worship, rather than to a worship book, is based, in part, on a comment that Gordon Lathrop once made to me in a conversation at a meeting of the North American Academy of Liturgy.

the celebration is a true and complete sign of the things which Baptism signifies.

Principle 26: Water is a sign of cleansing, dying, and new birth. It is used generously in Holy Baptism to symbolize God's power over sin and death.

Principle 27: A baptismal font filled with water, placed in the assembly's worship space, symbolizes the centrality of this sacrament for faith and life.

Principle 28: The laying on of hands and prayer for the Holy Spirit's gifts, the signing with the cross, and the anointing with oil help to appropriate the breadth of meanings in Baptism. Other symbolic acts also are appropriate such as the clothing with a baptismal garment and the giving of a lighted candle.

Liturgy of the Word and Eucharist:

Principle 6: Sunday, the day of Christ's resurrection and of the appearances to the disciples by the crucified and risen Christ is the primary day on which Christians gather to worship. Within this assembly, the Word is read and preached and the sacraments are celebrated.

Principle 7: The public reading of the Holy Scriptures is an indispensable part of worship constituting the basis for the public proclamation of the Gospel.

Application 7A: The use of ELCA-approved lectionaries serves the unity of the Church, the hearing of the breadth of the Scriptures, and the evangelical meaning of the church year. The *Revised Common Lectionary* and the lectionaries in *Lutheran Book of Worship* make three readings and a psalm available for every Sunday and festival.

Principle 9: The preaching of the Gospel of the crucified and risen Christ is rooted in the readings of the Scriptures in the assemblies for worship. Called and ordained ministers bear responsibility for the preached Word in the Church gathered for public worship.

Principle 10: The assembled congregation participates in proclaiming the Word of God with a common voice. It sings hymns and the texts of the liturgy. It confesses the Nicene or Apostles' Creed.

Principle 53: Because of the living Word of God, Christian assemblies for worship are occasions for intercessory prayer. On the grounds of the Word and promise of God the Church prays, in the power of the Spirit and in the name of Jesus Christ, for all the great needs of the world.

Principle 34: The two principal parts of the liturgy of Holy Communion, the proclamation of the Word of God and the celebration of the sacramental meal, are so intimately connected as to form one act of worship.

Principle 35: According to the Apology of the Augsburg Confession, Lutheran congregations celebrate the Holy Communion every Sunday and festival. *This confession remains the norm for our practice* [emphasis added].

Principle 43: The biblical words of institution declare God's action and invitation. *They are set within the context of the Great*

Thanksgiving. This eucharistic prayer proclaims and celebrates the gracious work of God in creation, redemption, and sanctification [emphasis added].

Anyone who follows what is stated above as principles regarding Baptism, word, and Eucharist (including even the preferred liturgical use of a Eucharistic Prayer) will easily come to the conclusion that the very liturgical life *officially* envisioned by the ELCA for its congregations is *precisely* that which is expressed already by the very contents of *LBW, WOV, ELW*, and so on. In other words, what Lutherans have here is a *lex credendi*, an official theological stance about what the ELCA believes regarding the centrality of word and sacrament, which, as adopted in 1997 to provide "guidance and practice,"[21] for congregations, implies, presupposes, and is actually based upon a particular *lex orandi*; in other words, not just a classic liturgical shape, *ordo*, or pattern, but a specific liturgical-doctrinal content already expressed in the liturgy of the various Lutheran worship books.

Conclusion

So, is anything normative in contemporary Lutheran worship or are Lutherans to be left with congregational creativity? I would argue that there is a great deal that can be interpreted as constituting a norm and that, indirectly, at least, this norm can be located precisely in *LBW* and *ELW*. That is, *The Use of the Means of Grace* may well be an official theological statement on liturgy in the ELCA. But, at the same time, the statement itself is little other than a commentary on liturgical practices already existing in *LBW* and *ELW*. Hence,

21. Ibid, 2.

in the context of the so-called modern Worship Wars, those who advocate the classic historic liturgy actually have official support from the ELCA itself. As *The Use of the Means of Grace* makes clear, the Mass, the Eucharistic Liturgy, the Holy Communion, whatever name is chosen and whatever liturgical style may be employed, is central in ELCA Sunday and other festival worship and the very structure of that liturgy—including even the Eucharistic Prayer—is exactly what is presented in *LBW* and *ELW* as a "resource" for liturgy. In fact, if there were no *LBW* or *ELW*, *The Use of the Means of Grace* suggests that someone would have to invent them.

6

———

Ordinary Time? The Time after Epiphany and Pentecost

Celebrating the Mystery of Christ in All Its Fullness

In the Roman Catholic "General Norms for the Liturgical Year and the Calendar," the following description of what English-speaking Roman Catholics now call *Ordinary Time*, and what is called *Time after Epiphany* and *Time after Pentecost* in *Evangelical Lutheran Worship* (*ELW*), is provided:

> Apart from the seasons of Easter, Lent, Christmas, and Advent, which have their own characteristics, there are thirty-three or thirty-four weeks in the course of the year, which celebrate no particular aspect of the mystery of Christ. Instead, especially on the last Sundays, the mystery of Christ in all its fullness is celebrated. *This period is known as Ordinary Time.* Ordinary time begins on Monday after the Sunday following January 6 and continues until Tuesday before Ash Wednesday inclusive. It begins again on Monday after Pentecost and ends before the first evening prayer of the First Sunday of Advent. The missal and breviary for Sundays and weekdays in this period follow the same plan.[1]

Immediately, we are confronted here with a problem of translation, which in turn reflects and continues to foster, the common, even officially accepted, Roman Catholic way in English of referring to this liturgical season as *Ordinary Time*. The problem is this. The Latin original of the *Ordo Lectionum Missae* (hereafter, *OLM*) does not use anything akin to *tempus ordinarius*, literally, "ordinary time," but, rather, *tempus per annum*, that is, simply, "time through the year."[2] In fact, in the 1970 English translation of the introduction to the *Lectionary for Mass*, the more literal translation of *tempus per annum* was employed, using either "Season 'of the Year,'" or Sunday or week "of the year,"[3] a designation consistent with *ELW*'s usage of "Time after Epiphany" and "Time after Pentecost." This 1970 translation was thus "corrected" with "Ordinary Time" replacing season, Sunday, or week "of the year."[4]

The issue here is far from mere semantics or simply a question of appropriate translation or grammar. The use of *ordinary*, as Martin Connell reminds us in his study of the liturgical year, is not readily understood by contemporary English speakers as referring to a liturgical season celebrated according to a regular order or pattern, an *ordo*, for example, but in regular usage rather as something "'commonplace,' 'usual,' even 'plain,' 'ugly,' and 'below the usual level.'"[5] Such a designation as *Ordinary Time*, then, seems hardly fitting for a season oriented to celebrating "the mystery of Christ in all its fullness," something that is, indeed, always "extraordinary."

1. United States Catholic Conference, *Roman Calendar: Text and Commentary* (Washington, DC: Publications Office, 1976), 10 (emphasis added).
2. *Ordo Lectionum Missae*, editio typica altera (Vatican City: Libreria Editrice Vaticana, 1998), V.I.15.
3. *Lectionary for Mass* (New York: Catholic Book Publishing Co., 1970), 13.
4. National Conference of Catholic Bishops, *Lectionary for Mass*, volume 1: *Study Edition* (Collegeville, MN: The Liturgical Press, 2000), xl–xli.
5. Martin Connell, *Eternity Today: On the Liturgical Year*, vol. 2: *Sunday, Lent, the Three Days, the Easter Season, Ordinary Time* (New York: Continuum, 2006), 239–40.

Hence, the issue is not simply one of translation but of theological import and meaning.

This chapter, with some attention to historical development, will focus primarily on the theology of this "extraordinary time," this season of celebrating the whole mystery of Christ. It will do so in three sections. First, Adolf Adam[6] directs our attention to the important description of this season by Pierre Jounel: "The thirty-four Sundays *per annum* . . . represent the ideal Christian Sunday, without any further specification. That is, each of them is a Lord's Day in its pure state as presented to us in the Church's tradition."[7] The first section then will be devoted to the theology of Sunday itself as the original Christian feast. Second, since the focus of an individual Sunday Eucharist is largely dependent upon the biblical readings that are proclaimed, the lectionaries for this season will be discussed, both the Roman Catholic *OLM* and the *Revised Common Lectionary* (*RCL*), the second of which is now used throughout much of contemporary Protestantism. And, third and finally, some brief attention will be given to the various solemnities, feasts, or lesser festivals of the Lord, Mary, and the saints that occur during this season, especially because some of them are assigned to Sundays and others may take precedence even over Sunday.

The Theology of "Ordinary Time" Is the Theology of Sunday

If the Sundays of this *tempus per annum* celebrate "the ideal Christian Sunday . . . the Lord's Day in a pure state," then the theology of the season of "Ordinary Time" must be the same as the theology

6. Adolf Adam, *The Liturgical Year: Its History & Its Meaning after the Reform of the Liturgy* (Collegeville, MN: The Liturgical Press, Pueblo, 1981), 160.
7. Pierre Jounel, "The Sundays of Ordinary Time," in *The Church at Prayer*, vol. 4: *The Liturgy and Time*, ed. A. G. Martimort, et. al. (Collegeville, MN: The Liturgical Press, 1986), 23.

of Sunday, the Lord's Day, itself. I can think of no one who has better articulated this theology than the late Mark Searle (1992) in his excellent 1984 essay, "Sunday: The Heart of the Liturgical Year."[8] In particular, Searle disabuses us of the widespread notion that Sunday is but the replacement or fulfillment of the Jewish Sabbath, an interpretation similarly underscored by Pope John Paul II in his 1998 apostolic exhortation, *Dies Domini*:

> Because the third commandment depends upon the remembrance of God's saving works and because Christians saw the definitive time inaugurated by Christ as a new beginning, they made the first day after the Sabbath a festive day, for that was the day on which the Lord rose from the dead. The Paschal Mystery of Christ is the full revelation of the mystery of the world's origin, the climax of the history of salvation and the anticipation of the eschatological fulfillment of the world. What God accomplished in creation and wrought for his people in the Exodus has found its fullest expression in Christ's death and resurrection, through which its definitive fulfillment will not come until the *Parousia*, when Christ returns in glory. In him, the "spiritual" meaning of the Sabbath is fully realized, as Saint Gregory the Great declares: "For us, the true Sabbath is the person of our Redeemer, our Lord Jesus Christ." . . . In the light of this mystery, the meaning of the Old Testament precept concerning the Lord's Day is recovered, perfected, and fully revealed in the glory, which shines on the face of the Risen Christ (cf. 2 Cor 4:6). We move from the "Sabbath" to the "first day after the Sabbath," from the seventh day to the first day: the *dies Domini* becomes the *dies Christi!*[9]

Hence, according to Searle, Sunday itself is like a multifaceted jewel or prism through which the whole mystery of Christ is refracted week after week. As such, the Christian celebration of Sunday, the

---

8. Mark Searle, "Sunday: The Heart of the Liturgical Year," in *The Church Gives Thanks and Remembers*, ed. Lawrence Johnson (Collegeville, MN: The Liturgical Press, 1984), 13–36; reprinted in *Between Memory and Hope: Readings on the Liturgical Year*, ed. Maxwell E. Johnson (Collegeville, MN: The Liturgical Press, Pueblo, 2000), 59–76, from where it will be quoted in this chapter.

9. John Paul II, *Dies Domini: On Keeping the Lord's Day Holy*, para. 18 (Boston: Pauline Books & Media, 1998), 25–26.

"original Christian feast," is the "day of the Lord," the "eighth day" (the day of new creation that transcends the seven-day cycle), the "first day" (of creation and new creation in Christ), the "day of resurrection" and, among other images, Sunday is the day of "encounter with the Risen Lord," in other words, a postresurrection appearance of Christ among his disciples through word and Eucharist in the liturgical assembly.

Searle shows a special preference for the last of these images, namely, that of the Sunday encounter, writing,

> Sunday, with its assembly, its preaching, its breaking of bread, is essentially a post-resurrection appearance of the Risen Christ in which he breathes his Spirit upon his disciples for the forgiveness of sins and for the life of the world. As such, it is the point at which the central images of the Christian life converge and, because the liturgical year is but the spinning out of these images from week to week, the Christian Sunday may properly be claimed as the heart, not only of the liturgical year, but of the Christian life itself.[10]

In other words, Sunday, and by implication "Ordinary Time" as a whole, may be interpreted as the prolongation of the Easter night—and "eight days later"—upper-room encounters with the Risen Christ, who by the wounds in his hands, feet, and side, remains always the crucified Christ (John 20:19–31). It is, similarly, the continuation of the encounter both on the way to Emmaus and at the table in Emmaus, where Christ is revealed in the word-based "warming" of human hearts and "in the breaking of the bread" (Luke 24:13–35). Gordon Lathrop underscores this point, saying, "All the Scriptures read in the assembly, especially on Sunday, are read as if we were with the disciples on the road to Emmaus, and so 'beginning with Moses and all the prophets' (Lk 24:27) we interpret in the Scriptures the things concerning Jesus Christ."[11]

---

10. Searle, "Sunday: The Heart of the Liturgical Year," 76.

If there is a "theme," then, to the Sundays of "Ordinary Time" that theme is nothing other than the Paschal Mystery itself understood in its complete sense of Jesus' death, resurrection, gift of the Spirit, and the resulting Christian community itself, formed as his body. In this way each Sunday is not a "little Easter," as is often erroneously claimed, but "Easter is a big Sunday." That is, what we celebrate on every Sunday is not simply the resurrection of Christ as a weekly memorial of a past event, but the real presence of and encounter with the crucified and Risen Christ, and the gift of the Holy Spirit. And this is nothing other than what we celebrate annually in a big way through the Paschal Triduum and the great Fifty Days of Easter.

The centrality of this Paschal Mystery in its fullness celebrated on Sundays is highlighted strongly within the various Eucharistic Prefaces provided in the *Roman Missal* for the Sundays in Ordinary Time.[12] Note the following as examples of this:

Sundays in Ordinary Time I:

For through his Paschal Mystery, he accomplished the marvelous deed, by which he has freed us from the yoke of sin and death, summoning us to the glory of being now called a chosen race, a royal priesthood, a holy nation, a people of your own possession, to proclaim everywhere your mighty works, for you have called us out of darkness into your own wonderful light.

Sundays in Ordinary Time II:

For out of compassion for the waywardness that is ours, he humbled himself and was born of the Virgin; by the passion of the Cross he freed us from unending death, and by rising from the dead he gave us life eternal.

11. Gordon Lathrop, "A Rebirth of Images: On the use of the Bible in Liturgy," *Worship* 58, no. 4 (1984): 301.

12. The following texts are from *The Roman Missal* (Collegeville, MN: The Liturgical Press, 2011), 572–75, 578, and 584. On the Eucharistic Prefaces used during Ordinary Time, see Adrian Nocent, *The Liturgical Year*, vol. 4: *Sundays Nine to Thirty-Four in Ordinary Time* (Collegeville, MN: The Liturgical Press, 1977), 19–30.

Sundays in Ordinary Time IV:

For by his birth he brought renewal to humanity's fallen state, and by his suffering cancelled our sins; by his rising from the dead he has opened the way to eternal life, and by ascending to you, O Father, he has unlocked the gates of heaven.

Sundays in Ordinary Time VII:

For you so loved the world that in your mercy you sent us the Redeemer, to live like us in all things but sin, so that you might love in us what you loved in your Son, by whose obedience we have been restored to those gifts of yours that, by sinning, we had lost in disobedience.

A similar emphasis appears in the Eucharistic Prefaces in the worship books of contemporary Lutherans and Episcopalians. In fact, the following preface is shared between them:

Through Jesus Christ our Lord; who on the first day of the week overcame death and the grave, and by his glorious resurrection opened to us the way of everlasting life.[13]

That it is to the various texts of the "ordinary" Sunday Eucharistic Liturgy one should turn in order to illustrate the overall focus of "Ordinary Time" ought not come as a surprise. For Sunday and Eucharist form a synthesis. As Robert Taft notes,

By the middle of the second century . . . the picture is clear: for the community synaxis, Sunday and Eucharist form a unity as the symbolic celebration of the presence of the Risen Lord amidst his own, a presence that signals the arrival of the New Age, and it is generally agreed that everyone present communicated.[14]

---

13. *The Book of Common Prayer* (New York: The Church Hymnal Corporation and Seabury Press, 1999), 377. For the Lutheran version of this preface, see *Evangelical Lutheran Worship*, Leader's Desk Edition (Minneapolis: Augsburg Fortress, 2006), 180.
14. Robert Taft, "The Frequency of the Celebration of the Eucharist throughout History," in *Beyond East and West: Problems in Liturgical Understanding*, 2nd rev. and enlarged ed. (Rome:

And, at the same time, it is precisely the celebration of the Sunday Eucharist, this unity of Sunday and Eucharist, that provides the proper liturgical-hermeneutical context for the biblical readings that are read and proclaimed. If, as per Lathrop's interpretation noted above, we in the liturgical assembly are somehow "with the disciples on the road to Emmaus, and so 'beginning with Moses and all the prophets' (Lk 24:27) we interpret in the Scriptures the things concerning Jesus Christ,"[15] then it is also true that we are with those same disciples at the "breaking of bread" in Emmaus. Lathrop continues,

> We read a text from the gospel, not in order to recapture the time when independent tradition units circulated in the Christian communities, but in order to set the pericope we read next to the passion and resurrection of Christ held forth now in the Supper. Hence reading the individual pericopes and then celebrating the Supper presents us with a skein of images reinterpreting images which is the very pattern of the gospel books themselves. The Sunday texts are not then understood aright unless they are understood as leading to that Supper. The hierarchy of readings in the Sunday Eucharist may then be thought of as a primary example of a skein of images reborn.[16]

The theology of *tempus per annum* as the theology of Sunday finds its core and ultimate meaning in the Eucharist itself, this foretaste of the paschal feast of heaven. This *tempus per annum*, then, affords us the opportunity week after week after week of being able to attend to the various dimensions and implications of our redemption in Christ as read and proclaimed in the assigned biblical readings and homily, but always coming back to the very centrality of the Paschal Mystery

---

Edizioni Orientalia Christiana, 1997), 87–110; reprinted in Johnson, *Between Memory and Hope*, 78, from which it is quoted here.
15. Lathrop, "A Rebirth of Images," 301.
16. Lathrop, ibid., 296.

itself as this is celebrated and made available in the Sunday Eucharist. Of this Paschal Mystery, Jean Cardinal Daniélou once wrote,

> The Christian faith has only one object, the mystery of Christ dead and risen. But this unique mystery subsists under different modes: it is prefigured in the Old Testament, it is accomplished historically in the earthly life of Christ, it is contained in mystery in the sacraments, it is lived mystically in souls, it is accomplished socially in the Church, it is consummated eschatologically in the heavenly kingdom. Thus the Christian has at his disposition several registers, a multi-dimensional symbolism, to express this unique reality. The whole of Christian culture consists in grasping the links that exist between Bible and liturgy, Gospel and eschatology, mysticism and liturgy. The application of this method to scripture is called exegesis; applied to liturgy it is called mystagogy. This consists in reading in the rites the mystery of Christ, and in contemplating beneath the symbols the invisible reality.[17]

This is what both Sunday and Ordinary Time celebrate, what Jounel called above this Lord's Day in its pure state. Or, as Adrian Nocent writes, "These Sundays [in Ordinary Time] simply celebrate the paschal mystery as it is being fulfilled in the Church and the world. Consequently, except for the theology of Sunday, there is no question of elaborating a theology of Ordinary Time."[18] Clearly, then, the theology of Ordinary Time is, as we have seen, the theology of Sunday itself.

The Lectionaries of the Time through the Year

If the season of Ordinary Time, theologically, is about Sunday and Eucharist par excellence, then it should certainly come as no surprise to learn that this *tempus per annum* was, historically, the last season

---

17. Jean Daniélou, "Le symbolisme des rites baptismaux," in *Dieu vivant* 1 (1948): 17; English translation by Robert Taft, "Toward a Theology of Christian Feast," in *Beyond East and West*, 28–29.
18. Nocent, *The Liturgical Year*, 1.

of the liturgical year to be organized and assigned specific lectionary readings. Matias Augé provides a helpful summary of the liturgical development of this season:

> The beginnings of Ordinary Time may be found simply by looking at Sunday celebrations that lacked additional liturgical specification. The number of ordinary Sundays (and weeks) was gradually reduced in the first centuries as the liturgical year began to be organized. In the earliest documents these Sundays had no specific title. So, for example, the *GeV* [*Gelasianum Vetus*] contains sixteen formulas for Masses with the generic title . . . *pro dominicis diebus* (nn. 1178–1241). Later, in the Gelasian of the eighth century and in other sources close to it, we find six Sundays *post Theophaniam* and between twenty-two and twenty-seven Sundays *post Pentecosten*. In the *MR1570* [*Missale Romanum* of 1570] there are from four to six Sundays *post Epiphaniam* and twenty-four Sundays *post Pentecosten*. These few historical data suffice to give one an idea of the profound rearrangement accomplished by Vatican II in this part of the liturgical year.[19]

And, since Augé goes on to state that the character of the Sundays in Ordinary Time is derived especially from the lectionary readings, it is important to be reminded of the following. Prior to the publication of the Roman Catholic *Ordo Lectionum Missae* of 1969, with its three-year cycle of Sunday readings, a one-year cycle had been employed in Roman Catholic (and in various Protestant) liturgies since the publication of the *Missale Romanum* of 1570, which limited the Sunday readings to two, an Epistle and Gospel.[20] With the

19. Matias Augé, "The Liturgical Year in the Roman Rite," in *Handbook for Liturgical Studies*, vol. 5: *Liturgical Time and Space*, ed. Anscar Chupungco (Collegeville, MN: The Liturgical Press, Pueblo, 2000), 204.

20. The most notable exception to this was the 1958 Lutheran *Service Book and Hymnal* (Minneapolis: Augsburg, 1958), which had already restored an "Old Testament Lesson" to its one-year lectionary cycle. See Luther Reed, *The Lutheran Liturgy: A Study of the Common Liturgy of the Lutheran Church in America*, rev. ed. (Philadelphia: Fortress Press, 1959), 288ff. Prior to this in Lutheran circles an occasional reading from the Prophets might be the "Epistle Lesson" for a given Sunday or festival. I wish to express here my thanks to Professor Thomas Schattauer of Wartburg Theological Seminary, Dubuque, IA, for reminding me of this in a recent conversation. Actually, a three-year cycle of Epistle and Gospel readings already

exception of the Easter Vigil and occasional Ember Days, readings from the First Testament tended to be excluded altogether.[21] Indeed, as Martin Connell writes of the Tridentine Lectionary, "Only 1 percent of the Old Testament was proclaimed, less than 17 percent of the New Testament, and for the whole Bible—Old Testament and New Testament together—only 6 percent was proclaimed, 1,530 verses of the canon's 33,001."[22]

In light of the above, it is surely no exaggeration to say that the greatest ecumenical-liturgical gift of the twentieth century from the Roman Catholic Church to much of Protestantism in general was, of course, the *OLM*, which since its publication has been adapted and used in various versions, the most recent being the *RCL* of 1992, by "some 70 percent of Protestant churches in the English-speaking world."[23] With regard to the *RCL*, Horace Allen has said that "it . . . marks the first time since the Reformation that Catholics and Protestants find themselves reading the scriptures together Sunday by Sunday. . . . Who would have thought that 450 years after the Reformation, Catholics would be teaching Protestants how to read scripture in worship?"[24] In fact, it is precisely the use and preaching of the lectionary in these 70 percent of Protestant churches in the English-speaking world that has led as well to the recovery and introduction of the liturgical year itself, even, rather ironically, in

appeared in the 1819 *Swedish Psalm Book*, used liturgically by those Swedish Lutherans in the United States who formed the Augustana Evangelical Lutheran Church (1860–1962), one of the predecessor bodies of the Lutheran Church in America (1962–1987) and now of the ELCA. See *Den Svenska Psalm boken af år 1819* (Rock Island: Augustana Book Concern, 1884).

21. I use *First Testament* rather than *Hebrew Bible*, since the Bible used by the churches through the first millennium was more often than not in Greek, Syriac, Latin, or Coptic and included books that the Hebrew canon does not. On terminology see Gail Ramshaw, "The First Testament in Christian Lectionaries," *Worship* 64, no. 6 (2006): 494–510.

22. Connell, *Eternity Today*, 227.

23. Horace Allen, as quoted by John Allen Jr., "Liturgist Says Ecumenical Dialogue Is 'Dead,'" *National Catholic Reporter* (May 24, 2002), http://natcath.org/NCR_Online/archives2/2002b/052402/052402u.htm.

24. Ibid.

those churches known historically for their rejection of calendars, feasts, and seasons.[25]

As is well known, the *OLM* is a *eucharistic* lectionary, organized around the Gospel readings of the three-year cycle according to a *lectio continua* manner with Matthew as the primary Gospel for Ordinary Time in Year A, Mark (and several pericopes from John 6) in Year B, and Luke in Year C. Since the second reading in each of these years is a similar *lectio continua* reading from the various Pauline and Catholic Epistles (especially James and Hebrews), any correlation between the Gospel reading and this reading on a given Sunday is purely coincidental. The readings from the First Testament, however, have been chosen thematically to correspond to the Gospel reading. This is clearly reflective of that liturgical "hierarchy of readings," referred to by Lathrop above, centered deliberately in the Gospel, by which we in the liturgical assembly are somehow "with the disciples on the road to Emmaus, and so 'beginning with Moses and all the prophets' (Lk 24:27) we interpret in the Scriptures the things concerning Jesus Christ."[26]

The principle at work in the relationship between the First Reading and Gospel Reading in the *OLM* is clearly the New Testament and patristic exegetical and liturgical principle of typology, that is, properly understood, as a principle of correspondence or harmony between the two Testaments.[27] Among contemporary liturgical scholars it is Geoffrey Wainwright, who, in seeking to defend this approach against numerous critics, writes,

It is difficult to see how Christians could, without undermining their

---

25. On this, see James White, "Protestant Public Worship in America: 1935–1995," in *Christian Worship in North America*, ed. James White (Collegeville, MN: The Liturgical Press, Pueblo, 1997), 129.

26. Lathrop, "A Rebirth of Images," 301.

27. On this, see Andrew Ciferni, "Typology/Harmony in the New Lectionary," *The Bible Today* 28, no. 2 (March 1990): 90–94.

own faith, give up the category of "the Christ" as their first identification of Jesus (Matt. 16:16; John 4:1; Acts 2:36; Rom. 1:17, etc.). The scriptures of Israel—and the history to which those scriptures bore witness—provided the earliest Christians with the framework, both real and literary, in which to confess and interpret Jesus. In return, the scriptures and history of Israel were given a christological interpretation. Like it or not, the early Church engaged in a "battle for the scriptures," and the scriptures of Israel became, in Christian eyes, the "Old Testament"—viewed positively in so far as it witnessed to God's purpose and promises, and yet as insufficient in the light of the events around Jesus that constituted the New Testament and to which the apostolic writings bore witness. . . . In my view, typology—precisely in that it respects the concrete history of salvation to which the scriptures bear literary witness—provides an appropriate, and even indispensable, though perhaps not the only, way of relating the Old Testament and the New.[28]

If, however, the typological principle is a given in relating the First and Gospel Readings together in the *OLM*, the challenge for contemporary Christians is how best to interpret this biblical harmony or correspondence. In an excellent essay, Lawrence Hull Stookey,[29] after stating clearly that typology is *not* the same as allegory, though often confused as such, offers four ways in which this relationship has been and often is understood: (1) revolutionary displacement; (2) revelationary replacement; (3) evolutionary progress; and (4) complementarity. These categories or principles denote not only the relationship between the First Reading and the Gospel, of course, but the interpretation of the relationship between Christianity and Judaism as reflected in the lectionary selections. So, the category of "revolutionary displacement" suggests that Christianity with its new covenant supersedes Judaism with its old

28. Geoffrey Wainwright, "'Bible et Liturgie': Daniélou's Work Revisited," *Studia Liturgica* 22 (1992): 157.
29. Lawrence Hull Stookey, "Marcion, Typology, and Lectionary Preaching," *Worship* 66, no. 3 (2006): 251–62, especially 255–58.

covenant, just as the category of "revelationary replacement" suggests that the relationship is one of prophecy and fulfillment, that the "Old" Testament is fulfilled in the New, with the church now replacing the synagogue as the "new Israel" or "new synagogue." If both of these categories may be seen as essentially supersessionary in ideology, the next two offer alternatives to this all too common approach. That is, the category of "evolutionary progress" asserts that Christianity clearly evolves from but is in continuity with Judaism, and although "'higher' on the evolutionary scale, it neither displaces nor replaces the synagogue."[30] And, the principle of "complementarity," certainly the one that Stookey favors most highly, claims that, while Christianity could not have developed apart from Judaism, both Judaism and Christianity, while distinct, are complementary with each possibly having "'superior' insights into different aspects of the faith."[31]

Whatever of the four approaches the original framers of the *OLM* may have had in mind in the selection of pericopes for the Eucharistic Liturgy, Stookey's category of "complementarity" clearly finds resonance in the contemporary scholarly approach to the historical development of early Christianity and Judaism. That is, the relationship between Judaism and early Christianity is viewed today not as that of parent-child but, rather, that of two children from the same family, twins one might say, growing up in increasing estrangement from each other.[32] But even this notion of increasing estrangement must be tempered by the growing scholarly awareness that, in spite of the polemical stance of various early Christian leaders (e.g., John Chrysostom in Antioch, criticizing Christians for attending the synagogue), Christians and Jews in some areas, at least,

30. Ibid., 256.
31. Ibid., 257.
32. See Paul Bradshaw, *Daily Prayer in the Early Church* (New York: Oxford University Press, 1982), 29–30.

were apparently maintaining close relationships for a longer time than previously imagined, including even some worship together. Rodney Stark has underscored this in his recent study:

> [A] wealth of archaeological findings in Italy (especially in Rome and Venosa) show that Jewish and Christian burials reflect an interdependent and closely related community of Jews and Christians in which clear marks of demarcation were blurred until the third and fourth centuries c.e.. Similarly, excavations in Capernaum on the shores of the Sea of Galilee reveal a Jewish synagogue and a Jewish-Christian house church on opposite sides of the street. . . . Following the strata and the structures, both communities apparently lived in harmony until the seventh century. . . . It is also worth noting that Origen mentioned having taken part in a theological debate with Jews before "umpires" sometime during the first half of the third century. This seems inconsistent with the assumption that church and synagogue had long been separated. Equally inconsistent is evidence that as late as the fourth century Christian theologians consulted rabbis about the interpretation of difficult Scriptural verses.[33]

An approach to the Sunday lectionary in Ordinary Time based on the "complementarity" of both Testaments and of Christianity and Judaism may well be one of the most helpful ways to deal with the readings homiletically and in teaching. But, as Stookey himself notes, this category brings with it the "danger of reductionism. It also has in it a possible uncertainty about any distinctive identity for the Church."[34] Similarly, although Stookey does not say this, it would also seem to bring with it the strong possibility of replacing a christological and Christocentric reading of the Scriptures in the Eucharistic Liturgy with a theocentric interpretation, underscoring the activity of God in both the Gospel and harmonized First Reading. While I do not mean here to say that a theocentric reading of

---

33. Rodney Stark, *Cities of God: The Real Story of How Christianity Became an Urban Movement and Conquered Rome* (San Francisco: Harper, 2006), 138–39.
34. Stookey, "Marcion, Typology, and Lectionary Preaching," 262.

both Testaments is a bad thing, the eucharistic hermeneutic of the lectionary suggests, as we have seen, precisely the christological or Christocentric approach. It is, of course, the *OLM*, the Order of Readings for Mass, and, as such, the Eucharist remains primary. As noted above, in the words of Lathrop, the readings and their proclamation place us "with the disciples on the road to Emmaus, and so 'beginning with Moses and all the prophets' (Lk 24:27) we interpret in the Scriptures the things concerning Jesus Christ," as we "set the pericope we read next to the passion and resurrection of Christ held forth now in the Supper," realizing that "the Sunday texts are not . . . understood aright unless they are understood as leading to that Supper."[35] Gail Ramshaw may provide the most helpful way out of this potential impasse:

> The task is obvious. We must first admit that the Bible enjoys different meanings within the Jewish, Christian, Islamic and secular scholarly communities. *Christians cannot avoid using the First Testament in a distinctively Christian way, toward a distinctively Christian meaning.* For example, Christians value far more and in a very different way the story of Adam and Eve than do Jews. However, even the various branches of Judaism use their ancient texts in fundamentally different ways. We cannot avoid hermeneutical distinctiveness. But we are required to halt an anti-Semitic replacement theology and to think more deeply about the prophecy-fulfillment formula. Whatever text from the First Testament we choose to read, at least the preacher, if not the lectionary revision committee, must face this issue.[36]

While the *OLM* was adapted early on by various Protestant churches, for example, by North American Lutherans in the 1978 *Lutheran Book of Worship* and by United States Episcopalians in the 1979 *Book of Common Prayer*, one of the great ecumenical stories in the English speaking world, thanks to the work of the Consultation

---

35. Lathrop, "A Rebirth of Images," 301, 296.
36. Ramshaw, "The First Testament in Christian Lectionaries," 502 (emphasis added).

on Common Texts (CCT) and the English Language Liturgical Consultation (ELLC), has been the development of the 1992 *RCL*.[37] Although based clearly on the *OLM*, the framers of the *RCL* attempted to address two issues that have been interpreted as problematic in that lectionary, namely, the relationship between the First Reading and Gospel, as noted above, and the lack of women's experiences and accomplishments in both Testaments reflected in the various pericope selections. With regard to the first issue, Martin Connell writes,

> While the original purpose of the Consultation [CCT] was a consensus regarding the use of the three-year Lectionary for Mass . . ., eventually the Consultation approved a different set of first readings . . . for the long span of Ordinary Time between Pentecost and the beginning of Advent. While this additional set of first readings in the second half of the liturgical year departs from the Roman schema, its introduction was occasioned by the potentially supersessionary interpretation. . . . Enough Protestant churches and ministers sought to distance themselves from the long history of anti-Jewish rhetoric in Christianity that the Consultation approved a second set of readings, a worthy addition to the tradition that moves away from the lamentable history of anti-Jewish theology in the church.[38]

What this means concretely is that for the Sundays between Pentecost and Advent Year A provides a *lectio continua* reading of Genesis through Joshua, Year B focuses on the narrative of kingship

---

37. On these ecumenical organizations and the development of the *Revised Common Lectionary*, see Horace Allen and Joseph Russell, *On Common Ground: The Story of the Revised Common Lectionary* (Norwich: The Canterbury Press, 1998); Fritz West, *Scripture and Memory: The Ecumenical Hermeneutic of the Three-Year Lectionaries* (Collegeville, MN: The Liturgical Press, Pueblo, 1997), especially 137–39; David Holeton, "Reading the Word of God Together: The Revised Common Lectionary," *Communio Viatorum* 48, no. 3 (2006): 223–43; and Martin Connell, *Eternity Today*, vol. 2, 234ff. For the lectionary itself see CCT, *The Revised Common Lectionary* (Nashville: Abingdon, 1992), and CCT, *The Revised Common Lectionary: 20th Anniversary Annotated Edition*, foreword by Gordon Lathrop (Minneapolis: Fortress Press, 2012).

38. Connell, *Eternity Today*, 235.

in Israel from 1 Samuel through 1 Kings, and Year C provides a more extensive reading of prophetic texts. The result of this, of course, is that, since in this lengthy period of time three readings based on this *lectio continua* principle are read, there is no necessary correlation between any of the biblical readings on a given Sunday. Nevertheless, certainly one of the most positive contributions of this change is that the use of this more complete biblical narrative may well contribute toward the presentation of what Fritz West calls "a fulsome account of the history of salvation."[39]

The second issue, that of what Ruth Fox has called "a disproportionate number of passages about women in the Bible . . . omitted" from the *OLM*, has been dealt with in two ways in the *RCL*.[40] First, most of the readings, both First Reading and Gospel, have been lengthened to include previously omitted verses, many of which tended to ignore *positive* elements associated with women in the various pericopes, with negative narratives also omitted. And, second, this lectionary "incorporated readings that the Church has tended to overlook, such as those about Sarah, Hagar, Rebekah, Leah, Miriam, Deborah, the capable wife, Hannah, the woman with the issue of blood, the Syrophoenician woman, Dorcas, and Lydia."[41] Such a move can only have positive results in the long run.

At the same time, it must be noted that the *RCL* is not simply an adaptation or "correction" of the *OLM*. In fact, it can be argued that the two lectionaries, at least for the Time after Pentecost, reflect two distinct theoretical foundations. That is, as Fritz West has stated so clearly,

> We must . . . draw a distinction between the three-year lectionaries and their use. While the lectionaries themselves build upon an ecumenical

39. West, *Scripture and Memory*, 177.
40. Ruth Fox, "Women in the Bible and the Lectionary," *Liturgy* 90 (1996): 5.
41. West, *Scripture and Memory*, 169.

hermeneutic, the interpretative frameworks by which congregations appropriate them are not always consonant with that hermeneutic. To get a handle on this problem, we must differentiate the liturgical forms Churches use from the liturgical paradigms they harbor. Liturgical paradigms are the ritual propensities and understandings a Church brings to bear upon the worship it celebrates. The Catholic liturgical paradigm is marked by weekly Eucharist, a balance of word and sacrament, a sacramental perspective on worship, an appreciation for ritual and symbol, an organic understanding of Church, and a veneration of tradition. The Protestant liturgical paradigm is a preaching tradition characterized by the centrality of the sermon and, in most cases, the infrequent celebration of the Lord's Supper. Other attributes include a preference for the verbal over the symbolic, an emphasis upon the local expressions of the Church . . ., and a more occasional appreciation for Church tradition.[42]

However intended by the framers of the *Revised Common Lectionary*, it would seem that those operating out of the "Protestant liturgical paradigm" may more likely be attracted to the *lectio-continua* series of First Readings since on any given Sunday in this season it provides three distinct, possible "sermon texts" from which a choice could be made. Such a "Protestant liturgical paradigm," or even an understanding that reading Scripture in liturgy is a form of religious education or "Bible study," I would argue is certainly the principle behind the "Narrative Lectionary"[43] produced by Luther Seminary, in which only one reading is actually assigned to a given Sunday in a nine-month period. But for those who operate out of the "Catholic liturgical paradigm," preaching itself is "liturgical preaching" and, as we have seen repeatedly, points to the Eucharist as its culmination. Such may well be the difference between preaching a "sermon" on the text(s) for the day and preaching a "homily" on the eucharistic readings. In fact, to accommodate those of the "Catholic liturgical

---

42. Ibid, 8–9.
43. See Rolf Jacobson, "Commentary on Introduction," https://www.workingpreacher.org/preaching.aspx?commentary_id=1081.

paradigm," most notably in this case, Lutherans and Anglicans/ Episcopalians, since this lectionary has not (yet) been accepted by Rome, another three-year alternative series of First Testament readings is actually provided for these Sundays between Pentecost and Advent. Although revised and longer, these readings reflect more closely the typological approach to the First Testament and Gospel in the *OLM*. Both the Evangelical Lutheran Church in America and The Episcopal Church, abandoning their earlier lectionary adaptations, have now accepted the *RCL* with this alternative series for what, at least, Lutherans now refer to as the *Time after Epiphany* and *Time after Pentecost*.[44] Interestingly enough, the adoption of the *RCL* with this alternative series of First Testament Readings has actually brought Lutherans, Episcopalians, and others closer to the *OLM* itself and has resolved what was before often a week or two discrepancy between them during this season.

There can be no question but that both of these lectionaries are remarkable achievements. But with two series of First Readings provided for the Sundays between Pentecost and Advent, of course, it is hard to speak of the *RCL* as really "common" if, for approximately half of the Sundays in a given year, those of a "Catholic liturgical paradigm" are following one series and those of a "Protestant liturgical paradigm" are following another.[45] The ecumenical nature of the *RCL* during Ordinary Time, given its possible alternatives, then, might best be expressed by the term *resource*, that is, what is ecumenical about it, including common Second Readings and Gospel pericopes, is that it provides a common lectionary resource during Ordinary Time for "a Church marked by unity-with-diversity."[46] At this time in history, until conditions are right for real ecumenical

44. See *Evangelical Lutheran Worship*, Leader's Desk Edition, 67–74, 92–119.
45. See Holeton, "Reading the Word of God Together," 234–37.
46. West, *Scripture and Memory*, 168.

liturgical work once again, this will have to suffice.

Feasts of the Lord, Mary, and the Saints and Ordinary Time

In addition to the *tempus per annum* being the celebration of Sunday itself in its "pure state" as the Lord's Day par excellence, there are various solemnities, feasts, or lesser festivals that either automatically occur on a Sunday or may be celebrated on a Sunday if the date of the solemnity, feast, or lesser festival happens to fall on a Sunday. In the Time after Pentecost, this period begins and ends with two festivals, namely, that of the Holy Trinity on the Sunday after Pentecost and that of Christ the King on the final Sunday of the liturgical year, that is, the Sunday immediately before the start of Advent. Two others of what Adolf Adam calls "moveable solemnities of Ordinary Time,"[47] moveable because, like Trinity Sunday, they are dependent on the annual date of Easter, are the Roman Catholic Solemnities of the Body and Blood of Christ (*Corpus Christi*) on the Thursday after Trinity Sunday, though often transferred to the following Sunday in many dioceses, and that of the Sacred Heart of Jesus on the third Friday after Pentecost. While Christ the King may certainly function as a fitting eschatological conclusion to the entire liturgical year, the two festivals, which begin and conclude this Time after Pentecost, have no real thematic connection to the period as a whole and, consequently, do not shape any overall liturgical emphasis.

Other solemnities and feasts on the Roman Catholic liturgical calendar that may take precedence over a Sunday in both periods of Ordinary Time, if the date coincides with a Sunday, include the Presentation of the Lord (February 2), the Chair of Peter (February 22), the Birth of John the Baptist (June 24), Peter and Paul, Apostles

47. Adam, *The Liturgical Year*, 167.

(June 29), the Transfiguration of the Lord (August 6), the Assumption of the Blessed Virgin Mary (August 15), the Triumph of the Cross (September 14), All Saints (November 1), All Souls (November 2), and the Dedication of the Lateran Basilica (November 9). Various Protestant churches also follow a similar pattern of celebrating "lesser festivals" on Sundays during these periods. In addition to those several feasts held in common with Roman Catholics, Lutherans, for example, might add also the Confession of Peter (January 18), the Conversion of Paul (January 25), Barnabas, Apostle (June 11), Mary Magdalene, Apostle (July 22), James, Apostle (July 25), Bartholomew, Apostle (August 24), Mathew, Apostle and Evangelist (September 21), Michael and All Angels (September 29), Luke, Evangelist (October 18), Simon and Jude, Apostles (October 28), and Reformation Day (October 31), which is almost always transferred to the last Sunday in October, no matter what the calendar date of the Sunday is. In fact, the celebration of Reformation Sunday at the end of October, commemorating the date when Luther posted his *95 Theses* on the door of the Castle Church in Wittenberg on October 31, 1517, was one of the factors that lead Pope Pius XI, in a less ecumenical time, to establish the solemnity of Christ the King originally on the last Sunday in October.[48] Interestingly enough, today Roman Catholics and many Protestants alike celebrate Christ the King as the last Sunday of the liturgical year, thanks to the Roman Catholic transfer of this feast from the end of October.

While a case can certainly be made for solemnities and feasts such as the Presentation of the Lord (February 2), Transfiguration (August 6), Assumption (August 15), and All Saints and All Souls (November 1 and 2) taking precedence if their dates occur on a Sunday, the sheer number of festivals in various liturgical traditions, for which this

---

48. See John Baldovin, "On Feasting the Saints," in Johnson, *Between Memory and Hope*, 379.

can be done certainly calls into question the overall theology of the *tempus per annum* itself as being the celebration of Sunday in its "pure state" as the Lord's Day par excellence. As Martin Connell notes,

> [A] factor . . . that keeps people from an awareness of the fundamental three-year cycle of the lectionary is that many solemnities and feasts displace Sundays in Ordinary Time. These celebrations have their own Gospel proclamations, not usually drawn from the particular Gospel of that year. . . . Since there are only a fixed number of Sundays in Ordinary Time, and many of these are displaced by [solemnities and feasts] . . ., the interruptions in some years can be many.[49]

Connell suggests that this is a problem more for Roman Catholics than for Protestants, but the fact of the matter is that it is equally, if not even more, problematic for some Protestant congregations. Lutherans, for example, following a Reformation-era principle about saints' feasts, may even "transfer" various lesser festivals to the nearest Sunday in the Time after the Epiphany or after Pentecost, whether the date falls on a Sunday or not. For the month of September in 2014, for example, September 14, Holy Cross Day, fell on a Sunday. So did September 21, Matthew, Apostle and Evangelist. As such, several Lutheran congregations replaced the corresponding Sundays after Pentecost with these two festivals. Further, the date of the next Sunday was September 28, or one day before the Lesser Festival of Michael and All Angels (September 29). Again, in several Lutheran places Michael and All Angels may well have been transferred to this Sunday and, with this, the Sundays of almost the entire month of September were displaced by three "Sunday" festivals, one after the other. And there is no reason why something like this could not happen in other years with the transfer of all three festivals to their nearest Sundays in the month.

---

49. Connell, *Eternity Today*, 242–43.

Unfortunately, this tendency of allowing solemnities and feasts to take precedence over Sundays has begun to enter into other seasons of the liturgical year as well. For Roman Catholics in North America it has now long been common to transfer the celebration of the Epiphany of the Lord, from its traditional date of January 6 (a date known since the time of Clement of Alexandria in the second century[50]), to the Sunday between January 2 and 8, which is now also an option provided in *Evangelical Lutheran Worship*.[51] By doing this in some years (if the Sunday in question is January 7 or 8), however, Roman Catholic usage also displaces the more ancient "Epiphany" or "Theophany," that is, the Baptism of the Lord from the Sunday *after* the Epiphany to the Monday after the Epiphany. More recently, a similar displacement has happened in many Roman Catholic dioceses of the United States with the Solemnity of the Ascension now transferred from the fortieth day of Easter, "Ascension *Thursday*," to the Seventh Sunday of Easter, thus essentially removing the Seventh Sunday of Easter from the liturgical year and raising the annual question of "Will Ascension Thursday be on a Sunday this year?" So much for the twelve days of Christmas and the vast biblical associations with the number forty!

This discussion of solemnities and feasts during Ordinary Time has a direct relationship to the first part of Ordinary Time, that is, the period between the Epiphany and the beginning of Lent. If the two Solemnities, which begin and conclude the period of Ordinary Time between Pentecost and Advent, do not shape the individual Sundays in that season, the opposite is somewhat true for this period. While for Roman Catholics the Baptism of the Lord now actually concludes the *Christmas* liturgical cycle, for those churches that follow the *Revised Common Lectionary*, and, hence, do not transfer the Epiphany

---

50. Clement of Alexandria, *Stromata* I.21.
51. *Evangelical Lutheran Worship*, Leader's Desk Edition, 66.

of the Lord from January 6 but retain the traditional date, the Baptism of the Lord is the *First* Sunday *after* the Epiphany or what is, in Roman Catholic terminology, the *First* Sunday in Ordinary Time. Further, while for Roman Catholics the Transfiguration of Jesus is the focus of the Gospel Readings for the Second Sunday of Lent, the *Revised Common Lectionary* follows the sixteenth-century Lutheran practice of celebrating the Transfiguration of the Lord on the last Sunday after the Epiphany, that is, the Sunday before Ash Wednesday. As such, the Transfiguration becomes the Epiphany or Theophany of all theophanies par excellence and provides a sort of preview of coming attractions at Easter before the start of the Lenten fast. If these two festal Sundays do provide bookends and an overall focus for this time "after the Epiphany" for some Christian traditions, the Presentation of the Lord on February 2 may be said to provide the overall epiphanic focus for this season in all Christian traditions. That is, the Canticle of Simeon (Luke 2:29–32), read as part of the Gospel for the Presentation, underscores that the various Sundays in this first "season" of Ordinary Time are, indeed, concerned with Christ who is light of "epiphany" for the Gentiles and the "glory of [God's] people, Israel," as that epiphany or manifestation is celebrated at the Jordan, at Cana, in the fulfillment of the Scriptures at the synagogue in Nazareth, in proclaiming the nearness of the kingdom of God, in signs and wonders, and, for some, in the brilliant light on the mount of Transfiguration. It is for this reason that several Christian traditions using the *Revised Common Lectionary* view Epiphany still as an integral liturgical season in its own right and as a time of focus on missionary work around the world.

Conclusion

As we have now seen in detail, the theology of the *tempus per annum*, "Ordinary Time," or "Time after Epiphany and Pentecost," especially for the period between Pentecost and Advent, is really nothing other than the theology of Sunday itself in all of its multiple dimensions as the continuation of the postresurrection appearances of the crucified and risen Christ in the power and gifts of his Holy Spirit among his own at word and table in the assembly. If some problems of the precise relationship of the two Testaments remain with regard to the selection of pericopes in either the *OLM* or the *RCL*, the following comment by Fritz West should be borne in mind:

> To maintain the coherency of Sunday's proclamation, the *Lectionary for Mass* gives up a fulsome account of the history of salvation. To give the biblical account of salvation the *Revised Common Lectionary* gives up Sunday coherency in the season after Pentecost. Although both assiduously sought a balance, the goal proved elusive. . . . The difficulty of the task only points to the importance of the problem. Just as the Church in its theology struggles to relate the Christ event to history, so does the Church in its lectionaries struggle to balance the Bible's account of the history of salvation with the use of the memory of the Christ event for reading it. In this effort, the *Lectionary for Mass* and *Revised Common Lectionary* are both to be commended for seeing the problem clearly and seeking solutions boldly.[52]

Further, as we have also seen, there are occasional problems with the encroachment of other feasts on the Sundays in Ordinary Time in several Christian traditions, which may well constitute unfortunate "interruptions" in the sequence of the Sunday readings. While in some cases Sunday solemnities and feasts may well provide an overall hermeneutical key to that section of Ordinary Time, it is the integrity of Sunday itself to which we ought to hold liturgically.

---

52. West, *Scripture and Memory*, 177.

Finally, a more serious threat to the overall integrity of Ordinary Time and its current lectionaries is the 2007 *motu proprio* of Benedict XVI in allowing greater use of the 1962 *Missale Romanum* with its own cycle of lectionary readings. Unless and until the current *OLM* is integrated with that "usage" of the "one" Roman Rite, this is but a movement forward into the past and a restoration of the very problematic use of the Bible in the liturgy that the *OLM* sought to and did reform! If the current lectionary may be accused at times of a supersessionary mentality, the former lectionary then merits the more serious charge of Marcionism, the complete denial of the First Testament altogether. Make no mistake. This issue is not about liturgy per se. It is about the First Testament and Christianity and, with it, the very relationship between Judaism and the church in the modern world, as we seek to celebrate the Mystery of Christ in its fullness and in the fullness of the biblical witness.

7

The Blessed Virgin Mary and Ecumenical Convergence in Doctrine, Doxology, and Devotion

The influential Lutheran theologian Wolfhart Pannenberg once said that "Mary is more important in the history of Christianity as a symbol than as an historical person,"[1] a statement reflected also in the work of Hugo Rahner, Karl Rahner's lesser-known brother and fellow Jesuit, in his comment that "Mary the mother of Jesus, in virtue of the ineffable dignity of being the Virgin Mother of God made Man, became the essential symbol of the Church, our Mother."[2] And, more recently, the late Jaroslav Pelikan also wrote in his wonderful book, *Mary Through the Centuries*,

It is probably safe to estimate that for nearly two thousand years "Mary"

---

1. Pannenberg, as quoted by Lawrence Cunningham, *Mother of God* (San Francisco: Harper & Row, 1982), 61.
2. Hugo Rahner, *Our Lady and the Church* (New York: Pantheon Books, 1961), 4.

has been the name most frequently given to girls at baptism, and through the exclamation "Jesus, Mary, and Joseph" (or just "Jezis Mária!" as I used to hear it in Slovak from my father's Lutheran parishioners during my childhood), and above all through the *Ave Maria*, which has been repeated literally millions of times every day, [Mary is] the female name that has been pronounced most often in the Western world. Almost certainly she has been portrayed in art and music more than any other woman in history. . . . The Virgin Mary has been more of an inspiration to more people than any other woman who ever lived. And she remains so in the twentieth century, despite its being conventionally regarded as secularistic by contrast with previous so-called ages of faith.[3]

The topic of the Blessed Virgin Mary is often considered to be a major stumbling block to Christian unity, a central church-dividing issue between Roman Catholic, Eastern and Oriental Orthodox, and Protestant Christians in terms of Christian doctrine, doxology, and devotion. After years of ecumenical dialogue, however, especially reflected in those dialogues conducted and produced by Anglicans and Roman Catholics,[4] Lutherans and Roman Catholics,[5] and even Evangelicals and Roman Catholics,[6] as well as numerous theological studies of Mary by theologians of various Christian traditions,[7] a

3. Jaroslav Pelikan, *Mary through the Centuries: Her Place in the History of Culture* (New Haven: Yale University Press, 1996), 1–2.

4. *The One Mediator, the Saints, and Mary*, ed. H. George Anderson, J. Francis Stafford, and Joseph A. Burgess, Lutherans and Catholics in Dialogue 8 (Minneapolis: Augsburg, 1992) (hereafter, *OMSM*).

5. Anglican and Roman Catholic International Commission, *Mary: Grace and Hope in Christ* (Harrisburg: Morehouse, 2005).

6. Evangelicals and Catholics Together, "Do Whatever He Tells You: The Blessed Virgin Mary in Christian Faith and Life," *First Things* (November, 2009), online edition at http://www.firstthings.com/article/2009/10/do-whatever-he-tells-you-the-blessed-virgin-mary-in-christian-faith-and-life.

7. In addition to Pelikan, n3 above, compare Alain Blancy, Maurice Jourjon, and the Dombes Group, *Mary in the Plan of God and in the Communion of Saints: Toward a Common Christian Understanding*, trans. Matthew J. O'Connell (Mahwah, NJ: Paulist Press, 2002); William McLoughlin and Jill Pinnock, eds., *Mary for Time and Eternity: Essays on Mary and Ecumenism* (Herefordshire: Gracewing, 2007); Elizabeth Johnson, *Truly Our Sister: A Theology of Mary in the Communion of Saints* (New York: Continuum, 2003); Beverly Roberts Gaventa and Cynthia L. Rigby, eds. *Blessed One: Protestant Perspectives on Mary* (Louisville: Westminster John Knox, 2002); Carl. E. Braaten and Robert W. Jenson, eds. *Mary, Mother of God* (Grand

remarkable convergence, if not consensus, in ecumenical thought is taking place today. That is, while issues of Marian doxology and devotion may be still somewhat divisive, at the level of Marian doctrine there has been enough ecumenical convergence to say that, properly understood and articulated, this needs no longer be a church-dividing issue.

In this chapter I will focus on each of these areas under the following subheadings: (1) Ecumenical Convergence on Marian Doctrine; (2) Ecumenical Convergence on Mary in Contemporary Liturgy and Doxology; and (3) Ecumenical Convergence in Devotion to the Blessed Virgin Mary. In all of these, it is perhaps part 3 that offers the greatest surprise.

Ecumenical Convergence on Marian Doctrine

In an ecumenical context, the topic of Marian doctrine or dogmatic formulation almost immediately raises the question of the two modern Roman Catholic dogmas of the Immaculate Conception and the Assumption of the Blessed Virgin Mary into heaven. But while this is the case and of great importance, it is crucial I believe to begin with the classic Marian doctrine shared both by the Christian East and West, namely, the christologically-motivated Marian title *Theotokos,* God-bearer, or Mother of God, accepted by the Council of Ephesus in 431, the title that safeguards the personhood of the

Rapids: Eerdmans, 2004); Sarah Jane Boss, *Mary: The Complete Resource* (New York: Oxford, 2007); Chris Maunder, ed., *The Origins of the Cult of the Virgin Mary* (London: Burns and Oates, 2008); George H. Tavard, *The Thousand Faces of the Virgin Mary* (Collegeville, MN: Michael Glazier, 1996); John Macquarrie, *Mary for All Christians* (Grand Rapids: Eerdmans, 1990); Tim Perry and Daniel Kendall, *The Blessed Virgin Mary* (Grand Rapids: Eerdmans, 2013); Virgil Elizondo, *Guadalupe: Mother of the New Creation* (Maryknoll: Orbis Books, 1997); Maxwell E. Johnson, *The Virgin of Guadalupe: Theological Reflections of an Anglo-Lutheran Liturgist,* Celebrating Faith: Explorations in Latino Spirituality and Theology Series (Landham, MD: Rowman and Littlefield, 2002); and Johnson, ed., *American Magnificat: Protestants on Mary of Guadalupe* (Collegeville, MN: The Liturgical Press, 2010).

divine and human Christ himself against the approach of Nestorius and his followers. It is important to begin here since even this central Marian doctrine has often died from woeful neglect within Protestant churches.

As an example of this, in my first year as a student at Wartburg Theological Seminary, Dubuque, Iowa, Professor Ralph Quere asked our class of future pastors in Early Church History whether we thought it appropriate to call Mary the Mother of God. Only two out of more than thirty of us raised our hands in agreement that it was. But of all Protestant churches it is the Lutherans who actually have a confessional statement in the *Formula of Concord* that boldly proclaims, "We believe, teach, and confess, that Mary did not conceive and bear a mere and ordinary human being, but the true Son of God; for that reason she is rightly called and in truth is the Mother of God."[8] Further, Luther's own high regard for Mary and rather warm piety directed to her has not always been well-known by Lutherans or has been dismissed in general as a bit of antiquated devotionalism from which he could not separate himself. With reference to his 1521 commentary on the *Magnificat*,[9] often called "the centerpiece of Luther's Marian views," Eric Gritsch summarizes his overall approach:

> Mary is the prototype of how God is to be "magnified." He is not to be "magnified" or praised for his distant, unchangeable majesty, but for his unconditional, graceful, and ever-present pursuit of his creatures. Thus Mary magnifies God for what he does rather than magnifying herself for what was done to her. . . . "Being regarded by God" is the truly blessed state of Mary. *She is the embodiment of God's grace,* by which others can see what kind of God the Father of Jesus Christ is. . . . [And] Mary is the "Mother of God" who experienced his unmerited grace. Her personal

8. Formula of Concord: "Epitome" VIII, 12 in *The Book of Concord*, ed. Theodore Tappert (Philadelphia: Fortress 1959), 488, and "Solid Declaration" VIII, 24 in ibid, 595.
9. See *The Magnificat: Luther's Commentary* (Minneapolis: Augsburg Publishing House, 1967).

experience of this grace is an example for all humankind that the mighty God cares for the lowly just as he cares for the exalted. . . . Thus she incites the faithful to trust in God's grace when they call on her.[10]

Consequently, according to Gritsch, "to Luther Mary was the prime example of the faithful—a *typus ecclesiae* embodying unmerited grace. Mary is a paradigm for the indefectibility of the church."[11]

However, while the writings and homilies of Luther do tend often to have Marian themes, references, or overtones, we should not think that such concerns belonged to Luther alone. Rather, as the Augustinian ecumenist George Tavard demonstrated in his 1996 study, *The Thousand Faces of the Virgin Mary*,[12] positive assessments of Mary as *Theotokos* and model are also to be noted in the writings of Ulrich Zwingli, Heinrich Bullinger, and John Calvin, with Zwingli even including the *Ave Maria* in the introduction to his reformed order of Mass and Bullinger accepting Mary's Assumption of body and soul into heaven centuries before such a dogma was promulgated by Rome. Indeed, even Mary's perpetual virginity, her sinlessness or purity at least at the moment of *Jesus'* conception, if not at her own "immaculate" conception, and her assumed (no pun intended) place in heaven, whether bodily or not, at the end of her life were widely held both by the Continental Reformers as well as by several within the Anglican Reformation.[13]

If much of this emphasis tended to disappear from center stage or lie dormant even within theological method and catechetical formation in much of Protestantism, there can be no question but that some of the major catalysts in provoking a reassessment of the place of Mary within Protestantism were the *Dogmatic Constitution on*

10. Eric Gritsch, "The Views of Luther and Lutheranism on the Veneration of Mary," in *OMSM*, 236–37 (emphasis added).
11. Ibid, 241.
12. Tavard, *The Thousand Faces of the Virgin Mary*, 103–33.
13. See ibid, 134ff.

the Church, Lumen Gentium, of the Second Vatican Council, where in chapter 8 Mary is included theologically *within* the church, rather than having her own independent document as some Marian maximalists hoped for at the time; the 1974 Apostolic Exhortation of Pope Paul VI, *Marialis cultus: For the Right Ordering and Development of Devotion to the Blessed Virgin Mary*; and the subsequent ecumenical dialogues on Mary.

With regard to the ecumenical dialogues in particular, the 1981 Final Report of the first multiyear Anglican-Roman Catholic International Commission (also known as ARCIC I), which had treated papal authority specifically, had this to say about Mary in the context of considering the dogmas of her Immaculate Conception and Assumption:

> Anglicans and Roman Catholics can agree in much of the truth that these two dogmas are designed to affirm. . . . Nevertheless the dogmas of the Immaculate Conception and the Assumption raise a special problem for those Anglicans who do not consider that the precise definitions given by these dogmas are sufficiently supported by Scripture. For many Anglicans the teaching authority of the bishop of Rome, independent of a council, is not recommended by the fact that through it these Marian doctrines were proclaimed as dogmas binding on all the faithful. Anglicans would also ask whether, in any future union between our two Churches, they would be required to subscribe to such dogmatic statements. One consequence of our separation has been a tendency for Anglicans and Roman Catholics alike to exaggerate the importance of the Marian dogmas in themselves at the expense of other truths more closely related to the foundation of the Christian faith.[14]

ARCIC II, however, under the title of *Mary: Grace and Hope in Christ*, published in 2004, reflects continued dialogue on these very issues and concludes that "the teaching about Mary in the two definitions

---

14. ARCIC I, para. 30, http://www.anglicancommunion.org/ministry/ecumenical/dialogues/catholic/arcic/docs/pdf/final_report_arcic_1.pdf.

of 1854 and 1950, understood within the biblical pattern of the economy of grace and hope outlined here, can be said to be consonant with the teaching of the Scriptures and the ancient common traditions."[15]

Similarly, two years earlier the eighth Lutheran-Roman Catholic dialogue in the United States, entitled *The One Mediator, the Saints, and Mary*, was able to challenge both communions as to whether it would be possible that

> 1. Lutheran churches could acknowledge that the Catholic teaching about the saints and Mary as set forth in the documents of Vatican Council II . . . does not promote idolatrous belief and is not opposed to the gospel? and

> 2. the Catholic Church could acknowledge that, in a closer but still incomplete fellowship, Lutherans, focusing on Christ the one Mediator, as set forth in Scripture, would not be obliged to invoke the saints or to affirm the two Marian dogmas?[16]

While I have criticized this conclusion elsewhere as a surprisingly weak challenge to Lutherans,[17] it is clear that Lutheran hesitations and fears with regard to Marian doctrine and piety were resolved especially by the clearer articulation of Catholic theology on the one mediatorship of Christ and a renewed conciliar and post-conciliar theology of Mary. That is,

> The statements of the Second Vatican Council . . . demonstrate that the sole mediatorship of Christ can be asserted and the role of Mary further interpreted by Roman Catholics in ways that the old Lutheran fears can be diminished. The Lutherans of this dialogue are of the opinion that, as

---

15. ARCIC II, 58, n60, http://www.anglicancommunion.org/ministry/ecumenical/dialogues/catholic/arcic/docs/pdf/mary_definitive_text.pdf.

16. *OMSM*, 62.

17. See my "*The One Mediator, the Saints, and Mary:* A Lutheran Reflection," *Worship* 6, no. 3 (May 1993): 226–38.

long as the sole mediatorship of Christ is clearly safeguarded, these two Marian dogmas need not divide our churches.[18]

It is perhaps not so surprising that the Anglican and Lutheran dialogues with Roman Catholics could be so positive in their general assessments. What *is* surprising however, is the amount of agreement between Evangelicals and Catholics in their 2009 statement, "Do Whatever He Tells You: The Blessed Virgin Mary in Christian Faith and Life," where, even the once controversial title of *Theotokos* is now jointly affirmed:

> We are agreed that it is appropriate, and indeed necessary, to call Mary *Theotokos*—the God-Bearer. *Theotokos* means "the one who gave birth to the One who is God," and the title, based on the clear witness of Scripture, was emphasized in the early Church to counter the heresy of Nestorius, who divided the human and divine natures of Christ.[19]

Nevertheless, while the Evangelical members of this statement were able to see various positive elements in other Marian dogmas, such as Mary's perpetual virginity, her Immaculate Conception, and Assumption, the fact that none of these are clearly supported by Scripture makes them still next to impossible for Evangelicals to affirm in any positive way.

There is no question but that an important factor in this contemporary ecumenical reassessment of Mary has been due to two factors. As Elizabeth Johnson notes in her recent groundbreaking study, *Truly Our Sister: A Theology of Mary in the Communion of Saints*,[20] the theology of Mary embedded in the documents of the Second Vatican Council reflects a return to the Mariology of the first Christian millennium, a return to the commonality in Marian doctrine and devotion shared between Eastern and Western

18. *OMSM*, 59.
19. Evangelicals and Catholics Together, "Do Whatever He Tells You."
20. See above, n7.

Christianity. And, second, together with this, contemporary Mariology has included a decided return to Mary in Scripture as its starting point, a focus clearly evident in Pope Paul VI's *Marialis cultus*, from which Johnson takes the title for her book, *Truly Our Sister*. Now what is most intriguing about this, according to her, is the minimal role that Mary's own *Magnificat* in Luke 2 actually played over the centuries in shaping Marian doctrine and devotion. In spite of the fact that it has been sung daily as the centerpiece of vespers for centuries, it is, with the notable exception of someone like Luther, only quite recently where her song has contributed toward a new approach to her identity and role, as not so much the weak, subservient, obedient handmaid of the Lord and as the model for a particular patriarchal view of women, but the strong prophet who dares to proclaim that the mighty are cast down, the lowly lifted up, and the hungry filled with good things. As Johnson notes,

> The church in Latin America more than any other is responsible for hearing this proclamation of hope in a newly refreshed way. The *Magnificat*'s message is so subversive that for a period during the 1980's the government of Guatemala banned its public recitation. Seeing the central point of this song to be the assertion of the holiness of God, Peruvian Gustavo Gutiérrez argues, "Any exegesis is fruitless that attempts to tone down what Mary's song tells us about preferential love of God for the lowly and the abused, and about the transformation of history that God's loving will implies."[21]

Indeed, the biblical Mary that is emerging today, thanks, in part, also to various forms of liberation theology, has titles ascribed to her based on the biblical witness, as in the following from a "Litany of Mary of Nazareth," published by Pax Christi:[22]

Mary, wellspring of peace . . .

21. *Truly Our Sister*, 269.
22. "Litany of Mary of Nazareth" (Erie, PA: Pax Christi, no date).

Model of strength
Model of gentleness
Model of trust
Model of courage
Model of patience
Model of risk
Model of openness
Model of perseverance

Mother of the liberator . . .
Mother of the homeless
Mother of the dying
Mother of the nonviolent
Mother of widowed mothers
Mother of unwed mothers
Mother of a political prisoner
Mother of the condemned
Mother of the executed criminal

Oppressed woman . . .

Liberator of the oppressed
Marginalized woman
Comforter of the afflicted

Sign of contradiction
Breaker of bondage
Political refugee
Seeker of sanctuary
First disciple
Sharer in Christ's passion

Seeker of God's will
Witness to Christ's resurrection

Woman of mercy . . .
Woman of faith
Woman of contemplation
Woman of vision
Woman of wisdom and understanding
Woman of grace and truth
Woman, pregnant with hope
Woman, centered in God

Part of Johnson's own mariological program, both in her earlier articles[23] and now in her major study, has been to retrieve from Mariology and restore to a broader theological understanding of God *in se* precisely those female images or attributes of the divine that, in the course of Western Christian history, became transferred from God and concretized explicitly in Mary. That is, according to Johnson, Marian images and devotions beginning in the late patristic period and coming to their full flowering in the Middle Ages, became the vehicle by which the often distant and transcendent patriarchically conceived God was made accessible under the images of maternity, divine compassion, liberating power and might, divine immanence or intimate presence, and re-creative energy. While Johnson notes that several of these images could be interpreted stereotypically from the perspective of the "patriarchal feminine," in other words, patriarchically based self-serving ways of defining women, she states that especially the

characteristics of mothering, compassion, and presence, so particular to

23. Elizabeth Johnson, "Mary and the Female Face of God," *Theological Studies* 50 (1989): 501–26; and "The Marian Tradition and the Reality of Women," in *The Catholic Faith: A Reader*, ed. Lawrence Cunningham (New York: Paulist Press, 1988), 97–123.

the historical experience of women, are being reclaimed, reimagined, and revalued by contemporary analysis in ways that liberate. . . . Each element . . . represents a missing or underdeveloped piece in our repertoire of references to God and, as shaped by women's experience, should be allowed to connote and evoke the whole of the divine mystery in tandem with a plethora of other images.[24]

And when this is accomplished, the very human Mary that emerges *within* the communion of saints is, much like the litany referred to above, Mary as the woman of the Spirit, the outsider and outcast, the refugee, the poor, the thinking mother, and, most importantly, Mary as the "friend of God and prophet."[25]

What, then, ecumenically, of the two Marian dogmas of her Immaculate Conception and Assumption of body and soul into heaven? Is there any way forward here? There is a theological core in both of these Marian dogmas that may well be acceptable to Protestant theology within a contemporary ecumenical context. This might especially be the case when one considers the close relationship that exists between Mariology and ecclesiology in contemporary Roman Catholic thought. Surely, on one level at least, the dogma of Mary's Immaculate Conception is nothing other than the proclamation of justification by "grace alone" since such redemption by Christ of Mary in the womb (and, according to Catholic teaching, it *is* a redemption) could come about through no other possible means. As Berard Marthaler states, "It is the symbol par excellence of 'free grace'—Mary was justified from the first instant of her existence independently of anything she desired or did (*ante praevisa merita*)."[26] Similarly, with regard to her bodily Assumption, it is important to note the necessary contrast between the technical terms *ascensio*

---

24. "Mary and Female Face of God," 525–26.
25. *Truly Our Sister*, chs. 10 and 11.
26. Berard Marthaler, *The Creed: The Apostolic Faith in Contemporary Theology*, rev. ed. (Mystic, CT: Twenty-Third Publications, 1993), 134.

("ascension") and *assumptio* ("Assumption"). If, as John Macquarrie notes in his sensitive *Mary for All Christians*, "ascension" implies an active role assigned to the one ascending (e.g., the *ascension* of Christ into heaven), "Assumption" can only be an act of God in which the one assumed (in this case, Mary) remains passive.[27] Consequently, Mary's Assumption, like the Immaculate Conception, is dependent completely upon God's grace alone and Mary remains a "recipient" of both divine actions. As Marthaler continues,

> Mary typifies, in a way that Jesus (who did not need redemption) could not, what it means to be redeemed in Christ. While neither the Immaculate Conception nor the Assumption are mentioned in Scripture, they nonetheless affirm truths that are clearly implied in the mystery of grace and election. They illustrate once again how church doctrine affirms more about human nature and needs than about the Godhead—an axiom that seems especially true of the Marian dogmas.[28]

And as the Official German Catholic-Lutheran Dialogue on the Church as the Communion of Saints exhorts Lutherans,

> Lutheran Christians should, for the sake of the . . . goal of the unity of the faith, honor the efforts of the Catholic side to establish the place of Mary christologically and ecclesiologically. They are invited to consider that for Catholic thought the Mother of Christ is the embodiment of the event of justification by grace alone and through faith. It is from that conception that the Marian dogmas of the nineteenth and twentieth centuries are derived: If God elects a person in such a way as Mary, then Christian thought realizes that such a calling seizes that person totally—it begins in the first moment of that person's existence and never abandons that person.[29]

27. See Macquarrie, *Mary for All Christians*, 81ff.
28. Marthaler, *The Creed*, 135.
29. Bilateral Working Group of the German National Bishops' Conference and the Church Leadership of the United Evangelical Lutheran Church of Germany, *Communio Sanctorum: The Church as the Communion of Saints*, Official German Catholic-Lutheran Dialogue, trans. Mark W. Jeske, Michael Root, and Daniel R. Smith (Collegeville, MN: The Liturgical Press, 2000), 87–88.

Indeed, with regard to how contemporary Roman Catholic theology sees in Marian doctrine and devotion a close relationship to ecclesiology, *Sacrosanctum concilium* V.103 states that "in [Mary] the Church admires and exalts the most excellent fruit of redemption, and joyfully contemplates, as in a faultless image, that which she herself desires and hopes wholly to be." Hence, whatever the Immaculate Conception and bodily Assumption might mean for Mary as an historical person, the symbolic importance of these dogmas has to do with what they mean for the nature and identity of the Church itself. And, if at their core what these dogmas assert has ultimately to do with justification by "grace alone," then the image of Mary becomes simultaneously the image of a graciously redeemed humanity and church. Mary thus becomes the prototype and paradigm of how human salvation in Christ takes place.

While Protestants and Orthodox might continue to lament the fact that both of these "pious and pleasing thoughts," as they are sometimes called, were elevated from the realm of piety and the church's *lex orandi* (or liturgical tradition) to the status of *lex credendi* or *de fide* dogmatic definitions in Roman Catholicism,[30] the theological core of what these dogmas imply about the redeemed themselves may well be ecumenically acceptable in light of contemporary ecumenical convergence on the doctrine of justification itself. Indeed, the wonderful irony of this might just be that, in spite of the church-dividing nature of these dogmatic formulations, they actually affirm precisely *within* Roman Catholicism (!) what Protestants have always taught is to be the central focus in proclaiming how God saves humanity. Like Mary, the church is but the recipient of God's grace alone! Clearly such an understanding is not far removed from Luther's own mariological

30. See Frank Senn, *Christian Worship and Its Cultural Setting* (Philadelphia: Fortress Press, 1983), 79–80.

concerns, for whom, as we have seen, Mary herself "was the prime example of the faithful—a *typus ecclesiae* embodying unmerited grace," [and] "a paradigm for the indefectibility of the church." Is it so surprising, then, that Luther himself, in distinction to many of his own sixteenth-century Roman Catholic contemporaries, even gave a positive evaluation and affirmation of both the Immaculate Conception and Assumption as long as they were not imposed on people as matters of faith?[31] Can we do any less?

Ecumenical Convergence on Mary in Contemporary Liturgy and Doxology

Recent studies of early Christianity, including studies of Mary, have been much more open to considering the influence of popular piety and liturgy in the shaping of doctrine more than earlier scholarship was able or willing to do.[32] With regard to the title *Theotokos* itself, while, of course, christological in a broad sense, it appears as a more general honorific title for Mary among diverse fourth-century authors with various christological positions! In other words, *Theotokos* as a title for Mary does not appear to be tied originally to a *particular* christological position as a banner of orthodoxy as it will come to be at and after the Council of Ephesus. Prior to that, it is simply one honorific way in which to refer to Mary.

Liturgically as well, the use of the title *Theotokos* itself, including our earliest Marian hymn or prayer, the *Sub tuum praesidium*, may well be mid third-century Alexandrian in origins. Origen himself, as testified to by Socrates, may well have been the first to have used this

---

31. See Gritsch, "The Views of Luther and Lutheranism on the Veneration of Mary," 241.
32. Cf. my "*Sub tuum praesidium*: The *Theotokos* in Christian Life and Worship Before Ephesus," in *The Place of Christ in Liturgical Prayer: Christology, Trinity and Liturgical Theology*, ed. Bryan Spinks (Collegeville, MN: The Liturgical Press, 2008), 243–67.

title in theological discourse, and the developing Eucharistic Prayer tradition appears to be consistent with the growing development of prayer and supplication to the saints, as testified to in general by the cult of the martyrs and by Origen in particular. Already by the end of the second century, the *Protoevangelium of James* reflects an interest in Mary herself and provides several Marian elements that will develop further and become, ultimately, the content of theological reflection, liturgical festal celebration, and popular devotion to her in the life of the church, with the earliest Marian feast on August 15 quite possibly being a commemoration of Jesus' conception within the earliest days of Christianity itself. Hence, even the "christological" doctrinal controversy with Nestorius of Constantinople is not merely about doctrine. Rather, in the context of the late fourth and early fifth centuries, where Marian devotion is witnessed to not only in Egypt but in Cappadocia (Gregory of Nyssa and Gregory Nazianzen) and Syria (Ephrem) as well, the controversy is also liturgical-devotional, as certainly indicated by what might be called the "Marian mysticism" of Atticus, Pulcheria, and Proclus in Constantinople.

In such a multifaceted way, then, does the Virgin Mary, as *Theotokos*, become the very doctrinal and liturgical safeguard of the identity and personhood of Christ as the God-Man for what is recognized as orthodox Christian theology. Or, to say that another way, even if Mariology is but an implicate of Christology, generally speaking, it is this orthodox Mariology that keeps Christology "orthodox." And, it is worth noting, it is especially within those liturgical traditions in both East and West, where Marian feasts, commemorations, prayers and devotions exist in abundance, that, officially, at least, such a high or orthodox Christology tends to be maintained.

In the Eastern Christian rites, Mary frequently appears in various litanies in both the Eucharist and in the Divine Office, especially in the hymns to Mary in Byzantine vespers and *Orthros* (matins) known as the *Theotokia*,[33] and in the conclusion to the various litanies in the Byzantine and Armenian rites: "Commemorating our all-holy, spotless most highly blessed and glorious Lady the Mother of God [*Theotokos*] and ever-virgin Mary with all the saints, let us commend ourselves and one another and our whole life to Christ our God."[34] She also appears in what is known as the Ninth Ode (sometimes called the *Megalynarion*) in Byzantine *Orthros* (morning prayer): "O higher than the Cherubim, and more glorious beyond compare than the Seraphim, you gave birth to God the Word in virginity. You are truly the Mother of God: you do we exalt."[35] And, of the Twelve Major Feasts of the liturgical year for, at least, the Byzantine churches, several of them are related either directly to Mary (her Nativity on September 8, her Presentation in the Temple on November 21, and her Dormition on August 15) or indirectly to her (The Annunciation of our Lord on March 25 and his Presentation in the Temple on February 2).

And, of course, in the Roman or Latin West, there is an abundance of Marian antiphons and other liturgical texts, such as the seasonal chants at the end of the Office of Compline: the *Alma Redemptoris Mater*, sung during Advent and Christmas; the *Ave Regina Caelorum*, sung during Lent; the *Regina Caeli*, during the Easter season; and the *Salve Regina*, occasionally alternating with the *Ave Maria* during what is now referred to as Ordinary Time. Similarly, the Roman Rite continues to celebrate several Solemnities, Memorials, and Optional Memorials of Mary, under various titles or as commemorations of events in her life throughout the liturgical year.

---

33. See J. Raya and J. de Vinck, *Byzantine Daily Worship: With Byzantine Breviary, The Three Liturgies, Propers of the Day, and Various Offices* (Allendale, NJ: Alleluia Press, 1969), 410–26.
34. Greek Text in F. E. Brightman, *Liturgies Eastern and Western*, vol. 1: *Eastern Liturgies* (Oxford: The Clarendon Press, 1896), 363.
35. Trans. adapted from Raya and de Vinck, *Byzantine Daily Worship*, 166.

Today Mary is also appearing more frequently in the liturgical texts, calendars, and hymns of other Christian traditions as well. Perhaps not surprisingly it is *The Hymnal 1982* of The Episcopal Church in this country where most of these are located. I have counted at least nine hymns therein that could easily be classified as "Marian." Four of these in particular stand out, and three of these also appear in contemporary Lutheran resources.

First, both *The Hymnal 1982* and *Lutheran Book of Worship*, but, alas, not the more recent *Evangelical Lutheran Worship*, contain a version of the *Stabat Mater Dolorosa* ("At the Cross, Her Station [or, Vigil] Keeping, Stood the Mournful Mother Weeping"), the traditional sequence for the Roman Catholic feast of Our Lady of Sorrows on September 15 and a hymn frequently sung by Roman Catholics and others between each of the stations of the cross. There can be no question but that this is precisely a devotional hymn commemorating Mary herself in which it is *her* faith and devotion that are to serve to inspire the worshiper on to a greater faith and trust in Christ Crucified:

> Who, on Christ's dear mother gazing,
> Pierced by anguish so amazing,
> Born of woman, would not weep?
> Who, on Christ's dear mother thinking,
> Such a cup of sorrow drinking,
> Would not share her sorrows deep?
> Jesus, may her deep devotion
> Stir in me the same emotion,
> Source of love, redeemer true.
> Let me thus, fresh ardor gaining
> And a purer love attaining,
> Consecrate my life to you.[36]

Second, the hymn "Sing of Mary, Pure and Lowly" also contained in the Lutheran resource *With One Voice*, but again not in *Evangelical Lutheran Worship*, even holds before us the image of the "heart" of the Virgin Mary as she praises God. According to George Tavard, it was actually the Reformer Ulrich Zwingli who anticipated Counter-Reformation Catholic devotion to the Immaculate Heart of Mary by drawing special attention to her contemplative heart where she felt "all the sufferings . . . of her son."[37]

> Sing of Mary, pure and lowly, virgin mother undefiled [or, wise and mild].
> Sing of God's own Son most holy, who became her little child.
> Fairest child of fairest mother, God the Lord who came to earth.
> Word made flesh, our very brother, takes our nature by his birth.
> Sing of Jesus, son of Mary, in the home at Nazareth.
> Toil and labor cannot weary love enduring unto death.
> Constant was the love he gave her, though he went forth from her side,
> forth to preach, and heal, and suffer, till on Calvary he died.
> Glory be to God the Father; glory be to God the Son;
> glory be to God the Spirit; glory to the Three in One.
> *From the heart of blessed Mary*, from all saints the song ascends,
> and the Church the strain re-echoes unto earth's remotest ends.[38]

Third, the hymn, "Sing We of the Blessed Mother," appearing only in *The Hymnal 1982*, proclaims the traditional seven joys and seven sorrows of the Virgin Mary in poetic form. Particularly intriguing from a doctrinal perspective is its final verse:

> Sing the chiefest joy of Mary when on earth her work was done,
> and the Lord of all creation brought her to his heavenly home;

---

36. "At the Cross Her Station [or vigil] Keeping," is hymn 159 in *The Hymnal 1982* (New York: The Church Hymnal Corporation, 1982) and hymn 110 in *Lutheran Book of Worship* (Minneapolis: Augsburg Fortress, 1978).
37. Tavard, *The Thousand Faces of the Virgin Mary*, 108.
38. "Sing of Mary, Pure and Lowly," hymn 277 in *The Hymnal 1982*, and hymn 634, in *With One Voice* (Minneapolis: Augsburg Fortress, 1995). Emphasis added.

where, raised high with saints and angels, in Jerusalem above,
she beholds her Son and Savior reigning as the Lord of love.[39]

Fourth and similarly, the classic Anglican hymn, "Ye Watchers and Ye Holy Ones," appearing also in *Evangelical Lutheran Worship*, addresses its second verse, based on the Byzantine *Megalynarion*, directly *to* Mary in heaven, saying, "O higher than the cherubim, More glorious than the seraphim, Lead their praises; 'Alleluia!' Thou bearer of the eternal Word, most gracious, magnify the Lord."[40] As in verse 3 of "Sing of Mary, Pure and Lowly," where the praise of God ascends from her heart, so in this hymn is Mary herself identified as one closely united to and leading the praises of both the heavenly and earthly chorus of the church around the throne of God. And, as the great Episcopalian New Testament scholar Reginald Fuller once noted, this verse of "Ye Watchers and Ye Holy Ones" is nothing other than a poetic description of Mary's Assumption.[41] The same could be said, undoubtedly, for the last verse of "Sing We Of the Blessed Mother."

Together with contemporary hymnody Mary has also appeared in a rather full cycle of commemorations in the liturgical calendars of various churches today. While Marian-related festivals of our Lord like the Annunciation, Presentation, and her Visitation have been traditionally included in the liturgical calendars, at least, of Anglicans and Lutherans, her August 15 festival under the titles of "Mary, Mother of our Lord" (ELCA Lutherans), "Saint Mary, Mother of our Lord" (Missouri Synod Lutherans), and "Saint Mary the Virgin, Mother of our Lord Jesus Christ" (Episcopalians) has been adapted, with the same Gospel reading (Luke 1:39–56) that is assigned to the

---

39. Hymn 278 in *The Hymnal 1982*.
40. Hymn 618 in *The Hymnal 1982* and hymn 175 in *Lutheran Book of Worship*.
41. Reginald H. Fuller, *Preaching the New Lectionary*, rev. ed. (Collegeville, MN: The Liturgical Press, 1984), 557.

Solemnity of the Assumption in the Roman Catholic *Ordo lectionum missae*. The opening prayer for this festival in the 1979 *Book of Common Prayer* can be taken to support some sort of Assumption interpretation:

> O God, you have taken to yourself the blessed Virgin Mary, mother of your incarnate Son: Grant that we, who have been redeemed by his blood, may share with her the glory of your eternal kingdom; through Jesus Christ our Lord, who lives and reigns with you, in the unity of the Holy Spirit, one God, now and for ever. *Amen.* [42]

That August 15 should be chosen for a festival of the Virgin Mary is no surprise, since already in the Jerusalem liturgy of the late fourth century this day was celebrated as "Mary-Theotokos," eventually becoming, as still in East, her Dormition, and is the most ancient Marian feast in East or West. What is surprising is that both Lutherans and Episcopalians, by using the title *Mother of our Lord* for this feast, have missed an ecumenical opportunity here to state clearly and explicitly their doctrinal acceptance of Mary as the *Theotokos,* God-bearer, and Mother of God. As we have seen, even Evangelicals today have voiced their acceptance of the title *Theotokos* and I find it rather amusing that Nestorius of Alexandria himself would have had no trouble using the phrase *Mother of our Lord*. Certainly Episcopalians and Lutherans could have used *Mary, Mother of God* as the title for this feast.

Other feasts of Mary are also spreading ecumenically today. The current liturgical calendar of the Church of England, as expressed, at least, in its *Common Worship*, now includes in addition to those noted above, "The Conception of Mary" on December 8 and her "Birth" on September 8. Here I am reminded of the words of the late Arthur

---

42. *The Book of Common Prayer* (New York: The Church Hymnal Corporation, 1979), 243.

Carl Piepkorn, himself a member of some of the very early Lutheran-Catholic dialogues, who noted in 1967

> the legitimacy of apostrophes to [Mary] in hymns and in the liturgy; the propriety of celebrating the Annunciation, the Visitation, and Purification for what they really are, feasts of our Lord, to which some non-Roman-Catholics, following the Church's example in the case of Saint John the Baptist, would be willing to add her Nativity on September 8 and Falling Asleep on August 15 . . . and the legitimacy of naming churches and church institutions after her and after the mysteries of her Annunciation, Visitation, Birth, and Falling Asleep.[43]

Also, Presbyterians in the United States, not known historically for their attention to the liturgical year in general, have now included the Presentation of the Lord on February 2, the Annunciation of the Lord on March 25, and the Visitation of Mary to Elizabeth on May 31.

What is most surprising, however, and somewhat controversial, is the growing frequency of the December 12 celebrations of the Mexican Virgin of Guadalupe, which, outside of the Roman Catholic liturgical calendar appears officially nowhere else. Due to the increasing Hispanicization or Latinization of American Christianity in general, celebrations of Guadalupe are appearing not only in Episcopalian and Lutheran contexts, where there are churches now even named for her under this title, such as in Irving, Texas, and Waukegan, Illinois, but even among Methodists.[44]

Liturgical theologians like to refer to the ancient principle called *lex orandi, lex credendi* as a way to talk about the relationship between what is prayed liturgically and what is believed doctrinally and about how worship tends to shape believing. Certainly at the level of what

---

43. Arthur Carl Piepkorn, "Mary's Place within the People of God according to Non-Roman-Catholics," *Marian Studies* 18 (1967): 79–81.
44. See Edgardo Colón-Emeric, "Wesleyans and Guadalupans: A Theological Reflection," in Johnson, *American Magnificat*, 107–26.

several churches sing and pray liturgically there is a kind of Marian *lex orandi* that seems to go somewhat beyond what many might want to say doctrinally. But, if how we pray and sing *is* how we believe then perhaps greater attention to this phenomenon suggests itself.

Ecumenical Convergence in Devotion to the Blessed Virgin Mary

Closely related to the question of Mary in contemporary liturgy and doxology, is, of course, her place, or lack thereof, in what we might call devotion or popular religion and piety. And even in this, in what is probably the most ecumenically controversial area, there is to be noted some contemporary ecumenical convergence. Here I want to highlight both a renewed attention to Marian art, especially iconography, in various churches, and some surprising theological treatment on the part of Protestants to the invocation of Mary.

Again, it was Piepkorn who also called for and supported "the devotional value of good, unsentimental representations of [Mary] in the arts, especially after the earliest surviving models which always show her with the holy Child."[45] And there is no question but that today images of Mary, especially Eastern Christian icons of her and the Christ Child, are becoming more present in some Protestant worship spaces. Indeed, from my own experience, at least, one cannot go into an Anglican Church in England, at least the major abbeys and cathedrals, without now seeing icons of the *Theotokos* complete with vigil light stands nearby. And Rowan Williams, former Archbishop of Canterbury, has written about prayer and icongraphy in his book, *Ponder These Things: Praying with Icons of the Virgin,*[46] in which he interprets three of the classic Eastern Christian icons of the *Theotokos.*

45. Piepkorn, "Mary's Place within the People of God," 81.
46. Rowan Williams, *Ponder These Things: Praying with Icons of the Virgin* (Norwich: Norwich Books and Music, 2002).

Such is rather common as well in the Episcopal Diocese of Northern Indiana, though in several of these parishes it is not so much icons, though there are some, as it is statues either of the traditional English Our Lady of Walsingham or even, most surprisingly, Our Lady of Grace, the traditional Roman Catholic Mary dressed in blue, with hands extended, standing on the head of a snake, the image often associated in Roman Catholicism with the Miraculous Medal and, hence, with Mary's Immaculate Conception. That image is the primary Marian image in the Episcopal Cathedral of Saint James in South Bend, Indiana. And, of course, even images of the Virgin of Guadalupe are appearing with increasing frequency in Episcopal parishes with an equally increasing Hispanic/Latino participation throughout the country.

If it is not all that surprising that images of Mary are to be found more frequently in Episcopal and other Anglican contexts, especially in my area of the country formerly known as the "Biretta Belt" of Anglo-Catholicism, what is new is the presence of similar images in Lutheran settings. At least two ELCA churches in South Bend have icons of the Virgin displayed. So also there are occasional or seasonal Marian icons in the Chapel at Luther Seminary in Saint Paul, Minnesota, and in the chapel at the ELCA headquarters in Chicago. But, not surprisingly, it is within especially Hispanic/Latino Lutheran and Methodist churches where images of the Virgin, especially Guadalupe are found, such as statues, icons, and banners, together with vigil lights, often those found either in Hispanic markets or in the Mexican foods section of other grocery stores. Again, the Hispanicization of American Christianity is bringing the controversial question of Mary to the forefront of theological reflection, both in support of but also against, since, as Justo Gonzalez has written,

The *Virgen de la Caridad del Cobre* may be very important for Cuban identity, and certainly for Cuban popular Catholicism; for Cuban popular Protestantism, however, she is at best a matter of historical and ethnographic interest, and at worst an idol the devil has produced to lead the Cuban people astray. . . . It is also true that still today for most Protestant Latinos—even those of Mexican origin—rejecting Guadalupe is an essential mark of being truly Christian! Indeed, in some Protestant churches I have heard renderings of the stories of Caridad and Guadalupe that can only be interpreted as counter-myths—stories of how the devil invented these and other national "Virgins" for his own satanic purposes.[47]

Given this, the case of a Methodist church in Chicago where an image of the Virgin of Guadalupe was displayed in the sanctuary and carried in procession in the neighborhood causing somewhat of an international Methodist incident is perhaps not surprising. In fact, the United Methodist episcopal leadership had to get involved and determined that such an image could be permitted in the church entrance but not near the altar or pulpit.[48] The bottom line, however, is that she stayed.

But what of the invocation of Mary in an ecumenical context? In his previously mentioned 1971 Apostolic Exhortation, *Marialis cultus*, Pope Paul VI advocated especially two traditional Marian devotions; namely, the daily recitation of the *Angelus* and the prayer and mysteries of the rosary. He advocated these two devotional practices because of their relationship to the very events of Christ's life (the *Angelus* as the memorial of the incarnation and the rosary as rehearsing by its mysteries the significant moments in the life of Christ) and as devotions compatible with the celebration of the liturgy, into which all devotions are to lead. Pope John Paul II's

---

47. Justo L. González, "Reinventing Dogmatics: A Footnote from a Reinvented Protestant," in *From the Heart of Our People: Latino/a Explorations in Catholic Systematic Theology*, ed. Orlando Espín and Miguel Diaz (Maryknoll, NY: Orbis, 1999), 224.

48. See Colón-Emeric, "Wesleyans and Guadalupans," 107–8.

2002 Apostolic Letter, *Rosarium Virginis Mariae* (On the most holy rosary), underscored that similar Christocentric orientation of the prayer and added to the traditional fifteen Joyful, Sorrowful, and Glorious Mysteries, five new "Luminous Mysteries," namely, Jesus' Baptism, his self-revelation at Cana, his preaching of the reign of God, his transfiguration, and his institution of the Eucharist. John Paul II's strong Christocentric interpretation of the rosary in this letter has certainly caught the attention of some Protestant theologians. Reformed evangelical professor of theology at Tübingen Stephen Tobler is quoted as saying, "I am convinced that if Catholics pray the rosary as proposed in this apostolic letter, and if evangelicals recognize and rediscover without prejudices this new way of conceiving the rosary, then it will be a favorable occasion. But we must work on it."[49]

But, since together with the Apostles' Creed, Lord's Prayer, and Glory Be to the Father, the primary repeated prayer of the rosary is the Ave Maria or Hail Mary, what of that prayer ecumenically? The sixteenth-century Protestant Reformers' own sense of Mary is often not known or has simply died from neglect. Martin Luther, for example, not only kept throughout his life both a crucifix and an image of the Virgin and Child in his study, but retained the traditional Hail Mary in his 1522 *Betbüchlein* or *Personal Prayer Book*. What was then the traditional Hail Mary, however, did not yet include the later added invocation, "Holy Mary, Mother of God, pray for us sinners now and at the hour of our death," but concluded with the words, "Blessed is the fruit of your womb, Jesus," or "Jesus Christ." This prayer book, in fact, continued to be published in various editions until 1545, that is, one year before his death, and is clearly indicative of some form of Marian devotion continuing

---

49. "Rosary May Contribute to Unity, Says Protestant Theologian," Zenit, Dec. 12, 2002, http://www.zenit.org/en/articles/rosary-may-contribute-to-unity-says-protestant-theologian.

in existence within early Lutheranism. In retaining the Hail Mary, Luther did not interpret this as a "prayer" *to* Mary or as an "invocation" *of* her, but, instead, as a *meditation* on God's unmerited grace showered *upon* her.

> Let not our hearts cleave to her, but through her penetrate to Christ and to God himself. Thus what the Hail Mary says is that all glory should be given to God. . . . You see that these words are not concerned with prayer but purely with giving praise and honor. . . . Therefore we should make the Hail Mary neither a prayer nor an invocation because it is improper to interpret the words beyond what they mean in themselves and beyond the meaning given them by the Holy Spirit. . . . But there are two things we can do. First we can use the Hail Mary as a meditation in which we recite what grace God has given her. Second, we should add a wish that everyone may know and respect her [as one blessed by God].[50]

Echoing this approach of Luther, it was again Piepkorn who in 1967 suggested that an ecumenical consensus could at that time be reached on a number of mariological themes. According to him, there could be agreement on

> a place for Mary in prophecy (although it would probably be somewhat more restricted than a Marian maximalist would rejoice at); the virgin conception and birth; the rightfulness of the title *theotokos;* the Virgin's place in the Church as the first of the redeemed; her role as the *kecharitomene* par excellence, uniquely endowed with God's favor; her paradigmatic piety, patience, humility, and faith; her status as the most blessed of women; her *fiat mihi* as the typical divinely empowered response that God elicits from all those of His children whom He calls to be in freedom workers together with Him; the analogy between the Blessed Virgin Mary and the Church that makes it possible for a Lutheran to use the *Magnificat* as the canticle at vespers and to say the first, pre-Counterreformation part of the *Ave Maria. . .* as memorials of the Incarnation; the probability of her intercession for the Church;

---

50. Martin Luther, *Personal Prayer Book,* in *Luther's Works,* vol. 43, Devotional Writings II, ed. Gustav K. Wiencke (Philadelphia: Fortress Press, 1968), 39–40.

the paradoxical parallel between the obedient Virgin Mary and the disobedient Virgin Eve that theologians have noted since the second century (although originally the thrust was Christological rather than Marian); Saint Mary's virginity certainly *ante partum* and *in partu* and fittingly *post partum*.[51]

More recently, two other Lutheran theologians have entered into this discussion and have actually gone beyond Piepkorn in advocating the appropriateness even of the invocation of Mary added later to the Hail Mary. From a Hispanic-Latino context, Professor José David Rodriguez of Lutheran School of Theology, Chicago, has written,

> Mary is not just the mother of the historical Jesus, but also of the incarnate God and in Jesus Christ the humanity and the divinity are present in perfect integrity, without distortions or confusions. For this reason it is right and salutary that we incorporate in our evangelical liturgy the angel's greeting to Mary, "Greetings favored one! The Lord is with you" (Luke 1:28), along with the words of her cousin Elizabeth full of God's Spirit that exclaimed to her with a loud cry, "Blessed are you among women and blessed is the fruit of your womb" (Luke 1:43), to conclude with the Hymn that the Church added at a later time "Holy Mary, Mother of God, pray for us sinners now and at the time of our death, amen," for we believe that the saints on earth and those in heaven are joined in the same communion and we need to pray one for each other.[52]

And in dialogue with the Lutheran confessional stance against the invocation of saints, Robert Jenson suggests instead that we can ask Mary as Mother of God to pray for us for two reasons:

> First, Mary is Israel in one person, as Temple and archprophet and guardian of Torah. To ask her to pray for me is to invoke all God's history with Israel at once, all his place-taking in this people, and all the faithfulness of God to this people as grounds for his faithfulness to

---

51. Piepkorn, "Mary's Place within the People of God," 79–81.
52. José David Rodriguez Jr., "The Virgin of Guadalupe from a Latino/a Protestant Perspective: A Dangerous Narrative to Counter Colonial and Imperialistic Power," in Johnson, *American Magnificat*, 131.

me. . . . "*Fiat mihi*," Mary said, giving her womb as space for God in this world. . . . This place is a person. To ask Mary to pray for us is to meet [God] there. Second. From the beginning of creation, heaven is God's space in his creation. As a created space for God there must be a mysterious sense in which Mary *is* heaven, the container not only of the uncontainable Son, but of all his sisters and brothers, of what Augustine called the *totus Christus,* the whole Christ, Christ with his body. But Mary is a person, not a sheer container. That she contains the whole company of heaven must mean that she personally is their presence. To ask Mary to pray for us is to ask "the whole company of heaven" to pray for us, not this saint or that but all of them together. It is to ask the church triumphant to pray for us. Interestingly, Luther and Melanchthon were happy to say that the saints as a company pray for us, that the church in heaven prays for the church on earth. To invoke Mary's prayer as the prayer of the *mater dei*, the prayer of the Container of the Uncontainable, is to invoke precisely this prayer. Perhaps, indeed, Mary's prayer, as the prayer of the whole company of heaven, is the one saint's prayer that even those should utter who otherwise accept Melanchthon's argument against invoking saints.[53]

With regard to art and devotion, therefore, we might say that Mary—even culturally specific images of her—is no longer off limits for Protestants in general, though the extent to which she is embraced will vary considerably. And, although my own references to contemporary authors on this subject tend to be Lutheran primarily, the topic of Marian devotion is by no means limited to Lutheran or Anglican authors or, as I have shown, to their experiences. Such beginning convergence in this area could not even have been dreamed of fifty years ago, when the Second Vatican Council was called. At that time, only Anglo-Catholics would have been willing to embrace what most would have considered as specific Roman Catholic practices of devotion. Though here, as I like to remind my students, one of the most popular books on the rosary, *Five for Sorrow, Ten for Joy*, was written by a Methodist, J. Neville Ward, in 1973.

53. Robert Jenson, "A Space for God," in Braaten and Jenson, *Mary, Mother of God*, 56–57.

Conclusion

The influential Swiss Reformed theologian Karl Barth once said, "Mariology is an excrescence, i.e., a diseased construct of theological thought. Excrescences must be excised."[54] While I suspect there are still those, perhaps many, who would share Barth's critique not only of Mariology but of the Catholicism itself that Barth saw Mariology as symbolizing par excellence, much has indeed changed ecumenically with regard to Mary in a variety of Christian traditions today. Doctrinally, not only is there an ecumenical convergence among Roman Catholics, Orthodox, and Magisterial Protestantism on Mary as *Theotokos*, but Evangelicals have also come to recognize this. Similarly, rightly understood in light of the centrality of Christ, even those Roman Catholic dogmas of Mary's Immaculate Conception and Assumption into heaven have, through official dialogues, come to be reckoned as no longer church dividing and not "opposed to the gospel." Further, on the liturgical level, including hymnody and other liturgical texts and calendars, Mary the *Theotokos* finds her place in heaven "higher than the cherubim, more glorious than the seraphim," as she leads the heavenly choir around God's throne. And, even in art and devotion, Mary is no longer the stranger she once was to Protestantism in general. As Presbyterian poet Kathleen Norris has written,

> There's a lot of room in Mary. A seminary professor, a Presbyterian, employs the language of the early church in telling a student struggling with family problems, "You can always go to *Theotokos* . . . because she understands suffering." A grieving Lutheran woman in South Dakota tells me, "I love Mary because she also knew what it is to lose a child." And an elderly Parsee woman in India proudly shows a visiting

54. Karl Barth, as quoted by Thomas A. O'Meara, *Mary in Protestant and Catholic Theology* (New York: Sheed and Ward, 1966), 17.

Benedictine nun her little shrine to Mary, saying, "I'm not a Christian but I love *her*."[55]

Far from being excised, various forms of Mariology are being embraced, even by those Reformed Christians who are the theological descendants of Barth himself. Perhaps the Roman Catholic response to the eighth United States Lutheran-Catholic dialogue can serve to summarize what many are beginning to discover in their theological and contemplative reflection on Mary:

> Jesus Christ alone is never merely alone. He is always found in the company of a whole range of his friends, both living and dead. It is a basic Catholic experience that when recognized and appealed to within a rightly ordered faith, these friends of Jesus Christ strengthen one's own sense of communion with Christ. It's all in a family, we might say; we are part of a people. Saints show us how the grace of God may work in a life; they give us bright patterns of holiness; they pray for us. Keeping company with the saints in the Spirit of Christ encourages our faith. It is simply part of what it means to be Catholic, bonded with millions of other people not only throughout the world, but also through time. Those who have gone on before us in faith are still living members of the body of Christ and in some unimaginable way we are all connected. Within a rightly ordered faith, both liturgical and private honoring of all the saints, of one saint, or of Saint Mary serves to keep our feet on the gospel path.[56]

---

55. Kathleen Norris, "Virgin Mary, Mother of God," in Johnson, *American Magnificat*, 165.
56. *OMSM*, 117.

8

The Virgin of Guadalupe in Ecumenical Context

The event and image of the Virgin of Guadalupe, *La Virgencita* ("the dear—or little—Virgin"), or *La Morena* or *La Morenita* (the "dark one"), are obviously Roman Catholic in general and clearly part of the self-understanding of Mexican and Mexican-American Roman Catholics. Why, then, would Protestants of any stripe, whether Anglo or Hispanic-Latino, want to celebrate or pay any attention whatsoever to her and to her story? That is the question I sought to address in my 2002 study, *The Virgin of Guadalupe: Theological Reflections of an Anglo-Lutheran Liturgist*,[1] and this is the question, I am pleased to note, other theologians from differing Protestant traditions joined me in pursuing in my 2010 *American Magnificat: Protestants on Mary of Guadalupe*.[2] For, as United States Roman

---

1. Maxwell E. Johnson, *The Virgin of Guadalupe: Theological Reflections of an Anglo-Lutheran Liturgist*, Celebrating Faith: Explorations in Latino Spirituality and Theology (Lanham, MD: Rowman & Littlefield, 2002).

Catholicism and Protestantism alike become intentionally more multicultural, and as we all seek to be open to the experiences and gifts of the other at our doors and at our borders, and as Hispanic-Latino people come in increasing numbers to all of our churches, is it not necessary for us to listen, even ecumenically, to their stories and to embrace their images and symbols? And, clearly, one of those central stories, images, and symbols is the Virgin of Guadalupe.

Hence, as our Christian identities become increasingly Latinized in this country, the story and image of Guadalupe is seeking and is actually finding a place among Protestant Christians, even among Anglos. Note, please, I did not say that Protestants should "use" the Virgin of Guadalupe in order to attract Roman Catholic Hispanic-Latinos to their churches or to try to make "converts" out of Hispanic-Latino Catholics, something that has certainly been alleged by Roman Catholics from time to time.[3] Such deceptive use of the cherished religious symbols of others has no place among Christians! But Mary of Guadalupe may well find her own home among Protestants as she comes along with others into their midst and into their congregations. In fact, there are signs throughout our country that she is already here, with one of the newest Evangelical Lutheran Church in America (ELCA) parishes in Irving, Texas, bearing the name of *La Iglesia Luterana Santa María de Guadalupe*; with the last official act of Archbishop George Carey, former Archbishop of Canterbury, being the consecration of Our Lady of Guadalupe Episcopal Church in Waukegan, Illinois; and with several parishes of diverse denominations now finding room for her image and celebrating her December 12 feast. Indeed, the Virgin of Guadalupe is appearing everywhere, it seems, as tattoos, jewelry, fine art, folk

2. *American Magnificat: Protestants on Mary of Guadalupe*, ed. Maxwell E. Johnson (Collegeville, MN: The Liturgical Press, 2010).

3. See the essay by Edgardo A. Colón-Emeric, "Wesleyans and Guadalapans: A Theological Reflection," in Johnson, *American Magnificat*, 107–26.

art, home altars, yard shrines, rugs, ornaments and decorations for cars, coffee mugs, baseball caps, T-shirts, *paños* (pieces of cloth or handkerchiefs painted by prison inmates to raise funds to help in supporting their families), computer mouse pads, murals on the side of buildings and homes, or *veladoras* (devotional candles) in grocery stores. How, then, might Protestants respond to her increasing presence among us all today?

After an introductory section on possible Protestant approaches, this chapter focuses on three ways in which various Protestant communities might appropriate the Virgin of Guadalupe and, more importantly, why they might do so. First, I shall suggest that Protestants can appropriate and celebrate in some way Mary of Guadalupe because she proclaims the gospel, the good news of God's salvation in Christ. Second, I shall suggest that Protestants can do this because the Virgin Mary, even in classic Protestant theology, embodies for us God's unmerited grace, and in a special way, the Virgin of Guadalupe becomes, as I have argued elsewhere, a "parable" of justification by grace. And third, I shall suggest that Protestants can appropriate and celebrate the Virgin of Guadalupe because, in a special way, she is a type and model of what the church is to be in the world, a *typus ecclesiae*. Here, as well, I shall make some suggestions for what this might mean even for Marian devotion.

Possible Protestant Approaches to the Virgin of Guadalupe

There are several approaches to the Virgin of Guadalupe that Protestantism might take. The first, of course, is an explicit rejection of any form of the Guadalupan narrative, image, and devotion whatsoever as absolutely inimical to Protestantism. This kind of rejection may take one of two extreme forms. On the one hand, it may be expressed by the ardent anti-Catholicism often characteristic of especially Protestant fundamentalism that, as United Methodist theologian Justo González has noted, may acknowledge even the credibility of the Guadalupan events themselves but interprets and proclaims those events as invented by the devil "for his own satanic purposes."[4] It is no secret, of course, that many of the smaller antique Central American and other *santos* (wooden saints), carved by indigenous folk artists, formerly present in homes on *altarcitos* and now sold today in shops for collectors throughout the United States and elsewhere, have been "rescued" from the literal fires of fundamentalist purges in their "evangelistic" endeavors to destroy the vestiges of Catholic "superstition," "paganism," and "satanism" from their converts.

In a highly polemical anti-Catholic book from the early 1960s with the rather suggestive title, *Romanism in the Light of Scripture*, Dwight L. Pentecost offered the following description and interpretation of the famous image on Juan Diego's *tilma* in the Basilica of Our Lady of Guadalupe in Mexico City:

> Some years ago it was my privilege to travel through the land of Mexico with my brother, who has been a missionary there for some years. We visited a number of the outstanding shrines and edifices erected by the Roman system to the praise and glory of Mary. On one occasion my brother said to me, "If you want to see the theology of Mary in the Roman Church, come with me to a church where over the altar is a scene which, more than volumes could say, reveals their actual belief concerning the position of Mary." He took me downtown and into a rather large church in the center of the old part of the city. We walked forward to the altar where we could look up and see a great painting based upon the twelfth chapter of the Book of the Revelation. . . . The chapter gives a number of cues to let us know that the Apostle John is depicting the nation Israel under the form of a woman. The man child

---

4. Justo González, "Reinventing Dogmatics: A Footnote from a Reinvented Protestant," in *From the Heart of Our People: Latino/a Explorations in Catholic Systematic Theology*, ed. Orland Espín and Miguel Diaz (Maryknoll, NY: Orbis Books, 1999), 224.

produced by that woman was none other than the Saviour, the Lord Jesus Christ. But there over the altar, as the center of attention in that edifice, was the scene of a great blazing sun, with a picture of the Virgin Mary in the midst of that sun. According to this artist's conception, the woman of Revelation 12 was none other than Mary. Under that blazing sun, in lesser glory and light, was painted a moon and on that moon was the face of the Lord Jesus Christ. Mary was standing in that sun with her feet upon the head of the Lord Jesus Christ and He was bowed in submission and subservience to Mary who stood above Him. . . . Mary was elevated above . . . the Son of God Himself. She was occupying the place of pre-eminence and authority as the sun of the day rules over the moon and the stars of the night.[5]

On the other hand, the rejection of Guadalupe may also take the form of an intellectual elitism, which similarly looks down at her and other similar popular symbols and forms of religious expression as but the intellectually "curious" expressions of an "unenlightened" faith with nothing to offer modern Christianity. The second form of this rejection is also characteristic of some within Roman Catholicism, while admittedly at the extremes; but both forms are ultimately destructive of culture.

A second possible Protestant approach to Guadalupe would be the exact opposite of the first. That is, the Virgin of Guadalupe might be employed either as a "conversion tactic" in the evangelism or the proselytizing of newly arrived Mexican and Central American immigrants to various Protestant traditions in the United States or, among those whose liturgical-sacramental traditions are very similar to those of Roman Catholicism, she might be used to give the impression that a particular Protestant congregation is actually a Roman Catholic one. If the first approach is destructive of culture, this second one, while certainly dishonest, also displays a serious misrepresentation of what it means to be a "Protestant" Christian. If

5. J. Dwight Pentecost, *Romanism in the Light of Scripture* (Chicago: Moody Press, 1962), 26–27.

a Hispanic-Latino member of a Protestant Christian denomination sees him- or herself as a Roman Catholic or views this Protestant congregation as a Roman Catholic one, something has been poorly communicated. And if the Virgin of Guadalupe is used as but an evangelistic tool or gimmick in such contexts, this is little more than a condescending manipulation of a highly cherished and revered symbol.

To be fair, however, many within those Protestant traditions, like Lutheranism and Episcopalianism, with a strong and central "catholic" liturgical-sacramental tradition, tend not to view themselves as really "Protestant" either in their denominational affiliation or theological outlook. Anglicanism, for example, has a long history of understanding its identity as representing a *via media* (or middle way) between Protestantism and Catholicism, and Lutheranism itself is understood by many of its adherents today as an "evangelical Catholicism." That is, many contemporary Lutherans see and express themselves as Catholic Christians committed to an ongoing reform of the church catholic or universal and of themselves on the basis of justification by grace through faith for the sake of Christ. Hence, if the presence of the image of the Virgin of Guadalupe or another popular saint in an Episcopal or Lutheran worship space gives the impression that this congregation is a Catholic congregation, that impression is not totally inaccurate! Being Catholic is not synonymous with being *Roman* Catholic, and this needs to be understood especially by those who would interpret the presence of Guadalupe in a Lutheran or Episcopal worship space as dishonest or as a misrepresentation of what the denominational affiliation of that congregation "really" is.

A third Protestant approach to Guadalupe may be one of "temporary toleration." In such an approach, the Virgin of Guadalupe and other forms of "popular religion" are but tolerated among

Hispanic-Latinos until such time that a more complete formation through catechesis can take place. While I suspect that this is the approach taken by many Roman Catholics in the United States today as well, it can also be rather condescending or elitist in orientation. If catechesis and Christian formation, especially for those immigrants who are often poor and illiterate, is absolutely essential, mere temporary toleration of popular religious symbols and practices is not the same as a serious and creative engagement with the content of what those symbols and practices express already. And, for that matter, the continuing influx of Mexican, Central American, and other immigrants across the southern borders of the United States suggests that the question of Guadalupe and Hispanic-Latino popular religion will not be a temporary question at all. Further, one does not simply tolerate a culture different from the dominant one by means of condescending or patronizing gestures masquerading as "hospitality" and "welcome."

Another approach should be possible. United Methodist theologian Justo González narrates the following anecdote from his own past experience as a Protestant seminarian, which suggests that a theological reevaluation of Guadalupe within Protestantism might well be in order today:

> When I was growing up, I was taught to think of such things as the Virgin of Guadalupe as pure superstition. Therefore, I remember how surprised I was at the reaction of a Mexican professor in seminary when one of my classmates made some disparaging remarks about Guadalupe. The professor, who was as Protestant as they come and who often stooped because he was then elderly, drew himself up, looked at my friend in the eye, and said: "Young man, in this class you are free to say anything you please. You may say anything about me. You certainly are welcome to say anything you wish about the pope and the priests. *But don't you touch my little Virgin!*" At that time, I took this to be an atavism of an old man who had been fed superstition in his mother's milk. But now I know better. What he was saying was that, in spite of

all that our North American friends had told us, in spite of the veneer of superstition, in spite of the horrendous things that took place every Sunday morning as people crawled to the shrine of Guadalupe, there was in there a kernel of truth that was very dear to his heart—and all the dearer, since so much of the religiosity that he knew, both Catholic and Protestant, denied it. For generation upon generation of oppressed Indian people, told by word and deed that they were inferior, the Virgin has been a reminder that there is vindication for the Juan Diegos. And that is indeed part of the gospel message, even if has not always been part of our own message.[6]

The problem, as González notes further, is precisely the relationship of religious faith and culture. Does one need to deny one's very culture in becoming or being Protestant, especially when that culture has already been shaped to a large extent by Roman Catholicism itself? He writes elsewhere that

there is in much of Latino Protestantism a sense of cultural alienation that is very similar to that produced by the much earlier Spanish colonization of the Americas. Just as Spanish Roman Catholicism told our native ancestors that their religion, and therefore much of their culture, was the work of the devil, so has Anglo Protestantism told us that the Catholic religion of our more immediate ancestors, and therefore much of our culture, must be rejected. . . . Just as native populations can accuse the earlier Catholic "evangelization" of undermining their culture and destroying their identity, so do some accuse the later Protestant "evangelization" of similar misdeeds. In many ways, just as for many natives in the sixteenth century it was necessary to abandon much of their cultural traditions in the process of becoming Catholic, so are many Latinas and Latinos forced away from their cultural roots as they become Protestant. And in both cases, this cultural alienation is depicted as good news!. . . . Yet many Latino/a Protestants refuse to abandon their culture and its traditions.[7]

---

6. Justo L. González, *Mañana: Christian Theology from a Hispanic Perspective* (Nashville: Abingdon, 1990), 61. Emphasis added.
7. Justo González, "Reinventing Dogmatics," 225.

Consequently, he continues,

> Caridad, Guadalupe, and novenas are not part of my more immediate tradition. Yet they are part of my culture. Does that mean that, like my native ancestors five centuries ago when faced by the initial Catholic "evangelization," I must renounce my cultural heritage in order to affirm my Christianity? I do not believe so.[8]

Protestants Can Celebrate Mary of Guadalupe Because She Proclaims the Gospel

First, I believe that Protestants can celebrate Mary of Guadalupe because, like Mary herself in her great New Testament hymn of God's praise, the *Magnificat*, she proclaims to us the gospel, the good news of our salvation in Christ, the good news of God who scatters the proud, exalts the lowly, fills the hungry with good things and remembers his promises to Abraham and his children forever. With regard to this, the great Roman Catholic New Testament scholar, the late Raymond Brown, once wrote regarding Guadalupan devotion,

> For a people downtrodden and oppressed, the devotion made it possible to see the significance that the Christian Gospel was meant to have. In the Indian tradition, when Mary appears in the ancient garb of the mother of the Indian gods, she promises to show forth love and compassion, defense and help to all the inhabitants of the land. Ten years before, the whole Indian nation, their gods and their tradition has been torn down. She hears their lamentations and remedies their miseries, their pains and their sufferings. In the devotion to the Lady, the Christian Gospel proclaims hope for the oppressed. When one looks at the first chapter of Luke one realizes how authentic a Gospel hope that is. . . . For Mary, the news about Jesus means that God has put down the mighty, and He has exalted the lowly. . . . The Gospel of God's Son means salvation for those who have nothing. That is the way Jesus translates it, and that is the way Mary translates it. . . . Luke

8. Ibid., 228.

presents Mary as a disciple not only because she said, "Be it done unto me according to your word," but because she understood what the word meant in terms of the life of the poor and the slaves of whom she is the representative. I think that is exactly what happened in the case of Our Lady of Guadalupe. She gave the hope of the Gospel to a whole people who had no other reason to see good news in what came from Spain. In their lives the devotion to Our Lady constituted an authentic development of the Gospel of discipleship.[9]

And, in the following manner, Rev. Bonnie Jensen, the former executive director of the Women of the ELCA, has also drawn attention to Mary of Guadalupe in "We Sing Mary's Song," originally a homily given at a Consultation on Justice and Justification held in Mexico City December 7–14, 1985, by the then–American Lutheran Church (now part of the ELCA):

It is risky for the mighty to sing the Magnificat. It might mean moving from the center to the fringes. It might mean leaving the theologically proper talk to engage in simple, frank discussions. Or it might mean risking tenured positions in our schools of theology, or jobs in the church bureaucracy, as we speak clearly and forthrightly about the implications of our faith. It might mean risking our intellectual credibility as we respect the visions of poor Indians of Guadalupe.

But we can take the risk! We can sing the Magnificat in faith, knowing that fear can lead us to repentance, and repentance prepares us for the coming reign of God. . . .

I was deeply moved by the story of the poor man's vision of the Lady of Guadalupe. I was struck by how lowly, insignificant people have to beg the church to regard them with the esteem with which God regards them. We are not sure whether Mary appeared in a vision to this poor man. Perhaps we have our Protestant doubts. Yet even if we question the vision, the tragic truth remains: the poor and lowly often have to beg the church to proclaim and live out its message of a merciful, compassionate God! Behind the vision's gilded cactus leaves, miraculous

9. Raymond E. Brown, "Mary in the New Testament and in Catholic Life," *America*, May 15, 1982, 378–79.

roses, and imprinted cloak is the longing for a God who comes, not in the might of military conquest, nor in the ecclesiastical forms and evangelism plans of a mighty church, but in simple compassionate respect and regard for the lowly, the hungry, the women, the poor, the children. . . .

We sing the Magnificat to comfort the lowly. We sing to put ourselves in solidarity with the lowly and those who suffer. We sing in order to bring in the reign and community of our Lord Jesus Christ. . . .

We keep announcing to one another the sort of God in which we believe: a God who has respect for the Marys of Nazareth, for vulnerable, pregnant, unmarried women; a God who rummages through the dump with the hungry; a God who cries when children are killed and women are raped; a God who sees visions with poor farmers and plants roses on their hillsides.[10]

Professor José David Rodriguez, Jr., of the Lutheran School of Theology, Chicago, writes of this connection, saying,

The true intent of the [Guadalupe] story is not to bring people to venerate an image of the Virgin. The purpose of the story is to challenge people then as well as today *to join in an ancient biblical tradition,* a very important and popular tradition, that the early Christian community attributed to the virgin Mary. It is the tradition that is so eloquently presented in the Magnificat. It is the tradition that has a pre-history in the Scriptures with the song of Miriam in Exodus 15, the song of Hannah in 1 Samuel 2, and the song of Deborah in Judges 5. It is a tradition of a God who loves all human beings. But for this love to be actualized, God "scatters the proud, puts down the mighty from their thrones and exalts those of low degree" (Luke 1:51-52). . . . God's liberation of the poor and oppressed also calls for the liberation of the rich and mighty. The oppressed are not called to take vengeance on the powerful but to liberate them from their own violence. The humble are not raised to dominate over others but to get rid of all forms of domination. Slaves are not liberated to put others in bondage but to rid the world of slavery. God became human in the son of Mary to transform us from arrogant and selfish beings to true "humanized"

10. Bonnie Jensen, "We Sing Mary's Song," *Word and World* 7, no. 1 (1987): 81–82.

beings. . . . The story of the Virgin of Guadalupe is part of a broader story of the great saving acts of God in history. The good news for us is that we are invited to be a part of that wonderful and meaningful story.[11]

Protestants can celebrate the Virgin of Mary of Guadalupe, then, because she proclaims to us the gospel and because the message of Mary of Guadalupe is the same as that of Mary's own *Magnificat* of praise in the Gospel of Luke. Indeed, in so many ways, the Virgin of Guadalupe is simply the Mary of the Bible! As Reformed theologian Rubén Rosario Rodríguez reminds us,

> It is through Guadalupe's mediation that Latino/a people come to know God's liberating message previously communicated in the *Magnificat* of Mary: "He has shown strength with his arm; he has scattered the proud in the thoughts of their hearts. He has brought down the powerful from their thrones, and lifted up the lowly; he has filled the hungry with good things, and sent the rich away empty" (Luke 1:51–52). Ultimately . . . the Guadalupan epiphany points away from itself to the liberating work of Christ through whom we come to know the true God. Thus, in spite of the historical development of the Guadalupan devotion into a national and cultural symbol, it is first and foremost a witness to the person and work of Jesus Christ.[12]

And, as Kathleen Norris has written,

> Mary's love and pity for her children seems to be what people treasure most about her, and what helps her to serve as a bridge between cultures. One great example of this took place in 1531, when the Virgin Mary appeared to an Indian peasant named Juan Diego on the mountain of Tepeyac, in Mexico, leaving behind a cloak, a tilma, imprinted with her image. The image has been immortalized as Our Lady of Guadalupe, and Mexican-American theologian Virgilio Elizondo argues, in *The Future is Mestizo*, that the significance of this image today is that Mary appeared as a "mestiza," or person of mixed race, a symbol of the union

---

11. José David Rodríguez Jr., with the assistance of Colleen R. Nelson, "The Virgin of Guadalupe," *Currents in Theology and Mission*, 13, no. 6 (December 1986): 369 (emphasis added).
12. Rubén Rosario Rodríguez, "Beyond Word and Sacrament: A Reformed Protestant Engagement of Guadalupan Devotion," in Johnson, *American Magnificat*, 97–98.

of the indigenous Aztec and Spanish invader. What was, and still is, the scandal of miscegenation was given a holy face and name. As a Protestant I'll say it all sounds suspiciously biblical to me, recalling the scandal of the Incarnation itself, the mixing together of human and divine in a young, unmarried woman.[13]

We Can Celebrate Mary of Guadalupe
Because She Embodies for Us God's Unmerited Grace

A second reason why Protestants might celebrate Mary of Guadalupe is because she embodies in a special way God's gracious act of salvation, God's own unmerited and free grace. How quickly even Lutherans seem to have forgotten Martin Luther's own high regard, esteem, and praise for the Blessed Virgin Mary in his life and writings, even long after the Reformation had begun. As noted in the previous chapter, contemporary Luther scholar Eric Gritsch summarizes Luther's views, noting that for him,

> Mary is the prototype of how God is to be "magnified." He is not to be "magnified" or praised for his distant, unchangeable majesty, but for his unconditional, graceful, and ever-present pursuit of his creatures. Thus Mary magnifies God for what he does rather than magnifying herself for what was done to her. . . . "Being regarded by God" is the truly blessed state of Mary. *She is the embodiment of God's grace*, by which others can see what kind of God the Father of Jesus Christ is. . . . Mary sees wisdom, might, and riches on one side and kindness, justice, and righteousness on the other. The former reflect human works, the latter the works of God. God uses his works to put down the works of [people], who are always tempted to deify themselves. God's works are "mercy" [Luke 1:50], "breaking spiritual pride" (v. 51), "putting down the mighty" (v. 52), "exalting the lowly" (v. 53), "filling the hungry with good things," and "sending the rich away empty" (v. 53). . . . [And] Mary is the "Mother of God" who experienced his unmerited grace. Her personal experience of this grace is an example for all humankind that the mighty

13. Kathleen Norris, "Virgen Mary, Mother of God," in Johnson, *American Magnificat,* 162.

> God cares for the lowly just as he cares for the exalted . . . . Thus she
> incites the faithful to trust in God's grace when they call on her.[14]

It is precisely the language of God's free grace that several
contemporary Catholic authors use to speak about the Virgin of
Guadalupe today. That is, according to them, the God proclaimed
in and by the Guadalupan story is none other than "the God-who-
is-for-us,"[15] characterized by "a maternal presence, consoling,
nurturing, offering unconditional love, comforting" and "brimming
over with gentleness, loving kindness, and forgiveness" as "an
unconditional and grace-filled gift to the people."[16] And, if so, then
the story of Mary of Guadalupe is precisely a proclamation of the God
who justifies "by grace alone." And that this gift is received "through
faith" is surely exemplified in the response of Juan Diego, who, like
Abraham and countless prophets in the Hebrew Bible before him,
interprets this encounter as a call to his own prophetic ministry both
to his own people and to the governing (ecclesiastical) authorities to
whom he was sent. It must be recalled here that in distinction from
several other visions of Mary throughout history, especially the more
modern ones, where some kind of ritual code is violated and a new
ritual is enjoined in order to correct this,[17] Mary of Guadalupe asks
for *nothing* to be done other than the building of what she calls a
"temple." And this temple is itself to be nothing other than a place or
"home" where all peoples might encounter divine love, compassion,
help, and protection, and where their laments would be heard and all

14. Eric Gritsch, "The Views of Luther and Lutheranism on the Veneration of Mary," in *The One
Mediator, The Saints, and Mary*, ed. H. G. Anderson, et. al., Lutherans and Catholics in Dialogue
8 (Minneapolis: Augsburg Fortress, 1992), 236–37 (emphasis added).

15. Orlando Espín, "An Exploration into the Theology of Grace and Sin," in Espín and Diaz, *From
the Heart of Our People*, 139

16. Jeannette Rodriguez, "Guadalupe: The Feminine Face of God," in *Goddess of the Americas, La
Diosa de las Americas*, ed. Ana Castillo (New York: Riverhead Books, 1996), 25–31.

17. Cf. Sandra L. Zimdars Swartz, *Encountering Mary: Visions of Mary from La Salette to
Medjugorje* (Princeton: Princeton University Press, 1991), 247ff.

their miseries, misfortunes, and sorrows would find remedy and cure. In other words, this "temple," this "Beth-El" (house of God) of the Americas was (and is) to be a place where the God of unconditional love, mercy, compassion, grace, and forgiveness is proclaimed and encountered.

Even the implications of the call for justice and liberation so often associated in a particular way with the Virgin of Guadalupe are also consistent with a Protestant understanding of justification by grace through faith. From within his Reformed theological perspective Daniel Migliore writes of the relationship between the sovereignty of grace and the pursuit of justice exemplified in Mary's *Magnificat*, saying,

> Neither the biblical portrayal of Mary's passion for justice expressed in the Magnificat nor the classical Reformed emphasis on the sovereignty of grace lead to passivity or complacency. On the contrary, acknowledgment of salvation by grace alone goes hand in hand with a passionate cry for justice and a transformed world. This passion for justice remains anchored in God; trust is not transferred to revolutionary ideologies. Nevertheless, zeal for God's honor and the manifestation of God's justice in all creation ignites a real rebellion and a spirit of resistance against all forces of injustice and all the powers and principalities that oppose God's redemptive purposes.[18]

If Migliore himself is not concerned specifically with Mary of Guadalupe in this context, the parallels are obvious. As in the *Magnificat*, so in Guadalupe is manifested Mary's own "zeal for God's honor," which, perhaps today more than ever, has led to a "real rebellion and a spirit of resistance" against racial, social, and economic injustice in the world. At times, that rebellion and resistance may indeed be transferred more to revolutionary ideologies than to the biblical *God* of justice and righteousness. But the persistent presence

18. Daniel L. Migliore, "Mary: A Reformed Theological Perspective," *Theology Today* 56, no. 3 (October 1999): 354.

of the Guadalupan image often associated with movements of rebellion and resistance nonetheless keeps open the possibility of hearing what Migliore calls "*God's* righteous concern for the poor" and its implications expressed so powerfully in Mary's own *biblical* proclamation, her *Magnificat*. To be justified by grace alone sets one free in the name of God to risk oneself and one's identity in the pursuit of God's own justice and righteousness for the world.

I would like to suggest that we might best appropriate the story and image of the Virgin of Guadalupe under the category of *parable*, that is, "the Virgin of Guadalupe as parable of Justification," or, "Mary of Guadalupe as parable of the reign of God." By the use of the word *parable*, I mean to draw attention to how the Guadalupan story actually functions. That is, as modern New Testament scholarship on the parables of Jesus has come to emphasize, parables function as "stories that defy religious conventions, overturn tradition, and subvert the hearer's expectations"[19] about how God is *supposed* to act in the world and, in so doing, "make room" for the inbreaking of God's reign. If contemporary biblical scholarship is correct, the parables of Jesus, as reversals that make room for the advent of the reign of God as surprising gift and invite the action of response to that reign, point unmistakably to Jesus as the Great Parable of God himself. Indeed, it is precisely the Crucified One who functions as the ultimate parable of divine reversal and salvation, especially as this is proclaimed by Saint Paul in 1 Cor. 1:27–31:

> God chose what is foolish in the world to shame the wise; God chose what is weak in the world to shame the strong; God chose what is low and despised in the world, things that are not, to reduce to nothing things that are, so that no one might boast in the presence of God. He is the source of your life in Christ Jesus, who became for us wisdom from

19. Nathan Mitchell, *Real Presence: The Work of Eucharist* (Chicago: Liturgy Training Publications, 1998), 48.

God, and righteousness and sanctification and redemption, in order that,
as it is written, "Let the one who boasts, boast in the Lord."

The narrative and the widespread presence of the image of Mary
of Guadalupe can certainly be interpreted then as functioning
parabolically in the same sense as the biblical parables themselves.
For the Guadalupan story is precisely a parable of the great reversals
of God, the subversion of both indigenous and Spanish cultural-
religious worldviews and assumptions, standing them on their heads,
in order to make room for something new. Juan Diego is none other
than precisely one of the "low and despised in the world," who, in this
encounter, becomes himself the prophet or messenger of the reign
of God even to the ecclesiastical authorities, and, as an indigenous
layperson, subverts even the heavily clerical leadership structure of
Spanish colonial church life. It is no wonder that, increasingly, Juan
Diego is becoming today the model for the ministry of the laity,
the concrete example of the priestly ministry of the baptized—the
"priesthood of all believers" in traditional Protestant
terminology—especially within Mexican and Mexican-American
contexts.[20]

Nor is it any wonder why early ecclesiastical responses to the
Guadalupe event would have been so strongly negative. Then, as
now, Guadalupe challenges the wise, the powerful, the noble, and
the strong to a new conversion to the presence of the reign of God
as located precisely in the weak, the lowly, the despised, and the
rejected. This is nothing other than what Lutherans like to call a
theologia crucis, a "theology of the cross." For, like the parables of
Jesus, the Virgin of Guadalupe, as parable of the reign of God, or
parable of justification, is connected to the great biblical stories of

---

20. See Roberto Piña, "The Laity in the Hispanic Church," in *The New Catholic World* (New York:
Paulist Press, 1980), 168–71.

reversal, which point, ultimately, to the great reversal of the cross. As such, the narrative and image of Guadalupe belong, most appropriately, in close association with images of the Crucified One himself. For it is only in light of the image of Christ crucified, in the image of the cross, where the meaning of Mary of Guadalupe as "the embodiment of God's grace" is best revealed and appropriated.

In this light, perhaps, Protestants can come to appreciate the following insights offered by Virgil Elizondo in this context: "Protestants tell me: 'But Christ alone is necessary for salvation.' And I say to them: 'You are absolutely right. That is precisely what makes Guadalupe so precious. Precisely because she is not necessary, she is so special! She is a gift of God's love.'"[21] And elsewhere, he writes,

What most people who have not experienced the Guadalupe tradition cannot understand is that to be a Guadalupano/a (one in whose heart Our Lady of Guadalupe reigns) is to be *an evangelical Christian*. It is to say that the Word became flesh in Euro-Native America and began its unifying task—"that all may be one." In Our Lady of Guadalupe, Christ became American. Yet because the gospel through Guadalupe was such a powerful force in the creation and formulation of the national consciousness and identity of the people as expressed, understood, and celebrated through their art, music, poetry, religious expression, preaching, political discourse, and cultural-religious expressions, its original meaning—that is, the original gospel of Jesus expressed in and through native Mexican terms—has become eclipsed. This has led some modern-day Christians—especially those whose Christianity is expressed through U.S. cultural terms—to see Guadalupe as pagan or as something opposed to the gospel. It is certainly true that just as the gospel was co-opted and domesticated by Constantine and subsequent "Christian-powers," so has Guadalupe been co-opted and domesticated by the powerful of Mexico, including the church. Yet neither the initial gospel nor the gospel expressed through Guadalupe has lost its original intent or force, a force that is being rediscovered as the poor, the marginated, and the rejected reclaim these foundational gospels as their chief

21. Elizondo & Friends, *A Retreat with Our Lady of Guadalupe and Juan Diego* (Cincinnati: St. Anthony Messenger Press, 1998), 81–82.

weapons of liberation and as sources of lifestyles that are different from those engendered by ecclesial and social structures that have marginalized, oppressed, and dehumanized them.[22]

Former Lutheran campus pastor Richard Q. Elvee at Gustavus Adolphus College, Saint Peter, Minnesota, has written,

> The power of the pregnant Virgin asking Native Americans in a native tongue to become bearers of the Good News of Jesus Christ to the Americas was a powerful experience. Native peoples, who were being exterminated by foreign disease and decimated by oppression and war, became the bearers of the news that Jesus Christ was waiting to be born in the Americas. The oppression of the conquistadors would not destroy the people. God's messenger, the mother of Jesus, came to give hope and strength to a people wandering in despair. These conquered people were to teach their European conquerors the meaning of God's call of faith. These seemingly hopeless people were to become the hope of a hemisphere. With Jesus waiting to be born in the Americas, the Mexican people were to give him a home.[23]

What could be more "evangelical" than that? Certainly, then, the Guadalupan event *can* be interpreted as "not just another Marian apparition" but as something having "to do with the very core of the gospel itself" (Elizondo) even as that gospel is understood specifically in a Protestant theological context. As such, it might surely be said that the way in which the Guadalupan image and narrative function in the particular cultural context of Hispanic-Latino "popular religion" is precisely an inculturation or incarnation of the gospel of justification itself.

---

22. Virgil Elizondo, *Guadalupe: Mother of the New Creation* (Maryknoll, NY: Orbis Books, 1997), 113–14. Emphasis added.

23. "Christmas in Christ Chapel, December 2, 3, and 4, 1994" (Saint Peter, MN: Gustavus Adolphus College, 1994), 1.

Protestants Can Celebrate Mary of Guadalupe
Because She is a Type and Model of What the Church
Is to Be in the World

It is not only that the Guadalupan story proclaims the unconditionally gracious, loving, merciful, and compassionate God who justifies the Juan Diegos of the world by grace alone through faith. In addition, the very image of Mary of Guadalupe is revelatory of the multiracial, multiethnic, multicultural, mestiza church that came to be incarnated as the result of the sixteenth-century cultural confrontation between Spain and Mexico and still struggles to be born in our own day. Both the person and the image of Mary of Guadalupe, we might say, function as a *typus ecclesiae*, a type, or image, or model of the church. As noted in the previous chapter, Eric Gritsch has written with regard to Luther's Marian theology, "To Luther Mary was the prime example of the faithful—a *typus ecclesiae* embodying unmerited grace. Mary is a paradigm for the indefectibility of the church."[24]

The third reason, then, why Protestants can celebrate the Virgin of Guadalupe is because she is a type and model of what the church is to be in the world. That is, if the narrative of Mary of Guadalupe can be interpreted correctly as being about justification by grace alone through faith, then the image—which depicts the *typus ecclesiae* herself as pregnant with the incarnate Word—can surely be seen as, in a mirror's reflection, what the church itself, thanks also to God's unmerited grace, is and is called to be, as similarly "pregnant" with the same incarnate Word for the life and salvation of the world. Indeed, for those who might object that it is precisely *Christ* who appears to be absent from this narrative and image of justification, the words of Virgil Elizondo need to be heard: "The innermost core of the apparition . . . is what she carries within her womb: the new

---

24. Gritsch, "The Views of Luther and Lutheranism on the Veneration of Mary," 241.

source and center of the new humanity that is about to be born. And that source and center is Christ as the light and life of the world."[25] And in this sense, then, Mary of Guadalupe is truly "of the gospel" because the narrative and image of Guadalupe is, ultimately, about *Christ*!

Indeed, the interpretation of the image of the Virgin of Guadalupe as an image and model of the church itself may be one of the most profound Guadalupan gifts that Mexican and Mexican-American spirituality can make to the whole church catholic in our day. For the church being called into existence is, more than ever before, one called to be clearly multicultural and mestizo in form, and such a church of the future appears to be already present proleptically in Mary of Guadalupe's mestiza face. To gaze contemplatively upon her image, then, is to gaze at the future church in the making, and to gaze at what we hope, by God's grace and Spirit, the church of Jesus Christ, racially, culturally, and even ecumenically, will become.

It is here where I would suggest that there may, indeed, be some room for the types of Marian-Guadalupan devotion among Protestants that were noted in the previous chapter. In the joint Lutheran-Roman Catholic statement, *The One Mediator, the Saints, and Mary* (1992), at least enough theological convergence and clarity was noted to state that the issue of "invocation" of Mary and the saints need no longer be "church dividing" in the continued quest toward full and visible communion. "Saints on earth ask one another to pray to God for each other through Christ. They are neither commanded *nor forbidden* to ask departed saints to pray for them."[26] Also in response to Luther's theology of Mary, including his interpretation of the Hail Mary,[27] George Tavard asked appropriately,

---

25. Elizondo, *Guadalupe: Mother of the New Creation*, 128–29.
26. Anderson, et. al., *The One Mediator, the Saints, and Mary*, 61 (emphasis added).
27. See above, 188-89.

"Is it not possible on the basis of justification by faith and on the strength of Luther's example to count as a permissible *adiaphoron* a contemplative attitude before the mother of Christ, made of gratitude, admiration, and love?"[28] Based on *The One Mediator, the Saints, and Mary* and Tavard, if then, the *message* of Guadalupe and, at least, some form of the *image* of the Virgin of Guadalupe might well be acceptable within a Protestant theological framework, a case could surely be made in a modern ecumenical context for recovering or redeveloping an evangelical interpretation of the two classic Western Christian Marian devotions as well, namely, some form of the *Angelus* and rosary. Interpreted as prayerful meditations on Christ and our salvation, like the biblical form of the Hail Mary itself, both the *Angelus* and the rosary, may well be compatible with justification by grace through faith.[29] Consequently, as such, there may yet be room in Protestantism for some form of Marian veneration and devotion.[30] Again, the late Arthur Carl Piepkorn claimed that Luther's "analogy between the Blessed Virgin and the church . . . makes it possible for a Lutheran to use the Magnificat as the canticle at vespers, *and to say* the first, pre-Counterreformation part of the *Ave Maria* . . . as memorials of the Incarnation."[31] Similarly, the late Lutheran theologian, Joseph Sittler, in a published sermon entitled "Ave Maria, Gratia Plena," once said,

If . . . the figure of Mary articulates in her song and demonstrates in her

---

28. George H. Tavard, *The Thousand Faces of the Virgin Mary* (Collegeville, MN: Michael Glazier, 1996), 117.

29. See the very evangelical interpretation given to the *Angelus* and the Rosary by Paul VI in his classic 1976 apostolic exhortation, *Marialis cultus*, and note John Paul II's christologically centered encyclical on the rosary, *Rosarium Virginia Mariae*.

30. While my examples in this section tend to be from Lutherans, see also Rubén Rosario Rodríguez, "Beyond Word and Sacrament: A Reformed Protestant Engagement of Guadalupan Devotion," in Johnson, *American Magnificat*, 77–106.

31. Arthur Carl Piepkorn, "Mary's Place within the People of God according to Non-Roman Catholics," *Marian Studies* 18 (1967): 80. Emphasis added.

quiet life powers and dimensions of the action of God and the response of [humans], both our thought and our worship are the poorer for the neglect of her. It is not strange, but right and proper, that her meaning should be declared and her praise be sung from a Protestant pulpit. If we can find it in our competence in this place to hail the witness to the faith of Augustine, of Luther, of Calvin, or Wesley, how grudging before the gifts of God never to utter an *Ave Maria*—Hail Mary![32]

And, as we saw in the previous chapter, Lutheran theologians José David Rodriguez[33] and Robert Jenson[34] have pushed the envelope even further on this by advocating that the addition of "Holy Mary, Mother of God, pray for us sinners now and at the hour of our death, Amen" would be suitable for Lutherans to use. Hence, if, in the words of *The One Mediator, the Saints, and Mary*, that Christians "are neither commanded *nor forbidden* to ask departed saints to pray for them,"[35] these contemporary theologians offer theological assistance to those who would delight in not being forbidden from asking Mary to pray for them. Indeed, adopting what Tavard called "a contemplative attitude before the mother of Christ, made of gratitude, admiration, and love"[36] before an icon of the Virgin of Guadalupe or another classic Marian image may well engender the response of "Hail Mary . . . . pray for us" among some Protestant Christians.

---

32. Joseph Sittler, "Ave Maria, Gratia Plena," in Idem, *The Care of the Earth and Other University Sermons* (Philadelphia: Fortress Press, 1964), 55–56, and 63.

33. José David Rodriguez, Jr., "The Virgin of Guadalupe from a Latino/a Protestant Perspective: A Dangerous Narrative to Counter Colonial and Imperialistic Power," in Johnson, *American Magnificat*.

34. Robert Jenson, "A Space for God," in *Mary, Mother of God*, ed. C. Braaten and R. Jenson (Grand Rapids: Eerdmans, 2004), 56–57.

35. Anderson, et. al., *The One Mediator, the Saints, and Mary*, 61 (emphasis added).

36. Tavard, *The Thousand Faces of the Virgin Mary*, 117.

Conclusion

As I have demonstrated in this chapter, there are at least three reasons why Protestant Christians can, and perhaps even should, celebrate the Blessed Virgin Mary under the title of the Virgin, or Our Lady, of Guadalupe. First, Protestants can celebrate Mary under this title because, like the portrayal of Mary herself in her great New Testament hymn of God's praise, the *Magnificat*, the Virgin of Guadalupe proclaims to us the gospel, the good news of our salvation in Christ, the good news of God who scatters the proud, exalts the lowly, fills the hungry with good things and remembers his promises to Abraham and his children forever. Second, Protestants can celebrate the Virgin of Guadalupe because the God proclaimed in and by the Guadalupan story is none other than "the God-who-is-for-us," characterized by "a maternal presence, consoling, nurturing, offering unconditional love, comforting" and "brimming over with gentleness, loving kindness, and forgiveness" as "an unconditional and grace-filled gift to the people," and so, then, precisely a proclamation of the God who justifies "by grace alone." And, third, Protestants can celebrate the Virgin of Guadalupe because, in a particular way, her story and image provide a *typus ecclesiae*, type and model of what the church is to be in the world.

If this is correct, then one simply ought never say to Hispanic-Latino Christians, raised in a particular Catholic cultural contexts, but now increasingly present within various forms of Protestantism, "Throw out your images, stop lighting candles, dismantle the *altarcitos* in your homes, stop wearing medals, and stop reciting rosaries and novenas because Protestants don't do those things." If this approach, undoubtedly, has been a characteristic of Latin American Protestantism in general, and one still vehemently supported by several Hispanic-Latino Protestants themselves, another approach must surely be possible at least in some Protestant circles such as Lutheran, Anglican, Methodist, and Reformed. And part of that approach may simply be attending again to the words of Martin Luther in one of his Christmas Eve sermons, where he said,

> This is the great joy, of which the angel speaks, this is the consolation and the superabundant goodness of God, that man (if he has this faith) may boast of such treasure as that Mary is his real mother, Christ his brother, and God his father. . . . See to it that you make [Christ's] birth your own, and that you make an exchange with him, so that you rid yourself of your birth and receive instead, his. This happens if you have this faith. By this token you sit assuredly in the Virgin Mary's lap and are her dear child.[37]

Perhaps, then, in the words of Luther himself, Protestants can celebrate Mary of Guadalupe, porque *"Ella es nuestra mamá, Ella es nuestra mamita"*; because, finally, in faith, "She is *our* Mom!"

---

37. Martin Luther, "The Gospel for Christmas Eve, Luke 2[:1–14]," in *Luther's Works*, vol. 52: *Sermons, II* (Philadelphia: Fortress Press, 1974), 15–16.

9

Satis est

Ecumenical Catalyst or Narrow Reductionism?

It is also taught among us that one holy Christian church will be and remain forever. This is the assembly of all believers [or "saints"] among whom the Gospel is preached in its purity and the holy sacraments are administered according to the Gospel. For it is sufficient [*satis est*] for the true unity of the Christian church that the Gospel be preached in conformity with a pure understanding of it and that the sacraments be administered in accordance with the divine Word [or, "are administered rightly"]. It is not necessary for the true unity of the Christian church that ceremonies instituted by men, should be observed uniformly in all places. It is as Paul says in Eph. 4:4, 5, "There is one body and one Spirit, just as you were called to the one hope that belongs to your call, one Lord, one faith, one baptism" (*Augustana* VII:1-4).[1]

Prior to 1997, when the Evangelical Lutheran Church in America (ELCA) was to vote on various full communion proposals both with The Episcopal Church (the former *Concordat of Unity*, as the defeated

---

1. Tappert, *The Book of Concord*, 32. The text cited above is from the German version. Words in brackets are added from the Latin.

document was called), and with various Reformed churches in the United States, as well as the *Joint Declaration on Justification* with the Roman Catholic Church, I wrote a short article in the *Lutheran Forum* in which I suggested that the phrase *satis est* from *Augustana* VII would be cited over and over again at various synodical assemblies both in favor of or in disagreement with these proposals. I also indicated that the contents of that appeal to *Augustana* VII would tend to differ widely according to the theological positions of those who made it. *Satis est* would be invoked both by those who see *Augustana* VII as a liberating catalyst for the further pursuit of visible communion between Lutherans and other ecclesial traditions and by those who view it in a more restrictive, limiting, or reductionist manner, according to which, nothing *other* than full *doctrinal* agreement with the Lutheran dogmatic position on the "purity" of the gospel and the "right" administration of the sacraments could serve as a unifying basis. Or, as we still hear it invoked today in some quarters of American Lutheranism, especially now in the aftermath of *Called to a Common Mission*, if the principle of *satis est* is true, then for Lutherans to embrace something like the historic episcopacy for the sake of Christian unity with another Christian ecclesial body, then the principle is being compromised. That is, "more" is being required than proclamation of the gospel and administration of the sacraments.

What has generally not been done in such contexts, however, is what I suggested then and continue to suggest; that is, a *liturgical* reading of *Augustana* VII. For, as I shall attempt to demonstrate in what follows, the description of the church and its unity in *Augustana* VII, primarily, is about the church's very self expression in its worship, in its word and sacrament liturgy. And because this is so, *Augustana* VII provides *liturgical*—not specifically dogmatic—criteria by which ecumenical relationships and proposals are to be discussed and evaluated. In other words, if my reading of *Augustana* VII is correct, it is primarily the living *lex orandi*, and only, secondarily, the official *lex credendi* of various ecclesial traditions—including our own—that must be taken into account in any ecumenical movements toward full communion. The title of this chapter, therefore, is purely rhetorical. I believe that the principle of *satis est* is not narrowly reductionist but should function as an ecumenical catalyst.

Augustana VII as a *Liturgical* Description of the Church

When liturgists read in *Augustana* VII that the church is "the assembly of all believers [or 'saints'] among whom the Gospel is preached in its purity and the holy sacraments are administered according to the Gospel," they recognize here what certainly might be called a liturgical ecclesiology. That is, the church itself is defined here in *liturgical* terms as an *assembly* for gospel *proclamation* and sacramental *celebration*. Such liturgical *acts*, that is, the Gospel as actually *proclaimed* and the sacraments as actually *administered* within and to the gathered *assembly*, are the marks of the church, the very *events* in which, through which, and by which the nature and identity of the church are revealed.

Lutherans themselves, however, are not always aware that there is nothing distinctly *Lutheran* about this definition of the church's identity as a liturgical assembly. In similar language, Article XIX of the *Articles of Religion* of the Church of England also says,

> The visible Church of Christ is a congregation of faithful men, in which the pure Word of God is preached, and the Sacraments be duly ministered according to Christ's ordinance, in all those things that of necessity are requisite to the same.[2]

223

And, while the Roman Catholic response to the *Augustana*, the *Confutation*, did indeed reject Article VII, it did so on the grounds of the use of the term *saints* or *believers* in defining the assembly, *not*, it must be noted, on the basis of the assembly, preaching, and sacraments themselves as constitutive of the church.[3] It is in defense of this term, *saints*—not the role of assembly, gospel, and sacraments—that Melanchthon writes in *Apology* VII and VIII.[4]

Indeed, how could the Roman *Confutation* quibble with such a liturgical definition of the church in general? From the Emmaus account in Luke 24, to the description of the primitive Jerusalem Christian community in Acts 2:42, to the sixteenth-century Reformation context, all the way to our own day, the identity and nature of the church is described in liturgical terms, that is, by its continual assembling around word and table for the proclamation of the gospel and the celebration of the sacraments. Because it is a liturgical definition, *Augustana* VII's *Lutheran* definition of the church, at heart, then, is already an *ecumenical* definition. As such, it bears a remarkable similarity to what is said about the relationship between liturgy and the church in the Roman Catholic *Constitution on the Sacred Liturgy* from Vatican Council II:

> It is the liturgy through which . . . "the work of our redemption is accomplished," and it is through the liturgy, especially, that the faithful are enabled to express in their lives and manifest to others the mystery of Christ and the *real nature* of the *true Church*. . . . The liturgy daily builds up those who are in the Church, making of them a holy temple of the Lord, a dwelling place for God in the Spirit, to the mature measure of the fullness of Christ. At the same time it marvelously increases their power to preach Christ and thus show forth the Church, a sign lifted

2. Cited from *The Book of Common Prayer* (New York: The Church Hymnal Corporation, 1979), 871.
3. See Tappert, *The Book of Concord*, 168n1.
4. Ibid., 168ff.

up among the nations, to those who are outside, a sign under which the scattered children of God may be gathered together until there is one fold and one shepherd.[5]

And again, as such, *Augustana* VII's definition also finds resonance within Eastern Christian theology. The great Russian Orthodox liturgical theologian, Alexander Schmemann wrote,

> Christian worship, by its nature, structure and content, is the revelation and realization by the Church of her own real nature. And this nature is the new life in Christ—union in Christ with God in the Holy Spirit, knowledge of the Truth, unity, love, grace, peace, salvation. . . . In this sense the Church cannot be equated or merged with "cult"; it is not the Church which exists for the "cult," but the cult for the Church, for her welfare, for her growth into the full measure of the "stature of Christ" (Eph. 4:13). Christ did not establish a society for the observance of worship, a "cultic society," but rather the Church as the way of salvation, as the new life of re-created mankind. This does not mean that worship is secondary to the Church. On the contrary, it is inseparable from the Church and without it there is no Church. But this is because its purpose is to express, form, or realize the Church—to be the source of *that grace which always makes the Church the Church*, the people, the Body of Christ, "a chosen race and a royal priesthood" (1 Peter 2:9).[6]

Liturgy, of course, is not all that the church does, but it is, nevertheless, the very word and sacrament *source* from where the church—which must live faithfully in the world in both *martyria* (witness) and *diakonia* (service)—finds revealed its identity and self understanding. On this basic issue there appears to be little difference among the various churches, a basic issue underscored by a liturgical reading of *Augustana* VII. While Lutherans may have a distinct theological understanding of the purity of the gospel and of what

5. *Constitution on the Sacred Liturgy*, introduction, para. 2, in *Vatican Council II: The Conciliar and Post Conciliar Documents*, ed. A. Flannery, new Rev. ed. (Collegeville, MN: Liturgical Press, 1975), 1–2. Emphasis added.
6. Alexander Schmemann, *Introduction to Liturgical Theology*, 2nd ed. (Crestwood, NY: St. Vladimir's Seminary Press, 1975), 23. Emphasis added.

constitutes the right administration of the sacraments, the very fact that such liturgical terminology is used to define the church points to what is clearly a common ecumenical focus and tradition.

Augustana VII as a Statement about Legitimate Liturgical Diversity in Unity

If it is the means of grace—the gospel as *preached* and the sacraments as *administered*—that defines the "assembly of believers" called church, then the next section of *Augustana* VII is perfectly logical:

> For it is sufficient [*satis est*] for the true unity of the Christian church that the Gospel be preached in conformity with a pure understanding of it and that the sacraments be administered in accordance with the divine Word [or, "are administered rightly"]. It is not necessary for the true unity of the Christian church that ceremonies instituted by men, should be observed uniformly in all places.

But it is here, primarily, where a liturgical reading of this article is most needed today in order to avoid confusion about what is and what is not being said.

Often times the second sentence of the above quote—"it is not necessary for the true unity of the Christian church that ceremonies instituted by men, should be observed uniformly in all places"—is taken as an independent theological "proof text" by itself, without paying attention either to the context of the Article itself or to the whole historical context out of which the *Augustana* arose. As such, this sentence has, at times, been interpreted as a kind of license for doing in worship whatever it is that one wants to do. For, after all, it does not matter, we hear it said; "We are *free* from such human ceremonies like liturgy and free to choose what we will or will not do in our worship." Or, we hear from others, who, at least, while not ignoring the first part of this article entirely, still say "it does not matter what we do as long as the gospel is preached and the sacraments administered." Correct as it may be, such a principle can only go so far since, of course, the actual *doing* of the preaching of the gospel and the administration of the sacraments *does* matter and it matters a great deal.

The gospel as *proclaimed* and the sacraments as *administered* do not take place within a ritual vacuum or in isolation from, but, rather, within the very context of the Christian *assembly* gathered together for that expressed purpose. After all, for the gospel to be preached, the Scriptures must be read and they must be read and preached to a gathered community; for the sacraments to be rightly administered they will have some kind of ritual context. There will be some kind of "ceremony," some kind of ritual. That is simply inescapable! At the very least, someone must be sure that water is ready for Baptism, someone must prepare bread and wine and set the table, someone must pray a prayer of thanksgiving with its interpretive words identifying and explaining what it is that is happening here and now, and somewhere in all this there will be some form of sharing the meal now identified as Christ's Body and Blood given and shed for us for forgiveness, life, and salvation. Indeed, as *Apology* XXIV reminds us, "A sacrament *is* a ceremony or act in which God offers us the content of the promise *joined to the ceremony.*"[7] In other words, one cannot truly speak of word and sacrament as disembodied entities floating somewhere above us, separated from their intended context; one cannot speak of word and sacrament as divorced from their liturgical setting in the assembly. Without preaching, the gospel is not proclaimed. Without the ceremony of washing, Baptism is not Baptism; without the ceremony of the ritual

---

7. Tappert, *The Book of Concord*, 252. Emphasis added.

Meal—eating and drinking in faith with praise and thanksgiving—the Lord's Supper is not the Lord's Supper, no matter how *pure* one's doctrinal positions on these issues may or may not be. Sacramental theology, our understanding and interpretation of the sacraments, cannot be separated from sacramental *practice*, from the actual *doing* of the sacraments—the great mistake from medieval Scholasticism to the present that thinks that we can actually talk about the meaning of the sacraments without realizing that we need to talk about the liturgy. *How* particular communities actually *do* this gospel preaching and sacramental administering may legitimately differ within the church—but the actual *doing* of it is confessionally nonnegotiable, and that does, indeed, imply that *some* ceremony, some ritual, will be *done!* The question, then, in *Augustana* VII is not with ceremonies per se, but, rather, with the proper identification of *which* ceremonies are to be observed.

In dealing with the *satis est* aspect of *Augustana* VII, Lutherans also tend not to notice that the principle enunciated here is, primarily, a *liturgical* principle and is a very catholic and even Roman Catholic principle about the legitimacy of diverse and distinct rites within the universal church. Yes, the gospel and the sacraments—of course not separated from their appropriate liturgical contexts—are *enough*, *satis est*, for the *true* unity of the church, both locally and universally. But because this is written in a *liturgical* context and the issue is the use or nonuse of particular "human" rites and ceremonies vis-à-vis the Church of Rome, it is important to underscore the actual point being made. That is, the *Augustana* was addressed to a situation in which the division of the Western church was threatened, but had not yet formally occurred and would not formally take place for another twenty-five years until the Peace of Augsburg (1555) ratified it. Hence, this "confession" is not that of a specific separate "church" but the statement of a group *within* the one Western Catholic Church in which the princes and magistrates of the free cities were defending the liturgical diversity brought about by their reforms, and claiming that such diversity was acceptable, as long as the gospel was preached in its *purity* and the sacraments administered *rightly*. In other words, these Lutheran Reformers were arguing that they did not need to use the *Roman Rite*, or any of the other numerous rites and usages that existed in the late sixteenth-century medieval Western church, in order to be in union with the Western church. And, by the way, at this time period of 1530 and 1531, the dates of the *Augustana* and *Apology*, respectively, the so-called *Roman* Rite for the Mass itself was in a period of great decadence and transition and would not be standardized or universally imposed until after the Council of Trent in 1570 (some forty years *after* the *Augustana*) when Pope Pius V promulgated what became known as the *Missale Romanum Tridentinum* (the Tridentine Roman Missal). But even here, this Missal—which remained in effect until the 1960s reforms of Vatican Council II—was *not* universally imposed on even those Western churches in union with Rome, or on religious communities, who could demonstrate a two-hundred year old tradition of their own distinct rite. Similarly, the *Rituale Romanum* (Roman ritual), containing the rites for other sacraments such as Baptism, did not become either standardized or universally normative for Roman Catholics until the official *editio typica* of 1614.[8] The Lutherans believed, then, that they had the freedom to become a separate *rite* themselves, not apart from, but *within* the church universal, whose own liturgical self-expressions would reflect their legitimate and distinct theological understanding of the gospel. Such a recognition

8. The best available summary of the development of the "Tridentine" liturgical books is that of H. Jedin, "Das Konzil von Trient und die Reform der liturgischen Bücher," in *Kirche des Glaubens, Kirche der Geschichte*, vol. 2 (Freiburg: Herder, 1966), 499–525.

of legitimate liturgical diversity, in fact, is granted by Rome to many of those ancient churches of the Christian East—not Orthodox but known widely as Eastern Catholic—who, while having entered into union with Rome, continue to live out their faith, govern their communities, and celebrate their liturgies according to Eastern, not Western or Roman, Christian doctrine and theology. One must be careful, then, about attributing a kind of sacramental or ceremonial minimalism to *Augustana* VII or seeing it as a license to do whatever one "wants" or "feels" like doing in worship. A *liturgical* reading of this article suggests that the issue is about legitimate *liturgical* diversity in the church as long as the central *ceremonies* of preaching and sacramental administration are done. In other words, the true unity of the church does not consist in a universal liturgical uniformity of human ceremonies. Its true unity already exists by God's gracious gift in word and sacrament, a gift that calls all churches to an ecumenical fidelity to this liturgical center where the gospel is proclaimed and the sacraments are administered. But this fidelity can be and is lived out in numerous and richly diverse ceremonial ways, in different rites—distinct ecclesial traditions—throughout the world. Here, again, it should be noted that there is nothing specifically *Lutheran* about this reference to the nonessential nature of human rites and ceremonies. *Article* XXXIV of the Church of England's *Articles of Religion* makes a similar point, saying,

> It is not necessary that Traditions and Ceremonies be in all places one, or utterly like; for at all times they have been divers, and may be changed according to the diversity of countries, times, and men's manners, so that nothing be ordained against God's Word.[9]

But let's go a step further. It is often assumed by contemporary Lutherans that the references in this Article to the "holy sacraments"

9. Cited from *The Book of Common Prayer*, 874.

being "administered according to the Gospel" or "administered in accordance with the divine Word [or, 'rightly']" are clear references to only Baptism and the Lord's Supper, as the two "evangelical sacraments," and to their "words of institution" as the proper "divine Word" in their administration.[10] But the contents of both the *Augustana* and the *Apology* suggest that a bit of caution should be exercised about such a narrow interpretation. Indeed, not only does *Augustana* XIII *not* bother to specify the precise *number* of sacraments in general, but, in response to the *Confutation*, Melanchthon's *Apology* XIII specifically lists "absolution (which is the sacrament of penitence)" as one of "the genuine sacraments," and suggests ways in which "ordination" and even "prayer," for that matter, might also be considered as "sacraments."[11] Regarding the relationship between the *satis est* and the "right administration" of the sacraments themselves in *Augustana* VII, then, the question appears to be more open-ended than is usually thought, and, indeed, open to a broader interpretation than simply Baptism and Lord's Supper. As Melanchthon himself notes, "No intelligent person will quibble about the number of sacraments or the terminology, so long as those things are kept which have God's command and promise."[12]

Within this context it is intriguing to look at the question of ordination itself in relationship to the *satis est* and the "sacraments." Regarding ordination, specifically, Melancthon writes,

If ordination is interpreted in relation to the ministry of the Word, we have no objection to calling ordination a sacrament. The ministry of the Word has *God's command and glorious promise*: "The Gospel is the power of God for salvation to every one who has faith" (Rom. 1:16), again, "My word that goes forth from my mouth shall not return to me empty, but it shall accomplish that which I purpose, and prosper in the thing

10. Cf. Edmund Schlink, *Theology of the Lutheran Confessions* (Philadelphia, 1961), 199.
11. Tappert, *The Book of Concord*, 212–13.
12. Ibid., 213.

for which I sent it" (Isa. 55:11). If ordination is interpreted this way, we shall not object either to calling the laying on of hands a sacrament. *The church has the command to appoint ministers; to this we must subscribe wholeheartedly, for we know that God approves this ministry and is present in it.*[13]

And, immediately before treating the issue of human rites and ceremonies in his defense of *Augustana* VII, Melanchthon makes the strongest argument ever made in Lutheranism regarding ordained ministers, saying, "They [i.e., the ordained] do not represent their own persons but the *person of Christ*, because of the church's call, as Christ testifies (Luke 10:16), 'He who hears you hears me.' When they offer the Word of Christ or the sacraments, they do so in *Christ's place* and *stead*."[14] Similarly, it is not without significance that within the sequence of Articles in the *Augustana* itself, Article V, called either "The Office of the Ministry" (German) or "The Ministry of the Church" (Latin), in which this office is explicitly identified as "The Gospel and the sacraments" themselves, actually *precedes* Article VII on the identity and unity of the church. And, while Article V does not refer specifically in this context to "ordained clergy," Article XXVIII, "The Power of Bishops," certainly identifies the "power" of the ordained with the exercise of this "office":

> Our teachers assert that according to the Gospel the power of keys or the power of bishops is a power and command of God to preach the Gospel, to forgive and retain sins, and to administer and distribute the sacraments. . . . This power of keys or of bishops is used and exercised only by teaching and preaching the Word of God and by administering the sacraments. . . . In this way are imparted not bodily but eternal things and gifts, namely, eternal righteousness, the Holy Spirit, and eternal life.

---

13. Ibid., 212. Emphasis added.
14. Ibid., 173. Emphasis added. This is about as close as one can come to an *in persona Christi* understanding of ordained ministry without using the explicit theological phrase from the medieval Scholastic tradition.

These gifts *cannot be obtained except through the office of preaching and of administering the sacraments.*[15]

Does the relationship between the *satis est* and the preaching or teaching of the gospel and the administration of the sacraments in *Augustana* VII, then, at least by implication, suppose and include also the "sacrament" of ordination itself, almost as a necessary precondition for gospel preaching and sacramental administration?[16] Whether it is called a "sacrament" or not, it does, after all, have "God's command and glorious promise," and the very gifts of God's salvation, according to *Augustana* XXVIII, "cannot be obtained" without it. Indeed, without the actual *preaching* of the gospel by *someone* and without the actual *administration* of the sacraments by *someone*, and that *someone*, according to the Lutheran Confessions, is an *ordained* person, there is neither gospel proclaimed nor sacraments administered! Such an interpretation, that the *satis est* in *Augustana* VII also implies the church's ministry in some form, seems plausible indeed. Talking about gospel *preaching* and sacramental *administration* implies that one must also talk about the *preacher* and *administrator*. As Roman Catholics like to say, "The Eucharist makes the church and the church makes the Eucharist." We Lutherans might say, "Word and sacrament make the church but, at the same time, it is the *church* that proclaims the word and celebrates the sacraments." If the church and its ministry result from word and sacrament, there is a certain sense in which it is a never-ending circle and church and ministry

---

15. Ibid., 81–82. Emphasis added.
16. According to Peter Brunner, "Sacerdotium und Ministerium," in *Bemühungen um die einigende Wahrheit* (Göttingen: Vandenhoeck & Ruprecht, 1977), 32, "The gospel cannot come on the scene at all without its concrete human bearer." So also Luther, *Weimarer Ausgabe*, 50:641, says, "The church cannot exist without bishops, pastors, preachers, and priests, and in turn they cannot exist without the church: they must be together with one another." English translations by David Yeago, "The Papal Office and the Burdens of History: A Lutheran View," in *Church Unity and the Papal Office*, ed. C. Braaten and R. Jenson (Grand Rapids: Eerdmans, 2001), 104.

precede the actual *doing* of word and sacrament! In other words, one cannot talk about word and sacrament without talking about who does word and sacrament! And if such an interpretation is correct, then ecclesial bodies in ecumenical dialogue with Lutherans and in proposals regarding full communion with Lutherans have every right to push Lutherans toward greater theological clarity and precision regarding this "office of ministry" and how this office is and is to be "ordered" in service to the gospel and sacraments.

The Ecumenical Implications of a *Liturgical* Reading of *Augustana* VII

The *liturgical* reading of *Augustana* VII that I have attempted to provide in the preceding paragraphs suggests that any appeal made to the *satis est* in ecumenical relationships and in evaluating various proposals for full communion between Lutherans and others should be done rather cautiously and in full awareness of its primary liturgical context about human *versus* divine rites and ceremonies vis-à-vis sixteenth-century Rome. In other words, one should be suspicious when this principle is taken out of that historical context and applied to every imaginable ecumenical situation in the church today. When, in response to the Roman *Confutation*, Melanchthon speaks about Christian unity, it does not appear that he has our modern *ecumenical* questions about *visible* or *structural* unity in mind. His concern is *not*, and simply *could* not be, about what may or may not be necessary in bringing about greater or full communion between churches visibly separated from each other for centuries. His overall concern, as it is clearly expressed in this section of the *Apology*, is with the spiritual unity of the church! He writes,

We are talking about *true spiritual unity*, without which there can be no faith in the heart nor righteousness in the heart before God. For *this* unity, we say, a similarity of human rites, whether universal or particular, *is not necessary*. The righteousness of faith is not a righteousness tied to certain traditions, as the righteousness of the law was tied to the Mosaic ceremonies, because this righteousness of the heart is something that quickens the heart.[17]

For *this* unity, which transcends all Christian divisions and already *unites* all Christians in the one body of Christ, the gospel and the sacraments indeed are "sufficient," *satis est*! Even Rome acknowledges this, at least in principle, saying, in Vatican II's *Decree on Ecumenism*, "In spite of [various obstacles] it remains true that all who have been justified by faith in Baptism are incorporated into Christ; they therefore have a right to be called Christians, and with good reason are accepted as brothers by the children of the Catholic Church."[18]

But to assume from this that when another ecclesial tradition, for example, makes something like Lutheran acceptance of the entrance of Lutheran bishops into the succession of the "historic episcopacy" a necessary precondition for full communion, Lutherans are somehow being forced to reject their *satis est* in favor of additional criteria for unity does not necessarily follow. Nor does it follow that the *satis est* would be rejected if, for the sake of furthering visible Christian unity with Rome, some form of communion with the Bishop of Rome himself would be expected as a condition. (Indeed, it can be assumed definitely that some form of such communion *would* be expected.[19]) While there may be good and legitimate theological reasons why Lutherans might not want to embrace either the historic episcopacy or some form of communion with the Bishop of Rome for the sake

---

17. Ibid., 174.
18. Flannery, *Vatican Council II*, 454. For additional references, see Pontifical Christian Unity Council, *The 1993 Directory for Ecumenism* in *Origins* 23, no. 9 (1993), and John Paul II, *Ut Unum Sint* in *Origins* 25, no. 4 (1995).
19. See John Paul II, *Ut Unum Sint*, para. 97–98, 70.

of visible Christian unity,[20] the *satis est* of Augustana VII should not be one of them. Why? If my reading of this Article is correct, or, at least, plausible, then the answer is simply that *Augustana* VII is not talking about *this* kind of *visible* unity, not about unity for the sake of common visible witness and service, but rather of the true and spiritual unity that *already* exists by God's own gracious favor and gift in word and sacrament. It is on the basis of *this* unity already given by God through the very sacramental-liturgical means of grace that Lutherans and others are not only enabled, but also called to find concrete and *visible* ways to express this unity together in a full and visible form of communion.

There is, of course, a "catch" in *Augustana* VII regarding ecumenical relationships, a catch that a liturgical reading of this Article underscores clearly. Since this Article appears to be concerned chiefly with a *liturgical* understanding of the church and with liturgical matters in general, it follows that it is *precisely* a *liturgical* criterion or test that must be operative in assessing the state of relationships between specific churches. That is, the question for Lutherans is not, primarily at least, about the *lex credendi*, the doctrinal stance of a particular ecclesial body. The primary question is about its *lex orandi*, that is, the liturgical expression of its faith. In other words, are word *and* sacrament visibly central? Are they constitutive of the life and mission of this assembly? In spite of what may or may not be said officially, is it the *gospel* that is proclaimed in their assemblies or is it something else? Are the sacraments celebrated and administered rightly as the very means of God's grace or are they not? This is not about sacramental *theology*, not even about the contents of liturgical books—though one might hope for a correlation here—but about sacramental-liturgical *practice*! For the *satis est* is about the

20. Personally, however, I cannot think of any.

gospel *preached* and the sacraments, however many there may be, *administered*, about the gospel and sacraments in the process of their being *done* in the gathered *assembly*. If there is, in fact, unity here, unity in the *satis est*, then it would be nothing short of sinful not to pursue that unity further, even if the implications of that unity for Lutherans might call for serious change in the very structure of their ecclesial life. But, if *Augustana* VII is to be used in this context, the existence of that essential unity of the church can only be determined by a *liturgical* test of the center of any church's life, including, perhaps especially, our own.

Conclusion

Augustana VII, primarily, is a carefully-worded *descriptive* statement about the liturgical identity of the church as *assembly* for the liturgical tasks of gospel *preaching* and sacramental *administration*. These means of grace are sufficient—*satis est*—for true, that is, spiritual unity in the body of Christ because these are the means by which salvation is mediated to human beings and by which they are united together as one in Christ. It is, thus, in, through, and by means of these liturgical ceremonies of gospel *preaching* and sacramental *administration*, not through "human" rites and ceremonies, where such true unity is given by God. As such, *Augustana* VII stands as the *first* word Lutherans speak in ecumenical relationships, not the final or only word. It is from this acknowledgment of the unifying centrality of the means of grace in the church that the quest for further unity arises.

If so, then *Augustana* VII is not a *prescriptive* norm for assessing contemporary ecumenical relationships and proposals and ought not be quoted this way. Rather, vis-à-vis Rome in the sixteenth century, it is the Reformers' justification, no pun intended, as to how and why they as Reformed Catholics could continue as a legitimate expression of the one church and in *union* with the one church. Even if they did not accept all of the "human" (*Roman*) ceremonies, they accepted what was essential, namely, the gospel and the sacraments themselves. For the *true* unity of the church does not consist in liturgical uniformity, and unity with Rome, *the* ecumenical question on the mind of the Reformers themselves, still does not require such uniformity on the part of distinct ecclesial traditions. But to take this Article out of context and turn it into a narrow dogmatic *norm*, which automatically excludes any proposals for visible unity that might have certain structural or organizational implications for Lutherans because they require more than the *satis est*, seems to be a questionable reading of the text, and, ultimately, based on a questionable ecclesiology. Since, as noted above, the historical context of the *Augustana* reflects a situation where formal division in the Western Catholic church had not yet occurred, it is very questionable, indeed, to apply *Augustana* VII to our own situation today where we are trying to overcome almost 450 years of formal schism!

What happens, I fear, is that in the appeals made to this Article two visions of Christian unity are often confused, that of the true and spiritual union already given to all Christians by the sufficiency of the gospel and the sacraments, and the ecumenical quest for *visible* unity or communion based on this prior unitive reality. It is important to keep both visions clearly in mind. But it is equally important to realize that the very unifying Source of the quest for *visible* Christian unity is at the same time the Goal of the quest. For the *assemblies* that gather for gospel *proclamation* and sacramental *administration* are public, *visible* assemblies already, assemblies that in their separate gatherings testify to the *divisions* of the one church. Even though the divine ceremonies that take place in these assemblies are enough—*satis est*—for the true unity of all the assemblies already, is not the ultimate goal, even while respecting legitimate diversity, the gathering together of one, visibly united, public liturgical assembly where the gospel is indeed *proclaimed* and the sacraments are rightly *administered* to *all* of Christ's baptized body? Does not the true and spiritual unity given by pure gospel proclamation and right sacramental administration, in fact, call for a concrete, incarnational, visible, and public expression of that unity so that the world, indeed, may "come to believe" (John 17:21)? If so, then, the question of what are we *going* to do ecumenically together becomes very important.

The principle of *satis est* is an ecumenical catalyst for the pursuit of Christian unity and not the goal! And because of the *satis est*, the church is already one in Christ. But because it is already one, the challenge and goal is to allow that oneness to come to expression even if it means that certain things must die in order for the church to be reborn. If, even officially, we can share ecumenically in the real communion of one Baptism, the real presence of Christ in prayer, and the real presence of Christ in the "audible sacrament" of the proclaimed word (especially now with Roman Catholics in light of the *Joint Declaration*), then how tragic and, indeed, scandalous, not to share in the real presence of Christ in the visible word of the Eucharist itself.

10

Christian Worship and Ecumenism

What Shall We Do Now?

Both prior to and in the now fifty-plus years since the overwhelming approval of the *Constitution on the Sacred Liturgy* (December 4, 1963) at the Second Vatican Council (1962–1965), liturgical scholarship has been and clearly is an ecumenical endeavor with multiple liturgical pastoral implications. This is seen especially in the *Revised Common Lectionary*, in the very shape and contents of the Eucharistic Liturgy, in the renewal of the Rites of Christian Initiation, and surely, among other elements, in the revisions of the liturgical year and calendar, including the Three Days and the Fifty Days of Pascha. In specific reference to this ecumenical process and the products of liturgical reform and renewal engendered by it in the twentieth century, Paul Bradshaw has noted that,

> This twentieth-century phenomenon stemmed from a number of different causes. The rise of modern liturgical scholarship was, of course, a major factor, particularly in its earlier—primarily historical—phase, which revealed the changing past that existed behind current forms of

public worship. This not only demonstrated how very different were the liturgical practices of all churches today from those of the first few centuries of Christians, but also appeared to point towards a unified way of worship among those early Christians that contrasted sharply with the diverse traditions of contemporary denominations. . . . Historical scholarship both gave birth to, and in turn was stimulated by the Liturgical Movement, which sought to bring renewal to Christian worship in large measure by a return to what was thought to be the pattern of worship in the early Church. But the movement also provided a common theology of worship to undergird the changes and supply a rationale for them. . . . One other great movement of the twentieth century—ecumenism—must be counted as both cause and effect of the phenomenon that we are considering. The desire to overcome the barriers that had for centuries divided one denomination from another inevitably led to an examination of the differences in liturgical customs that existed between the churches, and to the wish not to do separately what we could do together in the area of liturgical revision.[1]

In fact, the relationship between liturgy and ecumenism has been so close that in an oft-quoted statement, the late James White, himself clearly a prime example of this relationship, once asked, "Why teach ecumenism when I can teach liturgy?"[2]

This chapter, actually a synthesis and update of several of my essays on liturgy and ecumenism over the past several years,[3] offers here

---

1. P. Bradshaw, "The Homogenization of Christian Liturgy—Ancient and Modern: Presidential Address," *Studia Liturgica* 26 (1996): 6–8.
2. James F. White, "A Protestant Worship Manifesto," *Christian Century* 99, no. 3, January 27, 1982, p. 84.
3. See "The Loss of a Common Language: The End of Ecumenical-Liturgical Convergence?" The Aidan Kavanagh Lecture, October 10, 2006, *Colloquium: Music, Worship, and the Arts* (New Haven: Yale Institute of Sacred Music, 2010), 27–39 (Another version of this chapter appeared in *Studia Liturgica* 37 [2007] 55–72); "Building Christian Unity," in *The Oblate Life*, ed. Gervase Holdaway, OSB (Collegeville, MN: The Liturgical Press, 2008), 231–35; "Not 'Sheep Stealing': Christ Calls Us to Be One/No es Robar Ovejas: Cristo Nos Llama a la Unidad," ¡*Oye!* 2008 4 (August, 2007): 24–25; "'Satis Est': Ecumenical Catalyst or Narrow Reductionism?," *Institute of Liturgical Studies Occasional Papers #11: Liturgy in a New Millennium, 2000–2003*, ed. Rhoda Schuler (Valparaiso: Institute of Liturgical Studies, 2006), 158–72; "Liturgy and Ecumenism: Gifts, Challenges, and Hopes for a Renewed Vision," The Godfrey Diekmann Lecture, *Worship* 80, no. 1 (January 2006): 2–29; "Romans 6 and the Identity of the Church: Towards a Baptismal Ecclesiology," *Catechumenate: A Journal of Christian Initiation* 22, no. 5 (September

an overview of where we have been, what the current situation is, and where we might go from here from within a shared ecumenical-liturgical vision, especially in light of what might be considered various recent setbacks.

Where We Have Been

Viewed from this side of the liturgical reforms and renewal of the Second Vatican Council and the similar reforms that took place in so many churches since the 1960s and 70s, we are the recipients of a rich liturgical-ecumenical heritage and treasure that has shaped all of us, both directly and indirectly. Indeed, this heritage might be summarized again, as in chapter 3 above, by pointing to the following now-common characteristics or goals of what is generally agreed across denominational boundaries should take place in Christian worship; namely, that the focus of our identity and mission is our common Baptism into Christ, both for infants and for those adults formed by the restored catechumenate; that the word of God is to be proclaimed clearly, audibly, intelligibly, and with dignity by carefully prepared readers; that ministers, presiding and otherwise, know their particular roles in the assembly and might carry them out in a manner befitting the worship of the Trinitarian God; that bread that looks, smells, feels, and tastes like (and, of course, *is*) real bread is broken and shared and where wine, rich and good wine, is shared in common; that the other sacraments or "sacramental rites" are seen as corporate and communal events with the rich and abundant use of the sacramental signs of water and oil and the healing and benedictory gestures of hand laying and touch; that the Liturgy

2000): 22–36; "Let's Stop Making 'Converts' at Easter," *Catechumenate: A Journal of Christian Initiation* 21, no. 5 (September 1999): 10–20; and "Planning and Leading Liturgical Prayer in an Ecumenical Context," *Pro Ecclesia* 8, 2 (Spring 1999): 187–200.

of the Hours is the church in the act of being itself in its constant, prayerful, eschatological, intercessory, and expectant vigil; that the Paschal Triduum, especially the Great Vigil of Easter, prepared for by a renewing forty-day Lent that is baptismal in orientation, and an ensuing fifty-day period of paschal joy, are seen as the pulsating center and heartbeat not only of the liturgical year but of life in Christ; and that the community itself, both in assembling to do *leitourgia* and in scattering for its missions of *martyria* and *diakonia* knows itself—"fully, actively, and consciously"—as that body of Christ it receives and celebrates so that it may itself be broken for the life of the world.

Further, within this received ecumenical vision of liturgy, even the very style of how many of us "do" worship has also changed dramatically, so dramatically, in fact, that contemporary eucharistic celebrations among Lutherans, Roman Catholics, Episcopalians, and several others often look (architecture and vestments), sound (shared musical and other texts), and are, essentially, the same.

As we saw above in Chapter 6, the greatest ecumenical-liturgical gift has been the three-year lectionary, the Roman Catholic *Ordo Lectionum Missae* of 1969, which since then has been adapted and used in various versions, the most recent being the *Revised Common Lectionary* of 1992, by "some 70 percent of Protestant churches in the English-speaking world."[4]

Closely related to this common ecumenical approach to the reading and proclamation of Scripture in liturgy has been also a common liturgical language, at least throughout the English-speaking world. Thanks to the liturgical texts produced by the now much maligned, misinterpreted,[5] and demolished International Commission on English in the Liturgy (better known by its

4. Horace Allen, as quoted by John Allen Jr., "Liturgist Says Ecumenical Dialogue Is 'Dead,'" *National Catholic Reporter*, May 24, 2002.

abbreviation, ICEL), together with the International Commission on English Texts and the English Language Liturgical Consultation, English-speaking Christians throughout the world have been using essentially the same texts for what we used to call the "Ordinary of the Mass"; in other words, *Kyrie*, *Gloria*, *Credo*, *Sanctus*, and *Agnus Dei*, together with the dialogical responses and other acclamations of the liturgy. This, of course, has meant that Christians from one tradition might easily worship in another even without the need to have a text in their hands!

Common theologies of worship or rationales to undergird contemporary changes have been articulated as well. If in the 1960's and early 1970's there is no question but that base was provided by Gregory Dix's fourfold *Shape of the Liturgy*, which he took as stemming from rubrical directions based on the biblical accounts of the Last Supper ("taking," "thanking," "breaking," and "sharing"), that "shape" has now been largely abandoned as an hermeneutical or ordering principle. Here too, of course, must be the added the significant 1982 Faith and Order document of the World Council of Churches, *Baptism, Eucharist, Ministry,* which showed at that time a remarkable ecumenical convergence in rite and theological interpretation. As we saw in Chapter 5, in his *Holy Things: A Liturgical Theology*[6] and *What Are the Essentials of Christian Worship?*[7] Gordon Lathrop has suggested a liturgical *ordo* or overall "pattern" for the scheduled ritual of Christian worship, which is both ecumenical and transcultural. According to him, this *ordo* is easily discernible

---

5. No one really has much right to criticize the work of the former ICEL until they have read in detail the 1992 doctoral dissertation, unfortunately not published, of Jeffrey M. Kemper, *Behind the Text: A Study of the Principles and Procedures of Translation, Adaptation, and Composition of Original Texts by the International Commission on English in the Liturgy* (Notre Dame, IN: University of Notre Dame, 1992).

6. G. Lathrop, *Holy Things: A Liturgical Theology* (Minneapolis: Fortress Press, 1993).

7. G. Lathrop, *What Are The Essentials of Christian Worship?* (Minneapolis: Augsburg Fortress, 1994).

as the very common "core" of Christian worship throughout the ages.[8] Hence, ecumenical liturgists are increasingly asserting that the very *ordo* or core of Christian liturgy is constituted by the *Sunday* assembly of the *baptized*, who *gather*, hear the *word*, share the *Meal*, and are *sent* on mission in the world. Together with the concept of the *ordo*, it is also important to note that the writings of liturgical theologians like Russian Orthodox Alexander Schmemann, British Methodist Geoffrey Wainwright, Roman Catholics Aidan Kavanagh, Ed Kilmartin, and, more recently, Louis-Marie Chauvet, are read and discussed by everyone in the field.

In the past ten years or so, however, this common ecumenical vision has come under not only contemporary critique by some but also outright hostility by others. To that I now turn.

The Current Situation

Reference was made above to James White's question, "Why teach ecumenism when I can teach liturgy?"[9] But, unfortunately, this approach is becoming less likely or possible today and certainly the answer is much less obvious. The most serious ideological challenge to the above ecumenical-liturgical consensus and vision, in fact, was certainly the 2001 Vatican document on translation, *Liturgiam authenticam,* a source of frustration to so many both within and outside the Roman Catholic Church, which resulted in the new English translation of the third edition of the Missal of Paul VI, and which began to be used on the First Sunday of Advent, 2011. In what is taken as a clear repudiation of the work of the former ICEL and English-speaking ecumenical cooperation in general, the following

---

8. Lathrop, *Holy Things,* 33–83.
9. White, "A Protestant Worship Manifesto," 84.

statement in *Liturgiam authenticam* makes the relationship rather clear from Rome's perspective: "Great caution is to be taken to avoid a wording or style that the Catholic faithful would confuse with the manner of speech of non-Catholic ecclesial communities or of other religions, so that such a factor will not cause them confusion or discomfort."[10] Now, just what might this be? If the now-approved translation of the *Ordo Missae* is any indication, then "the manner of speech of non-Catholic ecclesial communities" must be that of liturgical greeting and response (e.g., "And also with you" as the response to "The Lord be with you") as well as the English texts of the *Gloria*, Creed, *Sanctus*, and *Agnus Dei* since these are now being rendered in a word-for-word equivalent translation. But these very texts in their earlier form appeared in the earlier English translation of the Missal of Paul VI in 1970 and in subsequent editions. The *Lutheran Book of Worship*, which employs similar texts, did not appear until 1978, and the American Episcopal *Book of Common Prayer*, which also employs similar texts, in 1979, with other churches preparing their worship books either at the same time or subsequent to these publications. More recent books, such as *Evangelical Lutheran Worship* in 2006, contain the most recent of those common texts. That is, "the manner of speech of non-Catholic ecclesial communities" in their liturgical language is based directly on the manner of *Catholic* liturgical speech because it is adapted directly *from* already existing Catholic liturgical speech! It is not and simply could not have been the other way around, even if for Roman Catholics ecumenical consultation had been a part of the process.

With regard to these and other sorts of claims in *Liturgiam authenticam* Presbyterian ecumenist and liturgist Horace Allen of Boston University has said,

---

10. *Liturgiam authenticam*, para. 40.

The politics of this document are quite obvious. The emphasis on required Vatican approval, the insistence on decisions by conferences of bishops, as opposed to the International Commission on English in the Liturgy, and the dismissive references to "Protestant ecclesial communities" and their representatives is clear. It signals the effective termination of the longstanding international partnership between the Catholic International Commission on English in the Liturgy on the one hand, and the Consultation on Common Texts and the English Language Liturgical Consultation on the other. Toward the end of this sad reversal of many years of happy and fruitful ecumenical collaboration, it is stated with what must be an extraordinarily sardonic note, "From the day on which this instruction is published, a new period begins" for the liturgical use of vernacular languages. It adds that the norms established apply to previous translations, "and any further delay in making such emendations is to be avoided." As a committed ecumenical liturgist of at least three decades, I can only say in response to *Liturgiam Authenticam*: No! And how sad.[11]

And he is quoted further as saying that as a result of this document, "the entire ecumenical liturgical conversation and dialogue is over—finished, dead, done."[12]

Until only quite recently, I had considered Allen's response to be an exaggeration based on his personal frustrations over the apparent end of years of the ecumenical-liturgical work he himself had done. But this anti-ecumenical sentiment, which he so strongly deplores, had clearly been in the works prior to *Liturgiam authenticam* itself in 2001. In his recent book, *It's The Eucharist, Thank God*, Bishop Maurice Taylor, former member of ICEL, describes in detail the demolition of the former ICEL and its replacement under the direct control of Rome rather than under the Conferences of Bishops that make it up. He refers to a statement in a 1999 letter to ICEL by then-head of the Congregation for Divine Worship and the Discipline of

---

11. Horace T. Allen Jr., "Ecumenist Calls Rome's Translation Norms Unrealistic, Authoritarian," *National Catholic Reporter* (June 29, 2001).

12. Ibid.

the Sacraments, Cardinal Medina, which says, "ICEL was forbidden to provide any more original texts and *was ordered to cease having contacts 'with bodies pertaining to non-Catholic ecclesial communities.'*"[13] Taylor writes,

> Our contacts with non-Catholic liturgical agencies had resulted in a number of agreed common texts for prayers etc. used by other Christians as well as Catholics; this ecumenical initiative was appreciated by non-Catholics and its prohibition by the Congregation for Divine Worship (*contrary to the founding conferences' instructions*) was a great disappointment to many non-Catholics and, in fact, also to the Holy See's Pontifical Council for the Promotion of Christian Unity.[14]

With this, therefore, it could not be clearer that the new translation of the Roman Missal has, as part of its operating principles and make up, a decidedly anti-ecumenical agenda! And this, no matter how one might evaluate the merits or demerits of the translation itself, constitutes a scandal in light of the past forty-plus years of common ecumenical liturgical work. At least at the level of shared liturgical texts Allen is completely correct: "The entire ecumenical liturgical conversation and dialogue is over—finished, dead, done."[15]

Listen also to Gordon Lathrop much more recently:

> My principal concern is this: the new missal translation has simply and unilaterally abandoned what had been our shared ecumenical texts. Amid all the other furor—about awkwardly Latinized English, for example, or about the reintroduction of yet more gendered language for the church and for humanity and God—I wonder if most people who have thought about this new translation have even noticed this loss. The now widely known English missal translation, the 1973 ICEL translation, made use of those texts of the "prayers we have in common" that had been hammered out earlier in the ecumenical International Consultation on English Texts and in ICEL itself, thus with widespread

---

13. Maurice Taylor, *It's the Eucharist, Thank God* (Decani Books, 2009), 52 (emphasis added).
14. Ibid., 53 (emphasis added).
15. Horace T. Allen Jr., "Ecumenist Calls Rome's Translation Norms Unrealistic, Authoritarian."

and significant participation in the hammering by Roman Catholic liturgists and linguists. The very same texts—of the Creeds, of the Gloria, of the Preface dialogue, of the Sanctus, of the Agnus Dei, of the Lord's Prayer—were used in the book of my church: the Lutheran Book of Worship of 1978. They were also used in the 1979 Book of Common Prayer of the Episcopal Church, as also in many other liturgical books prepared throughout the churches of the English speaking world in the 70's and 80's. The list of those books is long. Then, in 1988, the English Language Liturgical Consultation, the successor to ICET, again with significant Roman Catholic leadership, published Praying Together, an important and helpful revision of all of these texts, based on years of common use and on further scholarship. The revised sacramentary . . . utilized these 1988 revisions. So did the American Presbyterian Book of Common Worship of 1993. So did the recent revised book of my church, Evangelical Lutheran Worship of 2006. So did many, many other books throughout the English-speaking Christian world.

Not this new book. The common Gloria, Sanctus and Creed translations are gone here. So is the common translation of both the full Preface dialogue and the briefer presidential "Lord be with you" exchange. The ecumenical Lord's Prayer has never been given much of a chance among Roman Catholics, but this new missal does not even give it a nod by providing it as an alternative. No. None of them. We do still more or less share the Kyrie and the Agnus Dei, albeit with differences even there. I will take those two shared texts nonetheless as signifying a plea for mercy amid this loss.

For this absence is a huge loss. The sense of common prayer, the sense that our commonly recognized Baptism has incorporated us into a common confession of faith and common acts of praise, the belief that these foundations do give us a ground on which to stand as we continue in dialogue toward fuller communion and more manifest unity—all of this is significantly eroded. The sense will be, rather, that what happens in Roman Catholic worship is qualitatively other than what happens in the worship of other communities. If this is what you think, then this missal will serve and reinforce your conviction. If it is not what you think—if the Creeds we share really are shared confessions, for example, and if the ordo of the Mass is recognizable to you in the patterns of the service in many other places—I hope you will lament with me. Words matter.[16]

As such, *Liturgiam authenticam* and the current translation of the Missal find their logical place in connection to the 2000 Declaration of the Congregation for the Doctrine of the Faith, *Dominus Iesus*, which, unlike previous statements, defined what constitutes a "church," and which faith communities actually can be called churches by the Roman Catholic Church, in distinction to the ambiguous term, *ecclesial communities* (clearly a circumlocution for *church*). *Dominus Iesus* also boldly goes where no document had ever gone before and redefines *Lumen gentium* 15, which stated that *the* church of Jesus Christ fully *subsists in* the Catholic Church, while the preconciliar theology stated that *the* church *exists* fully in the Catholic Church. What was clearly forgotten (or deliberately ignored) in *Dominus Iesus* is that the term *ecclesial communities* was coined at Vatican II as a deliberately inclusive rather than exclusive term so that Christian traditions that did not consider themselves to be "churches" in the traditional sense (e.g., the Salvation Army and the Society of Friends), could still be included positively! It was not intended to be a Catholic decision defining who constitutes a church and who does not. Further, a similar inclusionary intent was behind the use of the phrase *subsists in*. That is, while saying something positive about the Roman Catholic Church, it was a way of including other Christian traditions within the one, although divided, body of Christ.[17] It would be difficult not to view Benedict XVI's 2007 *motu proprio, Summorum Pontificum*, especially the rather revisionist sounding claim that the pre-Vatican II Latin Mass had never been abrogated,[18] as

16. Gordon Lathrop, "Ecumenical Affirmation and Admonition Revisited," *PrayTell: Worship, Wit, and Wisdom* (October 12, 2010) at http://www.praytellblog.com/index.php/2010/10/12/ecumenical-affirmation-and-admonition-revisited/.

17. On both of these points, see the excellent study by Roman Catholic liturgical scholar Paul Turner, *When Other Christians Become Catholic* (Collegeville, MN: Pueblo, 2007), 116–21ff.

18. On this, see Mark Francis, "Beyond Language," *The Tablet* 14 (July, 2007), online edition; and Massimo Faggioli, *True Reform: Liturgy and Ecclesiology in Sacrosanctum Concilium* (Collegeville, MN: The Liturgical Press, Pueblo Books, 2012), 150.

belonging to the same kind of reinterpretation and expressed by the "sound bytes" or "talking points" of a hermeneutics of "continuity versus rupture" and a restorationist agenda called the "reform of the reform," according to the *real* meaning of Vatican II.[19] Indeed, it as though the bishops who had both approved and implemented the liturgical reforms, and had celebrated the Mass, office, and other sacraments in Latin throughout their lives, did not know and could not have possibly known or understood what they were doing. The issue appears, at some level, at least, to be one of maintaining a specific and particular kind of *Catholic* identity over and against not only the world but other forms of Christianity as well.

With regard to what can surely be called a changed situation reflected in *Dominus Iesus*, the ecumenical goal, as witnessed also perhaps in Benedict XVI's Apostolic Constitution, *Anglicanorum coetibus*, forming an Anglican Ordinariate within the Roman Catholic Church, seems no longer to be the full communion of *churches* based on several years of bilateral dialogues, as much as it is again a process of return to or entry into the Roman Catholic Church of individuals or groups, a "home to Rome" mentality, where the one church of Christ no longer *"subsists in"* but again "exists fully" only there.

For those of us formed and raised in the ecumenical-liturgical vision and spirit of the past fifty years since the approval of the Roman Catholic *Constitution on the Sacred Liturgy* (1963), it becomes rather easy to despair and lament this current situation and to be tempted even to give up the liturgical-ecumenical task entirely. Indeed, what Peter Jeffrey writes in his commentary on *Liturgiam authenticam* seems to be coming truer with each passing day:

---

19. See John Baldovin, *Reforming the Liturgy: A Response to the Critics* (Collegeville, MN: The Liturgical Press, Pueblo Books, 2008).

On the basis of documents like LA [*Liturgiam authenticam*] we could never bring back the Counter Reformation Church. . . . But we could erect a cruel caricature of it, vastly more impoverished and repressive than the original ever was. There are none-to-subtle indications that this is just what LA's talk of a "new era" [of liturgical renewal] really means.[20]

How, then, shall we respond to these developments without despairing? Where, indeed, shall we go from here regarding the relationship between ecumenism and liturgy? What shall we do? This will be addressed in the following section.

What Shall We Do Now?

The good news is that there is no turning back. The ecumenical spirit (Spirit?) unleashed by the World Council of Churches, the Second Vatican Council, and the modern liturgical reforms will not easily be silenced. Things are not as they were before the documents *Lumen gentium, Unitatis redintegratio,* and *Ut Unum sint,* as well as others (e.g., *Nostrae Aetate*) concerned with various facets of ecumenism within the Roman Catholic Church in relationship with other Christians and other world religions. Indeed, although there are several who claim that ecumenism and the ecumenical movement have largely disappeared or, at least have been put on the back burner, there have been signs of great progress in recent years both between East and West,[21] and in the West between Rome and certain Reformation traditions.[22] One might claim, in fact, that ecumenism is no longer

20. Peter Jeffrey, *Translating Tradition: A Chant Historian Reads* Liturgiam Authenticam (Collegeville, MN: The Liturgical Press, Pueblo Books, 2005), 97.
21. See Robert Taft, SJ, "Mass without Consecration? The Historic Agreement on the Eucharist between the Catholic Church and the Assyrian Church of the East Promulgated 26 October 2001," *Worship* 77, no. 6 (2003): 482–509.
22. See Lutheran World Federation and the Catholic Church, *Joint Declaration on the Doctrine of Justification,* 1999, available at http://www.vatican.va/roman_curia/pontifical_councils/chrstuni/documents/rc_pc_chrstuni_doc_31101999_cath-luth-joint-declaration_en.html.

the exception but the rule, that it has actually deepened and become simply a part of the way most contemporary Christians live in the world and in their churches today, in spite of what appear to be official steps leading away from this. Certainly it is in an ecumenical manner that reputable Christian scholars continue to work, especially in the field of liturgical studies. The words of Robert Taft, on the occasion of his receiving the *Berakah* award from the North American Academy of Liturgy several years ago, remain true:

> Ecumenism is not just a movement. It is a new way of being Christian. It is also a new way of being a scholar. Ecumenical scholarship means much more than scholarly objectivity, goes much further than just being honest and fair. It attempts to work disinterestedly, serving no cause but the truth wherever it is to be found. It seeks to see things from the other's point of view, to take seriously the other's critique of one's own communion and its historic errors and failings. . . . In short, it seeks to move Christian love into the realm of scholarship, and it is the implacable enemy of all forms of bigotry, intolerance, unfairness, selective reporting, and oblique comparisons that contrast the unrealized ideal of one's own church with the less-than-ideal reality of someone else's.[23]

Indeed, the continued study of liturgy will remain and must remain ecumenical in its approach. It was such ecumenical study of the sources East and West that brought about the contemporary liturgical reform and renewal in the first place. Various elements of that reform and renewal might be criticized today in the light of more recent scholarship (e.g., the hegemony of the so-called *Apostolic Tradition*, ascribed to Hippolytus of Rome, ca. 215, in modern reform, but which is probably neither Roman, Hippolytan, third-century, nor apostolic[24]), but this is nothing other than the result of the same

23. Robert Taft, SJ, "Response to the Berakah Award: Anamnesis," in *Beyond East and West: Problems in Liturgical Understanding*, 2nd ed. (Rome: Pontifical Oriental Institute, 2001), 287.
24. See Paul F. Bradshaw, Maxwell E. Johnson, and L. Edward Phillips, *The Apostolic Tradition: A Commentary*, Hermeneia (Minneapolis: Fortress Press, 2002).

kind of historical-critical-theological scholarship that has marked and will continue to mark the ecumenical endeavor. We abandon such a critical-ecumenical approach to liturgical study to our own peril and replace history and theology with ideology and mythology.

I still think that it is much too soon to make a generalization about the future of ecumenical-liturgical dialogue and conversation based on this. Although since the First Sunday in Advent, 2011, we no longer have common liturgical texts in English, churches of a similar liturgical-sacramental tradition will still be talking about that shared, ecumenical *ordo* of liturgy, a common *pattern* of worship, which, for many traditions is not necessarily bound to specific editions or books. That has not changed and, for that matter, we are not even talking about a *new* Roman Missal in this case; it is still the Missal of Pope Paul VI. The Latin texts of that Missal have not changed, other than, of course the inclusion of more recent feasts. Further, we *are* all still singing and praying the same basic texts as we always have, the same basic Western Eucharistic Liturgy, with slightly different language (maybe just enough to trip us up in each other's churches now). Indeed, everything I stated above about contemporary liturgy remains an accurate description with the lone exception now of a common language. Reputable graduate programs in liturgical studies will remain ecumenical in terms of faculty and student make-up. Liturgical organizations like the North American Academy of Liturgy, the international *Societas Liturgica*, and the more recently formed international Society of Oriental Liturgy, together with the standard English journals in the field like *Worship* and *Studia Liturgica* will remain ecumenical in their leadership, membership, editorial boards, and contributors. No, the loss of a common liturgical language for the Ordinary of the Mass may be a (temporary?) ecumenical setback and an end to some forms of convergence, but it is surely not yet the end of "ecumenical liturgical conversation and dialogue."

At the same time, we dare not so easily succumb to this current situation of disunity in liturgical texts and language. Again it is Robert Taft who has reminded us that liturgical language is not for God; it's for us. *God already knows all the languages!*[25] And because liturgical language is for us, I care a great deal about what was accomplished with our common liturgical texts in English and I invite you to be fully supportive of the English Language Liturgical Consultation's "Reims Statement: Praying with One Voice," adopted in August, 2011:

> For the first time in history, Christians in the English-speaking world are using common liturgical texts. In the process of coming to agreed common texts, scholars from different Christian traditions agreed on principles for the translation from the earliest sources. This in itself has been a gift. Despite only having been in existence for a relatively short time, these texts have been adopted freely by an ever increasing number of churches. We celebrate this. They are being experienced as a gift, a sign and a way to Christian unity in our diversity. As the churches continue to discover the riches of these shared texts, we believe further revision is inappropriate at the present time. We invite all who have not yet explored these texts, and those who have departed from their use, to join us in prayerful reflection on the value of common texts and careful consideration of the texts themselves. Prayed together, shared common texts become a part of the fabric of our being. They unite the hearts of Christians in giving glory to God as we undertake the mission of the Gospel.[26]

It is, of course, true that the ecumenical-liturgical movement, in spite of the best intentions and hard work, has not produced the sort of

---

25. See Robert Taft, "On Translating Liturgically," *Logos: A Journal of Eastern Christian Studies* 39, nos. 2–4 (1998): 162.

26. English Language Liturgical Consultation, "2. Common Texts," *The Reims Statement: Praying with One Voice: On Common Texts and Lectionary in the Life of the Churches* (Reims, France: 16 August, 2011).

new ecclesial-communal *persona* that so many of us hoped it would. But what it has contributed toward is the ecumenical formation and identity of those in the field of liturgical studies itself as well as in related fields of study (especially in Scripture and church history). As the 1982 "Methodist-Catholic Statement: The Eucharist and the Churches," says, "In respect to biblical, theological, and liturgical matters we may share more in common with our dialogue partners than we do with many persons within our own communions."[27] This is a rather common phenomenon, especially among liturgical scholars and students, constituting, as it were, a core following within various churches whose Christian identity, through academic study and liturgical participation, tends to transcend those ecclesial boundaries into situations of greater communion. Several years ago Jesuit theologian Karl Rahner urged theologians to take more seriously what he termed "actual faith" rather than "official faith" in the pursuit of Christian unity. At the level of the "actual faith" of Christians within differing traditions, Rahner said that,

> Their sense of faith . . . is identical with that of Christians belonging to another denomination. They believe in God; they entrust their lives to this living God of grace and forgiveness; they pray; they are baptized and celebrate the Lord's Supper; they recognize Jesus Christ, the crucified and risen Lord, as the definitive guarantor of God's saving bestowal of himself on them; they live the gospel; they know, too, that to be a Christian in this sense obliges them to participate in a corresponding *community* of faith, the Church. The traditional points of controversy between the Churches . . . are unknown to them, or are unimportant, or are at most noted and accepted as part of [a] provisional and relative character . . ., and which is accepted nowadays as belonging naturally to the historical contingency of the human situation.[28]

27. *Origins*, 11, 41 (25 March 1982): 651–59, here at 653. See also Gerard Austin, "Identity of a Eucharistic Church in an Ecumenical Age," *Worship* 72, no. 1 (1998): 26–35. See also my grateful response to him, "A Response to Gerard Austin's 'Identity of a Eucharistic Church in an Ecumenical Age,'" *Worship* 72, no. 1 (1998): 35–43.

THE CHURCH IN ACT

Elsewhere Rahner referred to this unity at the level of the "actual faith" of Christians as constituting a kind of "Third Church," that is, not a new denomination separate from the churches, but as constituting a common Christian ground *within* the churches seeking and moving toward further realization in a greater Christian unity.[29] This is, precisely, an apt description of those of who study and are formed by the ecumenical nature of the liturgy.

So what are we to do now? I would suggest that there is nothing new to do other than what we have been doing already. That is, we who have been formed by the ecumenical vision and spirit of liturgical study dare not let go of that vision and spirit since the full and visible unity of Christianity has not yet been accomplished. Shortly after his recent retirement, Walter Cardinal Kasper, former president of the Pontifical Council for the Promotion of Christian Unity, while expressing his thanks for the progress made between Lutherans and Roman Catholics, lamented the fact that at the end of his tenure the official sharing of the Eucharist together between Protestants and Catholics had not yet become a reality. And, in pointing toward this unfinished ecumenical agenda, he said, "We can no longer afford to stick to our differences."[30] And, indeed, it was Kasper himself who as recently as February, 2010, suggested the possibility of even an official ecumenical catechism, affirming "our common foundation in Jesus Christ and the Holy Trinity as expressed in our common creed and in the doctrine of the first ecumenical councils."[31]

---

28. Karl Rahner, "Is Church Union Dogmatically Possible?," in *Theological Investigations*, vol. 17: *Jesus, Man, and the Church* (New York: Crossroad, 1981), 209.

29. Karl Rahner, "Third Church?," in *Theological Investigations*, vol. 17, 215–27.

30. "Vatican Cardinal Says Lack of Shared Communion His Greatest Regret," see http://touchstonemag.com/merecomments/2010/07/cardinal-kasper-says-lack-of-shared-communion-his-greatest-regret.

31. "Cardinal Asks Dialogue Partners If an Ecumenical Catechism Might Work," *Catholic News Service* (Feb. 8, 2010) at http://www.catholicnews.com/data/stories/cns/1000540.htm.

Several years ago, ELCA Bishop Robert Rimbo gave one of the keynote presentations to the annual Center for Pastoral Liturgy Conference at Notre Dame, called *Eucharist without Walls*, in which he borrowed from an earlier version of my previous chapter on the *satis est*. I now return the favor. At the end of his presentation, he issued the following invitation to embrace what he called a "reverential iconoclasm" regarding ecumenical sharing of the Eucharist:

> Just as the liturgical movement began at a grassroots level, so we too cannot wait for the powers that be to approve of our understanding of what is sufficient or what shall be our practice of eucharistic hospitality. It is enough for the true unity of the church that the Gospel is preached and the Sacraments are administered according to the Gospel. *Satis est.* It is enough. It is time for a new liturgical movement, a movement away from liturgical archaeology and a movement toward action–reflection. It is time for us to think about our unity at the Table only after we have lived it. It is time for us to begin communing together at the one table of the one Lord as the one church and consider the consequences of such when God reveals them to us. It is the Lord's Table, it is the Lord's Supper, and I am profoundly convinced that the Lord is calling us to a Eucharist without Walls.[32]

I couldn't agree more with this proposal. But theologically, at least, we may be drawing close to this reality even on an official level. As was noted above in chapter 3, according to Karl Rahner and Heinrich Fries, there is already a "pulpit fellowship" shared between Roman Catholics and, at least, Lutherans:

> *Pulpit fellowship* is already being practiced in many cases; and it no longer presents a disquieting exception, even to Catholic Christians. But one really should think about this more than ever, *since it is precisely a pulpit fellowship which presupposes a community of faith.* Consider the reality of salvation of the Word of God; consider Christ's presence in

---

32. Quoted by permission.

its various forms, including the form of proclamation; finally consider the theological conformity of Word *and* Sacrament—sacrament as visible Word (*verbum visibile*), the Word as audible sacrament (*sacramentum audible*).[33]

And, in light of the continued ecumenical dialogues, even Roman Catholic recognition of Lutheran "orders" is not out of the question with regard to the "validity" of the Eucharist. The recent Lutheran-Catholic dialogue, *The Church as Koinonia of Salvation*, certainly shows that from a Catholic perspective there is even hope here for some kind of resolution. According to this statement,

> Catholic judgment on the authenticity of Lutheran ministry need not be of an all-or-nothing nature. The Decree on Ecumenism of Vatican II distinguished between relationships of full ecclesiastical communion and those of imperfect communion to reflect the varying degrees of differences with the Catholic Church. The communion of these separated communities with the Catholic Church is real, even though it is imperfect. Furthermore, the decree positively affirmed: "Our separated brothers and sisters also celebrate many sacred actions of the Christian religion. These most certainly can truly engender a life of grace in ways that vary according to the condition of each church or community, and must be held capable of giving access to that communion in which is salvation." Commenting on this point, Joseph Cardinal Ratzinger, prefect of the Congregation on the Doctrine of the Faith wrote in 1993 to Bavarian Lutheran bishop Johannes Hanselmann: "I count among the most important results of the ecumenical dialogues the insight that the issue of the Eucharist cannot be narrowed to the problem of 'validity.' Even a theology oriented to the concept of succession, such as that which holds in the Catholic and in the Orthodox church, need not in any way deny the salvation-granting presence of the Lord [*Heilschaffende Gegenwart des Herrn*] in a Lutheran [*evangelische*] Lord's Supper." If the actions of Lutheran pastors can be described by Catholics as "sacred actions" that "can truly engender a life of grace," if communities served by such ministers give "access to that communion

---

33. *Unity of the Churches: An Actual Possibility* (New York/Philadelphia: Paulist Press and Fortress Press, 1985), 125 (emphasis added).

in which is salvation," and if at a Eucharist at which a Lutheran pastor presides is to be found "the salvation-granting presence of the Lord," then Lutheran churches cannot be said simply to lack the ministry given to the church by Christ and the Spirit. In acknowledging the imperfect *koinonia* between our communities and the access to grace through the ministries of these communities, we also acknowledge a real although imperfect *koinonia* between our ministries.[34]

Further, again it was Walter Kasper who, in his 2004 study *Sacrament of Unity: The Eucharist and the Church*, drew attention to Pope John Paul II's 1995 encyclical on Christian unity, *Ut Unum Sint*, saying,

> The pope offered a more spiritual description of the meaning of the prescriptions of canon law: "It is a source of joy to note that Catholic ministers are able, in certain particular cases, to administer the sacraments of the Eucharist, Penance, and Anointing of the Sick to Christians who are not in full communion with the Catholic Church but who greatly desire to receive these sacraments, freely request them, and manifest the faith which the Catholic Church professes with regard to these sacraments" [*Ut unum sint*, para. 46]. It is clear that this affirmation was very important in the pope's eyes, for he repeated it literally eight years later in his encyclical on the Eucharist [*Ecclesia de Eucharistia*, para. 46].[35]

Not only did John Paul say that such a practice was a *source of joy*, but in both texts he even changed slightly the requirements of canon law by no longer specifying that one of the conditions for reception is that of being unable "to approach a minister of their own community."[36] Such a subtle and widely unknown change may truly be viewed as a sign of ecumenical hope, especially now within the

34. *The Church as Koinonia of Salvation: Its Structures and Ministries; Common Statement of the Tenth Round of the U.S. Lutheran-Roman Catholic Dialogue*, para. 107.
35. Walter Kasper, *Sacrament of Unity: The Eucharist and the Church* (New York: Crossroad Publishing Co., 2004), 72–73. See also R. Kevin Seasoltz, "One House, Many Dwellings: Open and Closed Communion," *Worship* 79, no. 5 (2005): 405–14.
36. *Code of Canon Law: Latin-English Edition* (Washington, DC: Canon Law Society of America, 1983), 321.

context of Roman Catholic leadership under Pope Francis, for whom the "joy of the gospel"[37] and the unconditional mercy of God appear to be higher priorities than the enforcement of law.

> If the Christian is a restorationist, a legalist, if he wants everything clear and safe, then he will find nothing. Tradition and memory of the past must help us to have the courage to open up new areas to God. Those who today always look for disciplinarian solutions, those who long for an exaggerated doctrinal "security," those who stubbornly try to recover a past that no longer exists—they have a static and inward-directed view of things. In this way, faith becomes an ideology among other ideologies.[38]

Indeed, as Seasoltz reminded us, within the 1983 Roman Catholic Code of Canon Law itself, the final canon states clearly, "The salvation of souls is the highest law (can. 1752)."[39]

Conclusion

In *Ut Unum Sint*, Pope John Paul II asked *the* ecumenical question, when he wrote,

> How is it possible to remain divided if we have been "buried" through Baptism in the Lord's death, in the very act by which God, through the death of his Son, has broken down the walls of division? Division openly contradicts the will of Christ, provides a stumbling block to the world and inflicts damage on the most holy cause of proclaiming the good news to every creature.[40]

---

37. See his Apostolic Exhortation, *Evangelii Gaudium*, available at https://w2.vatican.va/content/francesco/en/apost_exhortations/documents/papa-francesco_esortazione-ap_20131124_evangelii-gaudium.html.
38. "A Big Heart Open to God: The Exclusive Interview with Pope Francis, *America* (September 19, 2013), online edition at http://www.americamagazine.org/pope-interview.
39. Seasoltz, "One House, Many Dwellings," 415.
40. *Ut Unum Sint*, 6.

How is it possible, indeed? But before *Ut Unum Sint,* Roman Catholic and Lutheran theologians Rahner and Fries developed a series of theses articulating how possible it would be to could be establish full visible Christian unity in our age based on various theses emerging from the ecumenical dialogues on Creed, Baptism, Eucharist, and even the Office of Petrine Ministry in the church. At the same time, these theologians were realistic enough to state that they did not think such would happen. Why? The answer then and now remains rather frustrating, though not without hope:

> We think that all the churches act with too much tactical caution in the quest for actual unity. They do not really come out courageously with declarations as to what the conditions are under which they are really prepared to unite with other churches, even with sacrifice. Each church waits for the other church to take the initiative and to express very clearly what it could not truly relinquish without, in its own religious conscience, incurring guilt before God. Nor do they express what does not belong thereto and can, therefore, be relinquished in order to fulfill Jesus' commandment. . . . We ourselves are pessimistic with regard to the question of whether the officials of all these churches can bring about unity in the near future. . . . But we are convinced—and to that extent optimistic—that there is an objective possibility today for creating a satisfactory and speedy church unity.[41]

And in the conclusion of their study, they issued a challenge that must be taken still today with the utmost seriousness, especially in light of recent ecumenical setbacks:

> People can deny and close their minds to the call of grace and to the hour, to the signs of the times. People—expressed in human terms—have caused the separation of the Church into confessions. People can alter history and renew it; and they must do so if what happened was not good and if it brought harm and scandal. . . . The indispensable prayer to the Lord of the Church for the unity of Christians and of the churches

41. Karl Rahner and Heinrich Fries, *Unity of the Churches: An Actual Possibility* (Minneapolis: Fortress Press, 1985), 9–10.

must not be an alibi for human sloth and lack of imagination; instead, it must be the ever-new motivation to an attitude and mind-set which is expressed in the rule of Taizé: "Never be content with the scandal of separated Christendom. Have the passion for the unity of the body of Christ."[42]

Such passion for the unity of the body of Christ, indeed, for the ecumenical formation of all Christians remains the goal of all of our liturgical celebration and formation.

42. Ibid., 140.

Conclusion

So what? Other than offering my random thoughts on various ecumenical-liturgical issues over my career, is there anything that draws these chapters together into some coherent or logical plan? In other words, is there a point to all of this? Let me suggest that the essays updated for publication in this volume, while originally written at, and sometimes for, various occasions over the past twenty-plus years of teaching and writing, are directed toward several liturgical-sacramental issues actually being raised and addressed today within the ELCA, as well as in some other churches and communions. The first of these issues, addressed only indirectly in chapter 1, "Baptismal Spirituality in the Early Church and Its Implications for the Church Today," is whether or not eucharistic participation should be limited to the baptized or if *all* those in attendance, baptized or not, should be regularly welcomed and admitted to share in the Eucharist. While the bishops of The Episcopal Church voted overwhelmingly in 2012 to continue the traditional practice of Baptism before Eucharist as "normative" in their parishes and other institutions,[1] the conversation in the ELCA, under the terminology of "radical hospitality," has only recently

---

1. See "Baptism before Communion Is Still Church's Norm," Episcopal News Service, July 25, 2012, http://episcopaldigitalnetwork.com/ens/2012/07/25/baptism-before-communion-is-still-churchs-norm/.

begun, but both communions, including other ELCA partner churches, find a number of adherents arguing for significant change in this regard.

It will come as no surprise to readers of this volume to discover that my own position is that it is Baptism that regularly leads to Eucharist as the norm for Lutheran practice and theology, and not the other way around. Mennonite author Alan Kreider has drawn attention to the following characteristic of liturgy in early Christianity, demonstrating, in fact, that the unbaptized were not even part of the eucharistic assembly:

> Christian worship was designed to enable *Christians* to worship God. *It was not designed to attract non-Christians*; it was *not "seeker-sensitive."* For seekers were not allowed in. . . . Christian worship . . . assisted in the outreach of the churches indirectly, as a by-product, by shaping the lives and character of individual Christians and their communities so that they would be intriguing.[2]

And there is a decided logic to this. For, as ELCA liturgical theologian Thomas Schattauer at Wartburg Seminary has recently written,

> When we are committed to the baptismal logic of participation at Holy Communion, we are not committed to enforcing a rule about who is qualified to receive but to communicating persuasively the deep relation between welcome to the table and the welcome to baptism. When we understand that participation in the Supper involves a person in a costly discipleship in the way of Jesus, we are committed to inviting people into the baptismal community that shares that life.[3]

---

2. Alan Kreider, *The Change of Conversion and the Origin of Christendom* (Harrisburg, PA: Trinity Press International, 1999), 14. Emphasis added.
3. Thomas Schattauer, "Exploring the Baptismal Foundations of Eucharistic Hospitality," in *Table and Font: Who is welcome? An Invitation to Join the Conversation about Baptism and Communion*, available at http://download.elca.org/ELCA Resource Repository/Schattauer_Thomas.pdf

The issue here is closely related to the hard work of establishing the adult catechumenate in our synods and parishes. In chapter 1 I drew attention to this, saying that

> as several of our Roman Catholic colleagues, based on their experience with the RCIA, can testify, in those places where the adult catechumenate leading to full Christian initiation in water, chrism, and eucharistic table has been restored, and along with it the immense variety of lay ministries needed (e.g., catechists, sponsors, and the role of the entire faith community in general) to lead and assist in such a process of conversion, parishes themselves have experienced a renewal in faith and life, the recovery of the dignity of their Baptism, and a renewed sense of their own identity as church, as the body of Christ on mission in the world. That possibility awaits us as Lutherans as well . . . if, in the words of George Lindbeck, "rather than present *experience* being allowed to hold sway over the inherited tradition," we let "the inherited *tradition* shape and govern present experience.". . . . Even if rooted in the answers of the church in a much older historical context, the modern recovery of this patristic-based baptismal process can not be written off today as mere "Golden Age Romanticism" on the part of modern "High Church" armchair liturgists who might like to dress up in ancient costumes and "play church." The increasing numbers of unbaptized and "unchurched" adults today would seem, just as it did in the context of the fourth and fifth centuries, to call the church to assist in the evangelization and formation of new Christians with authenticity and integrity. . . . The need for an adult catechumenal process of formation should become increasingly obvious to us. The issue is *not* only liturgy but it is evangelism and formation in Christ and the church. And the great gift of our classic liturgical tradition is that we don't have to invent a new process for this but can receive it from our ancestors in the faith most gratefully.[4]

Further, a focus on Baptism as a prerequisite to eucharistic participation is hardly exclusionary; *au contraire*, it is radically inclusionary, the most radical hospitality leading to the eucharistic table that can be imagined, since, according to St Paul, it is *Baptism*

---

4. Above, 24-25.

that constitutes the church in which "there is no longer Jew or Greek . . . slave or free . . . male and female" (Gal. 3:28). The unbaptized are not excluded; Baptism is the way they are included. Consequently, I believe there is no reason in this context to go beyond the wise pastoral counsel offered in the ELCA's statement, *The Use of the Means of Grace*:

> When an unbaptized person comes to the table seeking Christ's presence and is inadvertently communed, neither that person nor the ministers of Communion need be ashamed. Rather, Christ's gift of love and mercy to all is praised. That person is invited to learn the faith of the Church, be baptized, and thereafter faithfully receive Holy Communion.[5]

Second, if the current conversation in the ELCA, and elsewhere, on the relationship between Baptism and Eucharist may help us in articulating more clearly our baptismal theology as the *inception* of life in Christ and the paschal pattern for baptismal living in the world, it should also raise for us the question of our theological understanding of the Eucharist itself. For, if the Eucharist is little other than a mere memorial meal, a communal commemoration, or intellectual remembering of Christ's redemptive act with the ritual sharing of bread and wine, then the question of who participates in it may well be understood differently than if we affirm our classic Lutheran theological stance "that in the Lord's Supper the body and blood of Christ are truly and *substantially* present and are truly offered with those things that are seen, bread and wine."[6] Or, as reflected in the 1967 Lutheran-Catholic dialogue on the *Eucharist as Sacrifice,* that "in the sacrament of the Lord's Supper Jesus Christ true God and true man, is present wholly and entirely, in his body and blood under

5. Evangelical Lutheran Church in America, *The Use of the Means of Grace: A Statement on the Practice of Word and* Sacrament (Evangelical Lutheran Church in America, 1997), Application 37G.

6. *Apology of the Augsburg Confession,* Art. X, in Tappert *The Book of Concord,* 179-80 (emphasis added).

the signs of bread and wine."[7] If the Eucharist *is*, in the words of Luther's *Small Catechism*, "the true body and blood of our Lord Jesus Christ, under the bread and wine, given to us Christians to eat and drink,"[8] and if that real presence of Christ there "in, with, and under" is objective and not dependent on the faith of the communicant, received by the believing Christian toward "forgiveness of sins, life, and salvation," but not so by the unbeliever,[9] then the question of who participates or not is placed on a different level than a position of "radical hospitality" at the altar might imply. Please understand. Regular exclusion of the unbaptized from the Eucharist is not to protect the Eucharist from some kind of profanation. The Eucharist *is* what it *is*, to use a modern cliché. Rather, exclusion of the unbaptized from eucharistic participation is out of pastoral care for the unbaptized themselves and to keep them from making a public statement or commitment about faith in Jesus Christ by receiving him in Holy Communion that they may be neither prepared nor ready to make! If, however, they have been catechized, are prepared and ready to make such a faith commitment, then why would they not be seeking Baptism? For, as Schattauer says above, "participation in the Supper involves a person in a costly discipleship in the way of Jesus." And the meaning of "costly discipleship" is best learned by what we might call apprenticeship in the community of faith through its formation process known as the catechumenate leading to baptism.

It seems to me, then, that the challenge facing the ELCA here, and, potentially, in relationship to the ELCA's now several full-

---

7. *The Eucharist as Sacrifice*, Lutherans and Catholics in Dialogue, I-III, ed. Paul C. Empie and T. Austin Murphy (Minneapolis: Augsburg Publishing House, 1965), 192.

8. Tappert, *The Book of Concord*, 351.

9. The classic Lutheran explanation here, of course, is that the unbeliever receives the Body and Blood of Christ to his or her own condemnation. See Martin Luther, *The Large Catechism*, ibid, 454.

communion partners, is not really what comes first, Baptism or Eucharist, at all. Rather, *the* question is, what is the meaning of the Eucharist and what are the implications of participating in the Eucharist for ongoing life in Christ? Hence, what is needed is a renewed articulation of the theology of the Eucharist in general along with our Lutheran confessional stance in the real presence of Christ in the Eucharist. Three of the chapters in this collection, chapters 2, 3, and 4, have dealt with that issue rather directly under different categories, namely, the role of the Holy Spirit in the Eucharist (chapter 2), the eucharistic presence of Christ in relationship to his other modes of "real presence" in the word, preaching, and liturgical assembly (chapter 3), and whether or not, in light of history, liturgical-sacramental theology, ecumenical dialogue, and newly composed rites for the taking of the Eucharist to those in special circumstances, Lutherans might be able to affirm today a practice of Eucharistic reservation of the elements for this purpose consistent with their confessional theology of sacramental union (chapter 4).

Third, to speak of a renewed articulation of the meaning of the Eucharist and our Lutheran confessional position about Christ's real presence therein, also means we cannot separate that theology from what is actually done liturgically. That is, while there may be many things that fall under the classic Lutheran category of *adiaphora* in liturgy, there are several foundational issues that do not. What do we do in worship and how does what we do shape us as Christian believers? Is the Eucharist central to the worship life of the ELCA? If so, what does that mean for liturgical practice?

Two recent worship experiences in different ELCA Lutheran settings raised that question for me in rather disturbing ways. The first experience was a festival Sunday worship at one of our ELCA schools in which both a choir and orchestra were employed to provide musical leadership for a gathering that included several alumni and current students. But apart from glorious music, though even here it was not clear what the relationship of the particular sacred music was to the liturgy being celebrated, the *only* reference to the Holy Trinity was the opening greeting, "The grace of our Lord Jesus Christ, the love of God, and the communion of the Holy Spirit be with you all." There was no creed professed, nor a renewal of Baptism done. The so-called "Great Thanksgiving" consisted of the introductory dialogue ("The Lord be with you . . . Lift up your hearts . . . Let us give thanks"), followed by some kind of makeshift (spontaneous?) Words of Institution "prayer" directed anomalously to Jesus (called a "Eucharistic Prayer" in the bulletin) and followed by the Lord's Prayer. The elements to be distributed at Holy Communion were not on the altar during the "prayer" (only the presider's host bowl and chalice were there) but on a table at some distance from the altar. There was no Proper Preface, no *Sanctus* ("Holy, holy, holy"), no *Agnus Dei* ("Lamb of God"), just as there had been no *Gloria in Excelsis* or *Worthy Is Christ* earlier in the Liturgy and, for that matter, no Old Testament reading, though the choir did sing an unrelated choral psalm at the place where that reading may have been expected, and, for that matter, the readings were not those assigned to that Sunday in the liturgical year but had been chosen for this particular event. And there was no final Trinitarian (or even Aaronic) blessing. In talking with several people afterwards, including retired Theology faculty at that institution, it was clear that many found the service to be a beautiful and inspiring one. I, however, wondered, and still do wonder, why a school of the ELCA with abundant musical and other talent could not provide a better model of Lutheran worship for such an event. At another large Lutheran church, where my second recent experience took place, the "Eucharistic" Liturgy followed *Evangelical Lutheran Worship* rather closely up to and including the Offertory Hymn, "Let the Vineyards

Be Fruitful." But the offertory prayer was not used and the pastor immediately began reciting the Words of Institution followed by the Lord's Prayer leading directly into the distribution of Communion. In both of these occasions not only was there not a Great Thanksgiving, properly speaking, but "thanks" were not really ever given!

I have no idea as to how normative my two experiences of Sunday Lutheran worship are throughout the ELCA, but I have enough experience, at least among Lutheran congregations in the Midwestern United States, to conclude that what I witnessed was not atypical. And I begin to wonder if our Lutheran confessional statement from *The Augsburg Confession* XXIV holds true any longer, that is, "our churches are falsely accused of abolishing the Mass. Actually, the Mass is retained among us and is celebrated with the greatest reverence. Almost all the customary ceremonies are also retained."[10] Indeed, would anyone even think to accuse those two liturgical assemblies in my above examples of retaining and celebrating the Mass of Western Christianity? I think not. At the very least, not that long ago, even if a full Eucharistic Prayer was not prayed regularly by all as part of the Great Thanksgiving, the Proper Preface, *Sanctus*, and *Agnus Dei* were regular parts of the Lutheran Communion Service, as were the *Kyrie, Gloria,* and either the Apostles' or Nicene Creeds. Even this, however, cannot obviously be counted on anymore, and I wonder if our churches are no longer "*falsely* accused of abolishing the Mass," since *abolishing* the Mass is precisely what we seem to have done, in spite of what our worship books and official statements say to the contrary!

It is to help in addressing this situation, and others like it, that chapter 5 on what is normative for Lutheran worship was written.

10. Ibid, 56.

And here I simply want to reiterate one of the points I made therein.[11] That is, what we do or do not do, say or do not say in our liturgies forms us as communities. Our liturgical words and our actions matter! Hence, a community that celebrates and receives Christ's Body and Blood in the Lord's Supper every Sunday, attends to the rubrical options and varieties already present in our liturgical book(s), faithfully proclaims the lectionary readings, and tenaciously keeps the feasts and seasons of the liturgical year week after week, year after year, will be a different sort of community than one that is continually experimenting with "worship alternatives" and searching for something "better" to meet the so-called needs of worshipers and potential seekers alike. And I dare say that the first type of community will, undoubtedly, be more "orthodox," more "Lutheran," in its doctrinal-theological outlook. Why? Because the issue is not about liturgical "style." The liturgy is not only about expressing our prayer and praise to God or hearing the word of God. Rather, as the very corporate expression of the self-identity and worldview of the worshiping community, the body of Christ in this time and place, expressed concretely in its liturgical texts and liturgical actions, the purpose of liturgy is not to permeate our lives with ritual but to permeate them with Christ for the very building up of his body, the church, and for the salvation and life of the world.[12] Further, the liturgy of the ELCA present in *ELW* and other worship books (*LBW*, *WOV*, etc.), bears the doctrinal weight and concrete expression of what is recognized to be a faithful representation of the Lutheran theological-doctrinal tradition in union with the catholic-ecumenical liturgical traditions of the church. Can the same be said for other worship "resources" or makeshift liturgies composed anew?

11. See above, 122-23.
12. See Robert Taft, "What Does Liturgy Do? Toward a Soteriology of Liturgical Celebration: Some Theses," *Worship* 66, no. 3 (1992): 194–211.

Fourth, together with this, of course, and addressed in detail in chapters 2, 3, and 5, is the related importance of using and, more importantly, *praying* the full Eucharistic Prayer as part of the Great Thanksgiving as the central prayer of the Liturgy. The best advice I ever received about being a faithful pastor was given to me by a Lutheran pastor in Decorah, Iowa, where I was doing my seminary internship in 1976. He said to me, "Always study the Sunday New Testament readings in Greek, always say something nice about the deceased at their funeral, and always, always, pray the full Eucharistic Prayer." Although I may not have always studied the lectionary readings in Greek when I was in full-time parish ministry (though I often did and still do), I have always managed to say something nice about the deceased at their funerals (sometimes more easily than at others), and since my ordination in 1978, I have never presided at the Lord's Supper without using either the Strodach-Reed prayer provided in the 1958 *Service Book and Hymnal*, or one of the several provided in *LBW* or *ELW*, or others in other contexts, including those of the 1979 *Book of Common Prayer* when I have presided in Episcopal contexts, which I often do on a regular basis today. But why is this important? As I argued in chapter 5,

> long before there was an Apostles' or Nicene Creed, or an explicit "doctrine" of the Trinity . . . it was through a Prayer of Thanksgiving over the baptismal waters, through the candidate's threefold profession of faith in the Father, Son, and Holy Spirit in the context of Baptism itself . . . and through the Great *Eucharistia* over the bread and cup of the Lord's Supper, consisting of *praise* to God for the work of creation and redemption, *thanksgiving* for the life, death, resurrection, and ascension of Christ, and *invocation* of the Holy Spirit, that the church professed its faith in the Trinity by means of *doxology* and *praise*. . . . What is done, sung, or said liturgically and what is held, thought, or confessed doctrinally are inseparable. How and what the church *prays* shapes and *is*, in a real sense, how and what the church *believes*.[13]

This is hardly *adiaphora*. What we say and do liturgically matters! We pray the Eucharistic Prayer, then, for the very simple reason that this central prayer of the Mass bears and professes the classic Trinitarian faith of the church in the very context of the proclamation of Christ's real presence. Our Trinitarian faith is prayed, not only professed! In fact, I would be so bold as to say that the renewal and vision of Christian worship expressed by both *LBW* and *ELW* will never come to fruition until Lutheran clergy begin to see as part of their public pastoral role that they are called to be prayers of the Great *Eucharistia* and that this prayer is to shape their identity, spirituality, and pastoral ministry in the church. Indeed, such Eucharistic Prayers should be memorized that they might shape even how pastors regularly pray! If a shorter service is needed, then attend to those rubrics that suggest the occasional omission of the *Kyrie* or Hymn of Praise, but not the Great Thanksgiving! And, if you have to omit one of the biblical readings, omit the second, never the first since, as we have seen, the first is chosen to correspond to the Gospel assigned to a given day.

Fifth, closely related to whether or not the Eucharist is central in the life of Lutheranism, or whether we are any longer *"falsely* accused of abandoning the Mass," is the question of the lectionary employed in worship. There is, of course, no standard or common lectionary used in Lutheranism worldwide, but the official lectionaries used by, at least, ELCA Lutherans in the United States, either the one provided in *LBW*, or more regularly now since *ELW*, the *Revised Common Lectionary*, are derived and adapted from the Roman Catholic *Ordo Lectionum Missae* of 1969, and are shared with much of English-speaking Protestantism in the United States and elsewhere. Like the Roman Catholic *OLM* itself, as chapter 6 demonstrates, the

13. Above, 124. See also my recent book, *Praying and Believing in Early Christianity; The Interplay between Christian Worship and Doctrine* (Collegeville, MN: Michael Glazier, 2013).

hermeneutical principle governing both the *LBW* lectionary and *RCL*, as adapted by Lutherans and Episcopalians, is what Fritz West has called a "Catholic liturgical paradigm," that is, a "Eucharistic hermeneutic," which assumes that the Eucharist is regularly celebrated as the culmination of the Liturgy of the Word, including the homily. As noted above, Gordon Lathrop underscored this hermeneutical approach over thirty years ago, writing,

> We read a text from the gospel, not in order to recapture the time when independent tradition units circulated in the Christian communities, but in order to set the pericope we read next to the passion and resurrection of Christ held forth now in the Supper. Hence reading the individual pericopes and then celebrating the Supper presents us with a skein of images reinterpreting images which is the very pattern of the gospel books themselves. The Sunday texts are not then understood aright unless they are understood as leading to that Supper. The hierarchy of readings in the Sunday Eucharist may then be thought of as a primary example of a skein of images reborn.[14]

In light of recent lectionary proposals for Lutheran use, the challenge, again, is whether Lutherans are decidedly eucharistic in their Sunday worship or not. If not, then the more recent development of lectionary cycles designed to teach the biblical narrative or to provide adult education or Bible Study at worship may well be preferred to the *RCL* or other adaptations. But if we are eucharistic in our approach to reading and preaching the Scriptures at Sunday worship then we cannot take lightly—nor so easily abandon—the ecumenical gift that the Roman Catholic Church has given to us all in the three-year lectionary. As we also saw above, Presbyterian liturgist Horace Allen has said it this way: The *RCL* "marks the first time since the Reformation that Catholics and Protestants find themselves reading the scriptures together Sunday by Sunday. . . . Who would have

14. Gordon Lathrop, "A Rebirth of Images: On the Use of the Bible in Liturgy," *Worship* 58, no. 4 (1984): 296.

thought that 450 years after the Reformation, Catholics would be teaching Protestants how to read scripture in worship?"[15]

Sixth, articulating a contemporary theology of Mary may not appear to be a particular cutting-edge issue within contemporary Lutheranism, the subject matter of chapters 7 and 8 specifically. The fact of the matter, however, is that ecumenical attention to Mary in general as well as specific multicultural issues surrounding her are being raised for contemporary Lutheranism in new ways as it seeks to minister more intentionally in, for example, Hispanic-Latino contexts within the changing face of contemporary American culture. As I have demonstrated in these two chapters, the issues are not simply doctrinal but, again, liturgical and devotional in nature. Is there a enlarged place for additional feasts of the Blessed Virgin Mary in the liturgical calendar, feasts like the Virgin of Guadalupe on December 12, or Mary's Conception on December 8 or her Nativity on September 8, the latter two of which appear now on the calendar of the Church of England and the former of which is occurring with some frequency among Episcopalians, Lutherans, and even some Methodists in this country? In light of Luther's own devotion to Mary, is there not room for some form of Marian devotion in contemporary Lutheranism? Is not Mary to be recovered iconographically as the *typus ecclesiae* par excellence? Do not icons and other images of her belong in our Lutheran places of worship, as is beginning again to happen in this country? Perhaps again the words of Joseph Sittler bear repeating here:

> [I]f . . . the figure of Mary articulates in her song and demonstrates in her quiet life powers and dimensions of the action of God and the response of [humans], both our thought and our worship are the poorer for the neglect of her. It is not strange, but right and proper, that her meaning should be declared and her praise be sung from a Protestant pulpit. If we

---

15. See above, Chapter 6, 145.

can find it in our competence in this place to hail the witness to the faith of Augustine, of Luther, of Calvin, or Wesley, how grudging before the gifts of God never to utter an *Ave Maria*—Hail Mary![16]

Seventh, and finally, the last two chapters, chapters 9 and 10, are concerned more directly with the overall focus of the entire book, that is, Lutheran liturgical theology in ecumenical conversation. But even here there are particular contemporary liturgical and sacramental questions that these chapters address with regard to issues within Lutheranism. The approach of chapter 9, for example, in attempting to offer a *liturgical* reading of the *satis est* of Article VII of The *Augsburg Confession*, especially as it came to focus, at least in part, on the theology and implications of ordination, may be of assistance as the ELCA now studies the possibility of another "ordained" office of ministry ("Entrance Rite") in the church, that is, an office of "Word and Service," or, as called elsewhere, the office of "Permanent Deacon." And chapter 10, together with being an *apologia* for the ecumenical liturgical vision expressed by both *LBW* and *ELW*, in spite of various challenges to that vision and its expression, provides a statement of hope and encouragement toward the greater realization of that vision. For, indeed, in almost all of the issues addressed in this book, it is striking that an ecumenical convergence and, often, even a consensus has been reached. May we receive this convergence and consensus as nothing other than a profound gift of the Holy Spirit!

---

16. Joseph Sittler, "Ave Maria, Gratia Plena," in *The Care of the Earth and Other University Sermons* (Philadelphia: Fortress Press, 1964), 55–56, and 63.